Everyday Life
in the
Muslim
Middle
East

Indiana Series in Arab and Islamic Studies

Salih J. Altoma, Iliya Harik, and Mark Tessler

GENERAL EDITORS

Everyday Life
in the
Muslim
Middle
East

EDITED BY

*Donna Lee Bowen and
Evelyn A. Early*

Indiana University Press
Bloomington and Indianapolis

Manufactured in the United States of America

Library of Congress Cataloging-in-Publication Data
Everyday life in the Muslim Middle East / edited by Donna Lee Bowen
and Evelyn A. Early.
    p.   cm. — (Indiana series in Arab and Islamic studies)
    Includes bibliographical references (p.   ) and index.
    ISBN 0-253-31253-1 (alk. paper). — ISBN 0-253-20779-7 (pbk. :
alk. paper)
    1. Middle East—Social life and customs. 2. Africa, North—Social
life and customs. I. Series. II. Series: Bowen, Donna Lee, date.
III. Series: Early, Evelyn A., date.
DS57.E94   1992
909'.04927—dc20   92-40710

4 5 6 7 8 03 02 01 00 99

For our parents
and for
Amelia Aleene

CONTENTS

Part II   Gender Relations

Part III   Home, Community, and Work

PREFACE

This anthology was inspired by the editors' frustration with the paucity of supplementary teaching materials for Middle East courses and by our conviction of the importance of literary and primary sources in teaching those courses. Our sources include texts regularly read by Middle Eastern Muslims—including the Quran, popular pamphlets sold in sidewalk kiosks, and contemporary literature, as well as personal narratives. Likewise, we sought fieldwork reports by scholars recently engaged in research.

From friends and colleagues from our graduate days and our fieldwork in the Middle East, we assembled a panel of Middle East scholars and solicited their ideas and reading lists. We were not surprised to see that almost everyone used paperback novels and short story collections translated from Arabic, Persian, Turkish, and other area languages. Nor were we surprised at complaints about the high cost of books, making it impossible for students to purchase a spectrum of books to cover a wide geographic and subject area.

We compiled a list of literature in translation and another of colleagues recently back from studying Islam in Iran, tribal poetry in Yemen, childrearing in Morocco, and so on. We actively solicited articles that we felt would fit the reader's focus. Compiling lists was easy; cutting them was not. There were many aspects of Middle Eastern Muslim life to cover, including family, gender roles and socialization, village, town, jobs, urban migration, religion, medicine, expressive arts, and more. Then there were the theoretical issues implicit in our courses: modernization, secularization, the demographic revolution, social and economic development, "dependency," high and low culture, everyday life.

We devised elaborate grids to determine the variety of our articles: rural/ urban, Sunni/Shiʻi, women/men; and at one point we had an article for each country in the Middle East. Then we worried about including every religious and ethnic group before determining that "representative" was more useful than "inclusive." We found that we had too many "women" articles and had to cut back and introduce some "men" ones. We also found that Morocco and Egypt predominated geographically; not only were they the countries of our own research, they were also among the countries where research was easier to undertake in the 1970s and 1980s. When we had finished the initial draft—including all that we thought necessary to introduce a university student or general reader to everyday life in the Middle East—we had a manuscript of more than 1,200 pages. Publishers advised us to cut material drastically.

Our next task was cutting the book down to size in order to achieve a shorter, balanced manuscript. In most cases we were able to save original solicited pieces and articles not previously published. But each cut was difficult; we were personally convinced of the worth of each selection and, moreover, that all students of the Middle East needed the information in each article.

We then considered different methods of organizing the material. After several experiments and helpful comments from reviewers, we assembled the articles, using the theme of everyday life—starting with growing up in a family. We discussed and drafted in several venues—which over the course of doing the book ranged over the continental United States and the Middle East as assignments took us away.

Our first thanks go to our panel, whom we queried in early days and some of whom sent us letter after letter with suggestions and feedback. We list the entire panel here, including members whose articles were subsequently included: Lois Beck, Anne Betteridge, Frederick M. Denny, Fred M. Donner, Elizabeth W. Fernea, Robert A. Fernea, Michael M. J. Fischer, Erika Friedl, Leonard Helfsott, Carl F. Petry, Marilyn R. Waldman.

Next we thank the National Endowment for the Humanities for their confidence in our initial proposal. We feel that our anthology provides the kind of humanistic information on the Middle East which is consonant with NEH's mission and that their grant (which provided crucial support for research, phone calls, photocopying, and consultants) was well spent. We, of course, assume responsibility for the different turn the manuscript has taken.

No project is possible without institutional support. We would like to thank David Leege, Director of the Center for the Study of Man, University of Notre Dame, for providing an institutional home and intellectual support for this project in its first two years. Research assistants Purnima Bose at Notre Dame and Kathleen Morrison and Kimberley Swartz at the University of Houston helped with Early's evaluation of reader materials in class.

We owe a great debt to Brigham Young University for generously facilitating the grant through its final year and for critical scholarly and monetary support in seeing the project through to completion. Carol Hardman of the Research Office at BYU, Martin B. Hickman, Stan Albrecht, Don Fleming, Joyce Penrod, and Marilyn Webb of the College of Family, Home and Social Sciences, and Marie Cornwall of the Women's Research Institute all gave practical help as well as encouragement. Kristine Manwaring devoted two years of work during her university education to this project and contributed invaluable assistance in the early stages. Sally Turner Johnson's skill with language improved the final draft. In addition, students in subsequent years of classes at BYU, Notre Dame, and the University of Houston criticized articles and aided in evaluating selections and introductions.

We are grateful beyond words to Elizabeth W. Fernea and Dale F. Eickelman, both scholars committed to further Western understanding of the Middle East. Whether that commitment or our friendship motivated them to spend hours and hours graciously reviewing and re-reviewing our manuscript, their effort resulted in suggestions critical to shaping this volume.

Many other colleagues and contributors provided insights and support along the way. Michael Sells went far beyond scholarly collegiality in writing on and discussing pre-Islamic values which shaped the subsequent Muslim world. Abdel-Salam Al Ujaili kindly reviewed the translation of his work included here. The critical eyes of Dorothy Andrake and Mary Hegland produced photographic insight into the Middle East. We appreciate the help, talent, and discernment of Mahmoud Ayoub, Bill Beeman, Juan Campo, Kathy Ewing, Jane Gaffney, Gary Leiser, Dil Parkinson, Marcie Patton, John Perry, and Robert Staab in suggesting sources, translating, writing, and criticizing the materials.

Janet Rabinowitch of the Indiana University Press offered much more than the customary services of an editor and is probably happier than we to see this project finished. Her patience and confidence were key to the project.

The problems of transliterating terms for this book vividly demonstrate the diversity of the Middle East. While there are standard transliteration systems for literary Arabic and Persian (for example, those used by the *International Journal of Middle Eastern Studies*), rendering colloquial dialects from a variety of areas is more problematic. Arabic colloquial dialects have no agreed-upon pattern of transliteration as pronunciation differs sufficiently to prevent any one standard transliteration for the variety of colloquial languages. No one system exists which resolves the transliteration conflicts between literary Arabic and colloquial dialects.

It was difficult for us to standardize the transliteration of Arabic and Persian words used in this book in a manner which would make the word clear to the lay reader and evocative of the written or spoken language for the linguist. We aim to make the terms recognizable to students of Arabic or Persian and understandable for readers new to the area. Our solution has been to systematize more than to standardize. We set comprehensive criteria as best we could, but did not attempt to make all terms conform to a single standard. We simplified the transliteration as much as possible while at the same time we preserved the sounds of language in the Middle East.

Various consonants in Arabic and Persian are not used in English. The most difficult to transliterate properly are the ʿayn and the hamza (at times a vowel, at times a glottal stop). We have transliterated the ʿayn as ʿ. The hamza is used only when the author made a point of including it—for example, *Quran* but *maʾmur*.

Arabic has three long vowels, which for the most part we have not represented. Also, we have not differentiated the emphatic consonants from the nonemphatic.

We transliterated terms from colloquial dialects to best represent the pronunciation of that area. The *gallabiya* of Egypt becomes the *jellaba* of Morocco. We transliterated some Arabic terms in a colloquial transliteration to reflect the pronunciation conventions described in a given article (*hsuma*, Moroccan Arabic). We note different pronunciations of the same word in Arabic and Persian (*qadi* in Arabic, *qazi* in Persian). The careful reader will also note words borrowed from European languages (*piastre*) and Arabic terms which have been absorbed into English or French (*bedouin* or *caid*). In each of these cases we have noted the derivation of the term in the glossary. Occasionally, we follow the author's use of words or names transliterated in the French convention—the French *Bou Chaib* as opposed to *Bou Shai'ib*.

We retain media conventions in the transliteration of person and place names familiar to readers in a certain form (Hussein, Quran, Nasser).

We trust that the specialists who read this book will appreciate the reason for discrepancies in our transliteration system. Too, we hope that the reader uninitiated in Middle Eastern languages will catch some of the flavor of literature and speech so vital to knowledge of the area.

Everyday Life
in the
Muslim
Middle
East

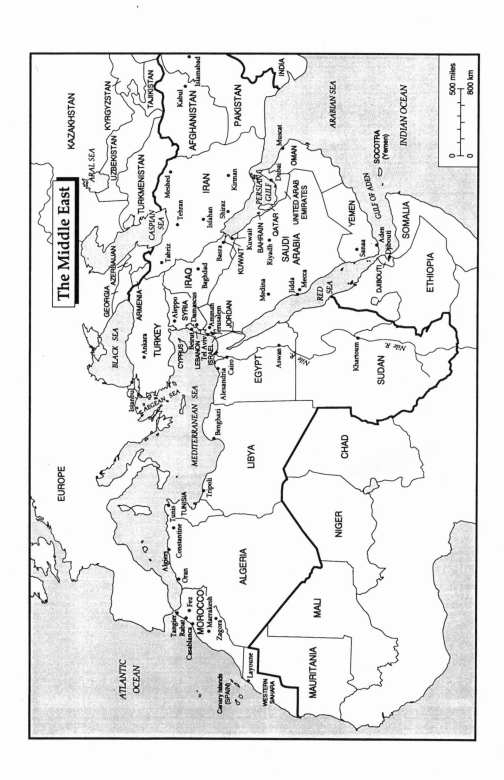

The Middle East

EUROPE

ATLANTIC OCEAN

KAZAKHSTAN

KYRGYZSTAN

ARAL SEA

UZBEKISTAN

TAJIKISTAN

TURKMENISTAN

GEORGIA

AZERBAIJAN

ARMENIA

CASPIAN SEA

• Meshed

• Islamabad

• Kabul

AFGHANISTAN

PAKISTAN

• INDIA

BLACK SEA

• Ankara

TURKEY

• Tabriz

• Tehran

IRAN

• Isfahan

• Kirman

• Shiraz

ARABIAN SEA

INDIAN OCEAN

• Muscat

OMAN

• Dubai

PERSIAN GULF

UNITED ARAB EMIRATES

SOCOTRA (Yemen)

GULF OF ADEN

Istanbul

CYPRUS

AEGEAN SEA

• Aleppo

SYRIA

• Damascus

LEBANON

Beirut

Tel Aviv

ISRAEL

Jerusalem

Amman

JORDAN

Baghdad

IRAQ

• Basra

Kuwait

KUWAIT

BAHRAIN

QATAR

Riyadh

SAUDI ARABIA

YEMEN

• Sanaa

Aden

Djibouti

DJIBOUTI

SOMALIA

MEDITERRANEAN SEA

• Benghazi

Alexandria

Cairo

• Aswan

EGYPT

Nile R.

Nile R.

• Medina

• Jidda

• Mecca

RED SEA

Khartoum

SUDAN

ETHIOPIA

• Tripoli

LIBYA

CHAD

• Tunis

TUNISIA

• Constantine

Algiers

• Oran

ALGERIA

NIGER

• Fez

Tangier

Rabat

MOROCCO

• Marrakesh

Casablanca

Zagora

MALI

Layoune

WESTERN SAHARA

MAURITANIA

Canary Islands (SPAIN)

0   500 miles

0   800 km

INTRODUCTION

This anthology is designed to give Western readers a sense of what it is like to live in the Middle East in the latter part of the twentieth century. The Middle East is perhaps the most difficult region of the world for Westerners to comprehend. We are more familiar with its stereotypes, often inaccurate, than with its specificity. The area seems rife with contradictions. Several factors are responsible for this: Westerners tend to be unfamiliar with the region itself, and they know few Middle Easterners personally. Media accounts emphasize the tangled politics and history of conflict in the area. We lack the more immediate image which might be garnered from an encounter with everyday life of ordinary Middle Easterners.

In preparing this book, we have worked from the assumption that one can learn much about another culture by examining the daily, simple acts that are performed by all people—often without their thinking or remarking upon the significance of these actions. The materials presented here emphasize life as Middle Easterners live it. We have chosen to focus on five areas: generations and life passages; gender relations; home, community, and work; religious expression; and performance and entertainment. To survey the region broadly, we include examples from Iran and Afghanistan in the East to Morocco in the West. Selections treat such varied topics as childrearing in a Moroccan town, the effects of war on children's lives in Lebanon and Afghanistan, an Afghani courtship and marriage, visiting rituals in the sheikhdoms of the United Arab Emirates, boasting and exaggeration in the Lebanese countryside, the working life of an editor on a Palestinian daily newspaper, and Syrian television comedy.

EVERYDAY LIFE

The approach used here has evolved as social scientists have focused on ordinary people's lives rather than on abstract theories of social action. Fernand Braudel, through his pioneering work in cosmopolitan history, has legitimated the historical study of everyday life. Henri LeFebvre's *La Vie Quo-*

tidienne opened a new chapter in modern social science. Scholars such as LeFebvre, Pierre Bourdieu, Lloyd A. Fallers, Clifford Geertz, and Victor W. Turner have emphasized how ordinary life is organized and what its cultural principles are. Everyday life studies demonstrate how abstract cultural principles may be used in analysis of data gathered on the ground. For example, such culture in praxis studies demonstrate what kinship or religiosity or nationalism means by considering what happens and what is said when someone marries, visits a shrine, seeks medical care, supports a leader, or undertakes community projects.

The everyday life approach is extremely helpful in understanding distinctions such as traditional and modern and in analyzing concepts such as patriarchy and honor. What, for instance, do we learn about traditional and modern medicine when a Muslim Middle Eastern woman concerned about infertility consults a doctor in a mother-child health clinic and then visits a shrine to vow that she will sacrifice a lamb if she becomes pregnant? She relies equally on clinical medicine and a local interpretation of her religion. Or, in another case, what can we conclude when a devout Muslim merchant strikes a business deal to import revealing sequinned Parisian dresses? Does he see a conflict between his religious belief and the sale of ostentatious products from Western material society?

In the readings that follow, individuals such as a Syrian physician and a Moroccan brotherhood leader decide how to use scientific and religious knowledge to cure disease and to deal with water shortages. Their decisions illustrate the complex cultural patterns of the Muslim Middle East. Whether their decisions are traditional or modern is hard to say. Most of everyday life is a mix of the old and the new. The cultural system that holds it all together for Muslim Middle Easterners is a rich tapestry woven with strands of Islamic and local customs in a historic framework. Everyday culture blends classic and local religious traditions to solve problems—finding a job, raising children, mending a quarreling community, combatting inflation. It is in this arena that people work out cultural conflicts between tradition and modernity or religiosity and secularism wrought by the rapid changes in the Middle East. They debate the merits of traditional irrigation canals and generator-energized pumps, of amulets and antibiotics, of family and state.

Only by examining the nuts and bolts of everyday life does one gain an appreciation of the overlap, the mix, of the old and the new. Lloyd A. Fallers, in a study of cultural life in Edremit, Turkey, notes how people live a routine which represents an implicit compromise between Muslim and secular ideologies:

> Ordinary people are not automatons. They are not guided through life by the conventions of "encoded" culture and patterned social relations in an utterly routine way. There are occasions when they reflect, decide, strive and succeed or fail in a highly self-conscious manner. But for most people,

most of the time, life is routine. Encoded culture informs their social action quite implicitly—which is why these systems of meaning are often difficult to get at—the social action informed by shared meaning flows along almost mechanically. (1974: 9–10)

As the people of Edremit juggle different cultural codes, so everyone selects which cultural codes or guidelines to follow as occasions arise: religious? nationalist? traditionalist? secularist? local? patriarchal? Life is lived as a cultural counterpoint between one's heritage and the pragmatic demands of one's life situation.

In the selections in this book, the ordinary and the mundane provide a key to understanding Middle Eastern culture. Situated social discourse—how people explain their unique experiences—affords insight into a person's view of his or her culture. Several selections are self-conscious studies of the personal discourse of reciting the Quran or the social discourse of poetry, folk tales, jokes, lies, and satires. For example, a Yemeni's poetry articulates the political situation. Egyptian bedouin women's poetry exposes personal emotions. Some accounts mix the Islamic with the local context. Traditional tales and heroes may be celebrated on television programs, at national cultural festivals, or in stories people tell one another.

MIDDLE EASTERN MUSLIM CULTURE

A major part of Middle Eastern experience has been said to be based on Muslim culture. But what is Muslim culture? As many Muslims say, Islam exists for all times and all places. Do the Quaranic laws and precepts of the seventh century offer a message limited in time and space, or are they universal in application? And if so, or if not, what does this mean in everyday religious and secular life?

Muslim Middle Easterners from myriad demographic backgrounds do not engage in social discourse, raise children, or practice rituals in the same way. The ideal or typical "Muslim family" may not really exist, given that some Muslims live in extended families in villages and others in nuclear families in cities. A "Muslim state" or "Muslim society" is difficult to define. Middle Eastern Muslims differ in terms of geography, ethnicity, religion, class, gender, and local custom. Ethnic variations as in Iraq, Turkey, and Iran, with their Kurdish populations, or in Morocco and Algeria, with their Arab and Berber groupings, may influence politics more than religion does. Upper-class Muslims may have more in common with members of their class (including Christians) in another country than they do with lower-class fellow nationals.

Differentiation by religion in the Middle East is tricky. While religious beliefs and sectarian allegiances run deep, large areas of commonality exist as well. Although this book concentrates on Muslims, many observations apply equally to Christians, Jews, and other religious groups long resident in Middle Eastern lands. The common cultural heritage, strong nationalist feelings—whether Arab, Turkish, Iranian, Kurdish, or nation-state loyalties—and similar political situations can blur religious differences. The sharp, politically based conflict between the Israelis and the Palestinians and other Arabs is now and has historically been tied more to politics, territorial rights, and nationalism than to religion.

Muslim Middle Easterners draw from varied sources of inspiration and knowledge. Religious sources include passages from the Quran or from prophetic tradition, as well as religious rituals such as the Quran-prescribed pilgrimage to Mecca and local customs such as visits to local shrines. Another important cultural source for such important Middle Eastern values as honor, bravery, hospitality, and generosity is pre-Islamic Arab poetry. Saudi Arabia is the home not only of the holy cities of Islam, but also of the "Arab" (bedouin) identity celebrated in that poetry. As Michael Sells explains:

> The pre-Islamic ode was infused with the bedouin ethos of honor, courage, generosity and the hero's refusal to let impending death distract him from the pleasure of the moment. . . . Though Islam was to change much of the bedouin ethos, banning the wine drinking and tribal warfare that were so much a part of it, the emphasis on generosity, upon the willingness to spend one's life rather than hoarding it . . . remain[ed]. (1988:3)

Pre-Islamic values of generosity and courage endure in the life of twentieth-century villagers in Lebanon, where young men carefully fashion an image of nobility (*karama*) and bravery, and among urban toughs in Cairo, where apocryphal tales of lads saving a family and its reputation abound. The pre-Islamic genre of satirical poetry directed at enemy tribes may be transformed into the political humor of cartoons, jokes, and comedies directed against contemporary governments. Pre-Islamic Arab values combine with Islamic values such as piety and reverence and with secular values such as patriarchy to form the rich, complex Middle Eastern Muslim culture we encounter in this collection.

THE HISTORICAL CONTEXT OF MIDDLE EASTERN LIFE

Individual lives tap into a kind of compressed history, a time tunnel which emphasizes certain periods of history and particular events. Most Middle Easterners speak often of two historical periods. The first, which serves to define themselves and their community, begins with the coming of Islam in the seventh century. Islam provides a safe, secure touchstone which ensures that today's Muslim is part of a long, illustrious, and well-defined tradition. The second and less secure period begins with the intrusion of the West.

Whether this event is dated from the eleventh century and the Crusades, from the end of the Second World War, or from some date in between, the import of Western incursion remains the same: a challenge to traditional patterns of action and thought, and—most important—a challenge to the supremacy of Islam as the unquestioned arbitrator of intellectual process and community guidance.

Although the revelations of Muhammad came in the seventh century, long after the appearance of Judaism and Christianity, they built upon the teachings of the Jewish Torah and the Christian New Testament. Muslims consider that Islam, as God's revelation, has guided men since the time of Father Adam. A popular Egyptian television serial, "There Is No God but God," entranced audiences throughout the Middle East a few years ago. Its major premise was that the belief in one god, *the* God, predated Muhammad and was taught through the traditions of the patriarchs as recorded in the Quran as well as in the Torah and the Gospels. Television audiences followed complicated subplots of intrigues by idolatrous Egyptian priests, romances in the royal family, and wars waged against Egypt. But the event which dominated the serial was the conversion of a pharaoh of Egypt to the true faith by believers in the one God of the monotheistic religions of Judaism, Christianity, and Islam.

Islam recognizes its debt to the teachings of the patriarchs of the Torah and the Gospels by calling adherents to Judaism, Christianity, and, later, Zoroastrianism the "People of the Book." The appellation is bestowed in recognition of their scriptures and affords them special status under Muslim rule. This confidence in an unbroken chain of prophets from Adam to Muhammad, in the oneness of the message of the prophets, and in Islam's emphasis upon a single deity established it as a world religion. Within a few decades of its appearance, Islam spread swiftly throughout the Byzantine and Sassanid empires and became a major world force both politically and intellectually.

A chain of victories which began with the conversion of the city of Mecca and of the rest of Arabia to Islam and was followed by the conquest of Syria, Iraq, Egypt, North Africa, Central Asia, parts of Spain, Anatolia, and the Balkans reinforced the sense of destiny of the Muslim community (*umma*). Within one or two centuries, however, the Islamic empire began to fracture into smaller, geographically distinct entities, some preaching sectarian differences. Rule by caliphs (*khulafa*; singular, *khalifa*) understood to be worthy successors of the Prophet Muhammad, was replaced by the rule of princes who were distinguished more by military prowess than by righteousness. Throughout the Middle East, North Africa, and into southern Asia, Muslim scholars and scientists built upon Greek philosophy and science as well as on the scientific traditions of other civilizations—India, Egypt, Mesopotamia, Iran—to establish a glorious civilization centered on the Quran and Islamic learning.

The second major historical reference point for Muslims, the challenge to

Islam, began in the eleventh century when the Crusaders mounted a success-ful campaign against Jerusalem, one of the three holy cities of Islam. Muslims were incredulous that uncultured Frankish barbarians could defeat a Muslim army. In the succeeding centuries, cracks in the facade of their highly pol-ished Muslim civilization widened as European armies laid siege to the capi-tal cities of the Middle East. Napoleon's landing in Egypt in 1798 signaled the era of European occupation and the dawn of imperialism and modernization. For Middle Easterners, the advent of the Europeans was simply the arrival of yet one more outside power ambitious to control the "crossroads of the world" and to exploit the region's natural resources, including local labor. In 1830 the French launched their conquest of Algeria, beginning a century-long wave of European conquest and political domination throughout the Middle East.

As the Ottoman Empire declined, special commercial courts guaranteed the rights of resident Europeans to pursue business interests. Europeans both shipped their manufactured goods to the Middle East and extracted the re-gion's resources. The French cultivated grapes in North Africa and, in later years, ran their factories with North African laborers. The British bought cot-ton from Egypt and Sudan and reexported it to the same countries as woven cloth from the British mills; French-run companies grew tobacco in Syria.

Muslim intellectuals realized that military defeats and European occupa-tions stemmed both from the weakness of Middle Eastern leaders and from the success of superior European weapons. Ultimately, the most serious threat was that posed by Western rationality and technology to traditional Muslim scholarship and belief systems. Muslim education centered on faith-ful use of Muslim texts: unquestioned obedience to revelation, steadfast ad-herence to the *sunna* and *hadith* (words and actions of Muhammad and his community), and study of the vast literature of Islamic jurisprudence and religious principles. Western education focused on empirical knowledge. The collision between reason and faith (in a system modulated over a millennium and a half to emphasize faith over reason) produced an intellectual dilemma. How does a tradition of faith compete in a world based on rationality?

Colonized Middle Easterners—Egyptians, Algerians, Syrians, Moroccans, and others—realized that they must understand, if not use, the sciences and systems of their rulers in order to expel them. Arab nationalism was originally a secular movement formed by both Christian and Muslim Arabs. Struggles for independence were often bitter. Algeria won freedom from France in 1962 after sustained warfare and heavy casualties. Palestine has yet to achieve independence. Most Middle Eastern countries see Israel, itself a na-tion which fought against the British mandate, as a Western implant which blocks Palestinian independence.

Independence which came in the 1950s and 1960s was heady, and new-found nationalism promised to overcome social, ethnic, economic, and reli-gious cleavage. But as years have passed and as governments have not fulfilled hopes for socioeconomic equity, divisions dominate the political arena. Wars, political assassinations, and coups d'etat have occurred in almost every country. Political instability is common. Middle Easterners are weary of disrupted lives, violent death, broken families, shattered economies, and ravaged croplands. For many, life is on hold.

Today, along with having to face problems of achieving political consensus, Middle Eastern countries lack the economic and technological infrastructures to deal with overpopulation, the fast growth of urban areas, and the resultant struggle over scarce resources. Economically, the presence, or absence, of oil reserves splits Middle Eastern countries into haves and have nots.

European influence, occupation, colonization, and, as many Arabs call the colonial period, the time of imperialism, are constant referents for Middle Easterners today. They are ambivalent, often opposing the West at the same time that they hope to emulate Western achievements and to avoid Western failures. Western success is measured in terms of prosperity, technological advancement, national strength, democratization and popular participation, and, in sum, the ability to go one's own way with one's beliefs intact without being influenced by outside forces. Western failure is gauged in terms of materialism, family breakdown, drugs, consumerism, and loss of religion—to name a few. Middle Easterners are puzzled by a Western society which does not care for its elder population. It seems to them that the moral core of Western society has collapsed.

Middle Eastern opposition to the West is fueled by memories of colonization coupled with such current realities as economic dependency, political vulnerability, and the series of military losses to Israel. From Algeria to Iran, indigenous Islamic political movements oppose Western influence and local political corruption. Islamic movements strive to create a uniquely Muslim society, epistemology, and technology—often through political action. Muslims frequently express a need to reunite the spiritual and religious side of life with the political and the commercial.

Westerners tend to lump all Islamic groups together under the rubric of "Islamic fundamentalism." The word "fundamentalism," which does not exist in Arabic, is defined by Christian religious groups as holding or returning to basic principles—in Christian terms to particular biblical teachings. Western application of the term to Islam confuses the issue. The misunderstanding is compounded by the way in which religious "fundamentalism" or activism has been associated with political violence. While fringe Muslim activist groups have grabbed headlines—the Hezbollah in Lebanon is an example—others have sought legitimate power through political organization and orderly recourse to the ballot box, as is the case of the Islamist party in Jordan. Other Muslim groups focus upon religious learning and are not politically motivated.

The application of Islam to an individual's life has taken many forms during the past decade. Iranians used Islam as a rallying point to eject their

Shah and set up a government predicated upon their understanding of Islam. Throughout the region some women have adopted Islamic dress to demonstrate personal modesty and piety. Islamic group members' search for religious roots includes such academic ventures as testing Prophetic medical cures in modern laboratories and debating the meaning of the Muslim community (*umma*) for the field of sociology. Muslims who are moved to political action are responding both to an interpretation of Islam and to an environment riddled with social and economic problems. At the same time, many Christian Middle Easterners feel threatened by Muslim activist political groups.

THE MIDDLE EAST: SOCIAL, DEMOGRAPHIC, AND INDUSTRIAL REVOLUTIONS

The Middle East is an ecologically diverse area with mountain ranges, pasture land, cultivated areas, deserts and oases, and urban areas. Fifty years ago, the majority of inhabitants were agriculturalists. Today, some Middle Eastern countries have a higher percentage of urban population than Europe. In Egypt it has reached 50 percent; in Saudi Arabia, 73 percent (World Bank, *Development Report, 1990*).

Urban migrants are as much pushed by land fragmentation as pulled by limited industrial opportunities. Until recently, migrants not finding jobs in urban areas have left their countries for Europe or the labor-hungry Gulf region. However, the 1991 Gulf war caused the exodus of thousands of well-trained Palestinians and millions of other migrant workers from host countries. Upheavals always spell difficult changes for workers, and this situation may take years to settle again—further straining already stretched economies in the meantime.

Urban areas are growing at a rate roughly double that of the population as a whole, and in most countries the urban population is jammed into one or two major cities. Adding to the demographic load, the population of the Middle East is young, with some 42 percent under the age of fifteen.

As politics occupies policy makers, a quieter but potentially more potent demographic revolution sweeps the Middle East. Decreased infant mortality brought by improved quality of life has yet to be counterbalanced by effective family planning. Current population growth will double populations within thirty to forty years. Economic and health planners who encourage family planning have now been joined by a few Muslim religious leaders who preach that the Muslim community should measure its strength by the quality, not the quantity, of its believers. For family planning to succeed, parents must become convinced that more children are a drain on family resources rather than insurance for one's old age or insurance against possible infant death. As educational levels rise and as public health services make contraception more readily available, attitudes about family planning are beginning to change.

In ancient times, the Middle East was a crossroads of commerce. Today, nation states of the area trade primarily in agricultural products, oil, and labor. Agricultural producers include Morocco, Syria, Egypt, Iraq, Turkey, and Iran. Oil exporters include Saudi Arabia, Iran, Iraq, Libya, Algeria, Kuwait, and the small states of the Persian Gulf. The oil-rich nations of Libya, Saudi Arabia, and the Gulf states import labor. Yemen, Egypt, Algeria, Tunisia, and Morocco export labor to Europe as well as to the oil states. The disparity in earning power between countries with oil and those without is dramatic. The per capita income in the United Arab Emirates for 1988 was $14,410 while in Egypt it was $760.

Industrialization may be the greatest challenge to tradition faced by the Middle East. Traditional economies where household cottage industries and agriculture were the main modes of production are giving way to the wage labor of industrial production and agribusiness. The vast majority of urban unemployed are unskilled laborers who may find occasional work in the large informal economic sector. Overeducated college graduates often wait years for placement in overstaffed public-sector bureaucracies while blue-collar skilled-labor jobs go begging. Egyptian office workers moonlight by driving taxis or working in coffee shops. Egyptian professors offer multiple evening tutorials to beat inflation and augment their meager salary.

Many skilled workers have left their native countries for more lucrative employment in the Gulf, Libya, or Europe. North African migrants returning home from France, urban-educated children returning to the village, young professionals imbued with the ideas of Western universities—all experience the strain of readjusting to the communities in which they grew up. Those left behind face major adjustments as well. Women left at home take on new responsibilities running their farms and workshops; children miss their absent fathers.

The social dislocation as a result of migration and overburdened urban infrastructures is challenging the entire traditional system and is providing additional fuel for nationalist, Islamic, and other movements of social discontent. Change, on both individual and societal levels, seems to be the order of the day. Given the challenges of the late twentieth century, how do Middle Easterners keep going? What values—family, religion, honor, generosity— serve as guideposts for their lives? What strengths do Middle Easterners draw from the patterns of their everyday lives? One must not lose sight of the fact that, in the face of all the upheaval, most Middle Easterners worry most of the time about their families and their communities. As long as these are threatened, the area will not be peaceful. Thus, it is with the family, with generations and life passages, that this anthology begins.

REFERENCES

Braudel, Fernand. 1981. *Civilization and Capitalism: 15th–18th Century*, trans. Sian Reynolds. Volume 1, *The Structures of Everyday Life*. Volume 2, *The Limits of the Possible*. New York: Harper and Row.

Fallers, Lloyd. 1974. *The Social Anthropology of the Nation State*. Chicago: Aldine Publishing Co.

LeFebvre, Henri. 1971. *Everyday Life in the Modern World*, trans. Sacha Rabinovich. New York: Harper and Row.

Sells, Michael. 1988. "The Heritage of the Desert." Unpublished manuscript.

World Bank. *Development Report, 1990*. Washington D.C.: World Bank.

PART ONE

Generations and Life Passages

INTRODUCTION

Family life, the arena for the passage from birth through circumcision, adolescence, marriage, and death, varies less by country than it does by locale. Bedouins and villagers usually live a more traditional life in extended families with all the sons and wives under one roof. More attuned to the rhythm of the seasons and less rushed by the daily press of commuting to jobs and the eight-hour workday, rural people focus on family ties as a basis for activities—home, work, socializing, entertainment. Urbanites often live in separate, nuclear families. Newly arrived migrants to large cities, separated from grandmother, mother, father, and siblings, search out neighbors to help them adjust to their new surroundings. The diversions offered by city living are often poor substitutes for the support system of an extended family. National and international labor migration has disrupted households while simultaneously placing peasants and day laborers in an international market of remittances and consumerism.

BIRTH

Children are valuable, and their birth is celebrated. At a seven-day naming ceremony in traditional quarters of Cairo, the newborn is shaken in a sieve while the midwife admonishes the child to obey his or her parents. As a proud American father hands out cigars, so the traditional Egyptian mother distributes packets of dried nuts, symbolic of fertility, to her well-wishers.

Children ensure continuation of the family and community; they are, as one *hadith* (religious tradition) states, "the delight of life." Families dote on children, and a toddler amid a group of adolescents or adults is overwhelmed with affection. Susan Schaefer Davis, in her article on childrearing, describes role models particular to Morocco.

Muslims are expected (not by religious commandment, but by strong recommendation) to marry and to produce progeny to increase the Muslim community and to bless their own family. An unmarried person is a social, not an economic, misfit and is shielded by family members from want or deprivation. The family into which one is born, the natal family, is the most important social group in one's life. It provides protection, food, shelter, income, reputation, and honor. The family is the reference for assistance as one grows up, finds a spouse, job, and home, raises one's own family, and adjusts to changing social circumstances. The family mediates between the individual and the outside world, and Middle Easterners naturally assume that relatives will be favored. One's family name is a ready-made identification which reveals to all both one's reputation and one's access to assistance.

Position within a family—whether married, single, divorced, widowed, a parent or childless—also defines one's social status in the community. A man is autonomous upon reaching adulthood, usually at age eighteen, but he is expected to support his natal as well as his own family. Traditionally a woman gains status when she gives birth to a male child, and she pours immense energy into his upbringing. When the first son is born, both parents are renamed "mother" (*um*) and "father of Muhammad" (*abu*). The mother-son tie, which some say is the most powerful a woman or man will ever have, is typically a close and loving emotional relationship of strong dependency. Whereas daughters marry and leave the family, sons support their parents in old age.

The tie between brother and sister runs a close second to the mother-son relation. Ideally, a brother will defend sisters in need throughout their lives, just as a sister will care for brothers as a kind of second mother. Although a woman may marry out of her natal family, she generally carries its name, continues to be close to her brothers—sometimes closer than to her husband—and remains a potential source of dishonor to them.

Circumcision, which occurs between infancy and age ten, is the main rite of passage between birth and marriage. In countries such as Egypt and Morocco, it is celebrated with parties and many congratulations. In traditional quarters of Cairo, there is a striking juxtaposition of a solemn religious event and a carnival. Young boys to be circumcised are dressed in white in the manner of a *hajj* returning from pilgrimage. Mounted on a horse, the boys proceed from the mosque at the time of the sunset prayer. Among the throngs of family, friends, and strangers watching and cheering them on are vendors of sweets and multicolored paper hats. Children who have not been circumcised receive a paper hat as a consolation prize.

War, in its many forms no stranger to the Middle East, has forced many children to age rapidly. Louise Berdal describes how children fare in the war zones of Beirut and Afghanistan.

MARRIAGE

Marriage is a milestone whose romantic intrigues and festivities provide major entertainment for all. Young Middle Eastern men and woman, contemplating their marriages, whisper about potential spouses and about whether romantic or traditionally arranged marriages are better. They eagerly await wedding parties where young and old crowd in to listen to music and drink thick sweet *sharbat*. Even luxurious hotel weddings assume the informality of home as children cavort and women ululate. Despite all this celebration, families take marriage seriously. Marriage is an economic contract negotiated by older males of the two families. They determine the bride price (*mahr* or *sadaq*) paid to the woman's father, as well as clothes, jewelry, and furnishings to be given by each side. The bride price ideally includes a sum of money to be set aside and paid to the wife in case of divorce.

Once the couple is "engaged" via a legally binding marriage contract, they may visit each other at home and may date. The wedding party and consummation may occur months or even years later. After the party, the couple sets up housekeeping together. Courtship, engagement, and marriage customs differ significantly by location, education, and social status. In Afghanistan—as Margaret A. Mills illustrates with the story "Of the Dust and the Wind"—the bride and groom may not have met before the wedding. In some Berber areas of southern Morocco, the bride lives chastely with the groom's family for months before the wedding in order to become familiar with the routine of the family. In the wealthy strata of Lebanon, Egypt, and Tunisia, wedding guests wearing French designer dresses and holding glasses of Scotch whiskey circulate around a hotel ballroom and toast the young couple's health.

OLD AGE AND DEATH

Within the shelter of the family, old age is a time of reaping what one has sown. Traditionally, younger adults consult their elders on decisions about medical treatments, business deals, marriages, and political alliances. Responsibility, but not authority, passes to adult children. A mother is often de facto household head long after her husband is dead and the oldest son has gray hair.

Death is accepted as a natural part of life. Customarily, the funeral procession of wailing women and silent men carries the shrouded body to be buried facing Mecca before the first sunset following the death. It is traditional for the family to receive condolences afterward, either in arabesque tents set up for the occasion (as in Egypt) or at home. Guests read the *Fatiha* (the first verse of the Quran), drink tea or coffee, and listen to Quranic recitation. Women normally receive condolences during the day at home. As in the story excerpted here from a novel by Driss Chraibi, funerals, by invoking emotions with Quranic readings, tie death to the forces of life.

PASSAGES THROUGH LIFE
DIFFERENT LOCALES

Passages through life are determined by family and by custom. Childhood, marriage, parenting, old age—each is shaped by biology and society. The

Middle East embroiders different designs for the rituals marking each stage. Erika Friedl's "Traditional Songs from Boir Ahmad" shows one design in the songs and poetry with which Iranian villagers honor passages of life. Yusuf Abu Haggag's memoirs evoke Cairo street society's ideas of adulthood and virility against a background of street gangs and neighborhood butchershops.

All societies value the family, but not every society values patriarchy and family honor as in the Middle East. Even societies with a strong sense of honor may not believe that women's actions can dishonor the family in the way that Middle Easterners traditionally do. It is such cultural themes as honor and shame which shape the social drama of everyday life.

Until recently, the Middle Eastern family was not beset by Western social problems such as runaway children, the youth drug culture (which, however, has made inroads in the Middle East), and the neglected elderly. Indeed, many Middle Easterners still question how Western society can abandon unwanted children or grandparents at the time when they most need family care. Middle Easterners exposed to Western mores while working abroad may, as in Chraibi's "The Son's Return," experience difficulty in shifting gears from one culture to another.

As we read about different ceremonies, different family expectations for puberty and dating, different definitions of "adulthood," we may ask: What is distinctive about growing up in the Middle East? Has the Middle East escaped the younger generation's rebellion and the neglect of the elderly? Or are its values already changing? Is Islam critical to the strength of the family, or is something else—such as a strong patriarchy or the centrality of family identity—the linchpin? The details of the individual lives presented in the following selections address such broad cultural questions.

Traditional Songs from Boir Ahmad

Collected and Translated by Erika Friedl

The following songs about childbirth, marriage, and death are sung by women of the Boir Ahmad tribe in southwestern Iran during times of life crises. The metaphors range from young women's mascara to daily herding duties. —Eds.

BIRTH

Oh, the red-lipped beauty is in labor pains.
May God make it a boy.

Oh, my dear, oh, my sister,
your baby boy is crying.

WEDDING

The songs below comment on the events from courtship to actual wedding and were traditionally sung at the different stages of a wedding. Since the Islamic Revolution in Iran, singing of such songs is forbidden. There is no music at all at weddings in Iran now.

The first seven songs are love songs that could be sung at many occasions, not just at weddings.

Three things I ask of God:
a good horse, a good rifle, and a pair of brown eyes.

Oh, my uncles, are you heathens?
Speak up for me to get me the red-lipped beauty.

I wish I was your mascara brush
inside your jacket
next to your breasts.

I wish I was your rifle—
on your shoulder by day
and at night under your shawl.

(A woman is speaking.)

And if you went up in the sky
to hide behind rainclouds,
my eyes would play in yours.

Tell your mother I am at your service—
The beads around your neck have set me afire.

Last night while you carried your water sack,
  I saw your hips.
If your father asks a thousand Toman for you,
  I'll give him more.

Lucky the man who has a strong horse, a good rifle,
a soft-spoken mother-in-law and a pretty bride.

Tomorrow morning we'll fetch the bride
for the lion-groom's pleasure.

How nice it is to mount a brown horse
and ride from morning to night for the bride.

Get up, blossom, put on your shoes, it's time to go.
His horsemen are here, it is time to be bashful.

I tell you, dear, keep your house well.
The bride is crying—I am so young, I won't marry.

(A young bride and her mother are speaking.)

Mother of the bride, why are you crying?
On your daughter's cap are a hundred Toman worth
  of gold.

*(The gold refers to the gold coins which traditionally were
sewn on a bride's cap.)*

The orange blossom stepped out of her house
when her lion-groom's bridewealth appeared
out of the shade.

My God, how long am I to wait in the crowd
outside his house?

The moon is fading and the morning star is high.

*(A bride is complaining about having to wait in front of her
groom's house—her entourage is singing.)*

The bridal chamber is ready, a rich bridal chamber.
In it the lion-groom is playing with a tiger.

How pleasant is your bride chamber's fragrance.
The lion-groom's hands are in his bride's braids.

You have a rich skirt and a red scarf on your head,
and your husband will take care of all your troubles.

(Sung for a bride.)

If you want your husband to like you, swing your hips,
and early in the morning sprinkle rosewater on the bed.

(Sung for a bride.)

DEATH

*Songs of mourning are still sung by Iranian women, but only in private, no longer
at funerals.*

Angel of Death, give me time, I haven't yet finished
two tasks:
My oldest I haven't given a wife, my baby I
haven't brought up.

(For a woman with young children.)

She was pregnant and asked for a cradle,
   but her brother had no plain wood.
For her, he wanted to use the best sandalwood.

   (For a pregnant woman, or one who dies in childbirth)

I went to her house, but she wasn't there.
She left for the high mountain spring to wash
   her cotton skirt.

   (This and the following eight songs are for women, praising their beauty, wealth, and industry)

I looked down from the hilltop: she was
   about to milk her herd.
The swing rod on her buttering stand was
   of fragrant wood, tied with bright cotton.

Don't let her tent come down, it has forty ropes,
   all in place.
Tighten them firmly, clouds are in the sky.

The tents were still pitched up in the winter camp, but
she packed for the camp in the mountains.

Don't leave: spin a little more on your spindle, your
dowry isn't yet complete.

   (This song is sung mostly for young unmarried women.)

Fold your nice scarf, your pretty shirt, and put them
   in the bundle.
It is time to break camp and move up to the mountains.

The beautiful woman's necklace broke.
The beads of coral and gold dropped into her lap.

The woman left for her mother's so fast,
that neither a horseman nor a bird can catch up with her.

The two of us sisters went to pick flowers,
but rain and snow came down hard and we lost
   sight of each other.

Child, like a tree with roots in loose gravel,
like a tree, all dried up, you haven't born fruit.

(There are few mourning songs for children. It is said that mourning for children is harmful to the dead child's soul.)

The master hunter went on a hunt. Night fell, but he
didn't come back.
Either the tiger got his dog, or the night took him by
surprise.

(For a hunter, but also for any man.)

I saw your rifle, its butt full of blood.
Is it yours or that of a wild buck?

(For a hunter who died of bullet wounds, usually in a battle.)

A partridge with two chicks left them
    and sat down on a rock.
It has not come back all summer,
    and the eagle at the young.

(For a hunter who leaves young children.)

The lad with the fine white cap disappeared
    over the pass.
Don't call him, maybe he'll come back by himself.

(For a young man.)

This fine young man they put on a stretcher.
His hair has the fragrance of mountain flowers.

(For a young man.)

The gorge is filled with the thunder of gunshots.
The young man was killed there by a pair of tigers.

(For a young man killed in battle.)

Bang, bang, from the river comes the noise of battle.
The young men spoil for a fight.

(For a young man killed in battle.)

Boir Ahmad boy, let us look at you. A ten-bullet
   rifle is on your shoulder,
and a red flower-bullet wound is on your white shirt.

(For a young fighter.)

The girl's tears tinkle like bells. I don't know:
does she cry out of her own misery, or for her brother?

(Sung by a woman for her dead brother.)

Growing Up in Morocco

Susan Schaefer Davis

After observing childrearing in a north central Moroccan town in the mid-1970s, Susan Schaefer Davis concluded that children are much more durable than Americans consider them to be. She notes the critical importance of gender and the family patriline in childrearing. Males are preferred for social and economic reasons more than for religious considerations. —Eds.

INFANCY

Male babies are preferred to females in Morocco. The preference is based on the function of each sex within the family. Since Morocco is a patrilineal society (in which descent is traced through males), the son will remain a part of the family and eventually be responsible for the support of his mother and father in their old age. The daughter, on the other hand, will marry and reside outside the group and is considered as someone who will be lost to the family at marriage.[1]

Further, having a daughter is less desirable because the female offspring are considered a threat to the family honor, as was quite clearly revealed in an incident which occurred a few years prior to our residence in a Moroccan village. The daughter of one family had become pregnant by the son of the family next door. While both families seldom mentioned the incident, it was clear from local gossip that the girl was believed to be at fault and that her family had been more dishonored. The boy had left the village to study (his family was embarrassed enough to remove him from the scene), but his family suffered no great stigma. The girl had also left the area and was raising her baby in the city. Meanwhile, her mother and sisters were "snubbed" by the

Adapted from Susan Schaefer Davis, *Patience and Power: Women's Lives in a Moroccan Village.* Boston: Schenkman Books, 1983.

neighborhood women's groups and seldom participated in their activities, but rather spent most of their time isolated inside their home.

At birth, preference for males is indicated by the larger celebration held for the naming ceremony of a boy. Otherwise, boys and girls are treated quite similarly from birth to two years of age. Both are constantly in the company of their mothers; baby sitters are an unknown institution. True, a small baby may be left in the care of a young girl for a few minutes, but only infrequently.

Since nearly all babies are breastfed (I saw perhaps three baby bottles during my stay in the village), they are never far from their mothers. When the mother is working or walking, she carries the baby on her back in a cloth sling, which is tied in front, one end over the shoulder, the other under the opposite breast. This leaves her hands free for work or carrying and the baby seems to cause no inconvenience. Children are carried in this way, or ride on the hip of a younger sister when they are old enough, until they can walk well. Thus they are in nearly constant contact with their mothers and other members of the family.

When they are sitting and visiting, women lay babies across their laps or on a cushion next to them; they are seldom held in the arms except when nursing. One is amazed when one sees several children sound asleep during an evening women's party with loud music and conversation, but they have learned early to sleep in any atmosphere.

It is interesting that, despite constant contact with her child, the mother appears to harbor no resentment toward it. One has no sense that she feels it a burden or that it hinders her from doing other things; whatever she does, the baby comes along, as do everyone's babies. Such tolerance may be partially due to the fact that babies do not appear to be a problem or nuisance. They are fed on demand (even three or four times an hour) and are never allowed to cry more than a few seconds without being pacified, usually with the breast. The baby is frequently wrapped with a cloth, used as a diaper but without pins, which is changed when soiled. Because of the almost constant bodily contact, mothers also learn to sense when babies are about to urinate or defecate and may then remove them from the back and hold them out over the (usually dirt) floor. One mother claimed that her son had been "trained" at six months—that is, he urinated and defecated only at specific times, and only when he had been "put aside" to do so. Accidents did occur, but women never seemed irritated or upset about their soiled jellabas.

One of the few times when babies do cry is when they are teased, and this usually does not occur until near the end of infancy; they are not teasable until that age. Adults seem to enjoy frustrating a child, perhaps holding a toy just out of reach until it bursts into tears, and then giving it both the toy and a big, warm hug. One does not have the sense they want to hurt the child or see it suffer but that the reaction to such teasing is one of the few varieties of behavior exhibited by the child and they want to see it perform. The hugs afterward are always very reassuring, and the child is never left to cry un-comforted.

When a child is in a group of people with its mother, it becomes the object of everyone's attention only if there is nothing else to talk about—that is, the baby will be held and cuddled and briefly admired, but it is not the focal interest of the group. Even when alone with its mother, the child is always attended to when it makes a demand, but otherwise it takes second place to other activities. One seldom observes women saying "Ma-ma, Ma-ma" and encouraging the child to repeat, or helping a child to stand and take its first steps. The child does these things when it is ready; it is not pressured or encouraged to be precocious. Conversations based on the accomplishments of one's children, so common among women in America, are not heard in Morocco. To a degree, Moroccan women do realize themselves through their children, especially their sons, but they place less emphasis on the process of childrearing than Americans do.

In infancy both sexes are dressed identically, in a little smock in the sum-mer, with a sweater and long pants added in the winter. Babies also usually wear bonnets on their heads, knit in the winter, cotton with a ruffle (for boys and girls) against the sun in the summer. One must inquire to determine the sex of a child, and a mistake does not upset or offend the mother (which is surprising, in view of the great sex role differentiation of the society). In fact, what seemed most offensive to mothers was to be told that their baby was lovely; this was the only situation in which they would openly disagree with a visitor. Initially I thought a woman lacked affection for her child when in response to a compliment she replied, "She's not pretty at all. Look how wrinkled she is, and just as black as her father!" But when one understands the susceptibility of small babies to illness caused by "the evil eye," one learns either to agree with the mother that the baby is not perfect or to pref-ace a compliment with the protective phrase *tbarek Allah* ("God bless").

EARLY CHILDHOOD

The early childhood period includes the second through fifth years in the child's life, when it is more mobile than the infant yet spends most of its time within the household rather than outdoors playing with peers. During this time the differential treatment of the sexes begins, the child learns to *hshim* (behave properly), and the events (important in traditional socialization stud-ies) of weaning and toilet training occur.

Weaning could be said to occur in either infancy or early childhood, since it usually happens very close to two years of age. By the time of weaning most children are also eating bits of food from the table, but doing so occurs late in comparison to the American practice. A few children who were ob-served refused to ingest anything except their mother's milk; they spat out any other food offered. Only one such child appeared obviously malnourished; he was very scrawny and unable to walk although he was over two years old.

Because breastfeeding is believed to prevent pregnancy (a belief which has some basis in fact), it is continued as long as possible before the child is two, although I heard of (never observed) cases in which a child nursed until it was six or eight years old. Weaning also occurs when a woman becomes pregnant and her milk supply decreases. It is recognized that weaning is difficult for the child, and it often occurs on a holiday (*'id as-seghir*), on which it is felt to be easier, or with a new moon. Nevertheless, women say of a newly weaned child, "Now he knows that *ghder* [treachery, betrayal] exists in the world." The feeling that before this time children are very close to the angels and unaware of worldly hardships in fact reflects, in metaphor, the real situation.

The process of weaning is very abrupt; the mother chooses a day, paints her breasts with liver bile or hot pepper to discourage the child, and from that point does not nurse it again. She binds up her breasts or wears her dress with the opening in back to be sure the child will not "steal" a sip while sleeping next to her. One might expect mothers to relent when they see how unhappy and upset the child is, but the culture bolsters their resolution through the common belief that their milk spoils and will poison the child once they stop nursing. One woman described how her baby girl had died at the time of weaning for just that reason. Although she had not given in and nursed the child, she thought the baby must have "stolen" some milk during the night. The next day the baby had diarrhea—her mother assumed it was from the "poison"—and she died a few days later. I suspect that diarrhea may indeed often occur with weaning, not from poisoned milk but because the infant is then more likely to drink the local water, which contains various germs. Adults are immune to most of them, and also strong enough to endure a round of dysentery, but the babies are much more susceptible.

Children will be fussy for the first few days after weaning, and some mothers try to pacify them with candy or cookies. Others object, however, saying that the children will then always crave sweets and not eat properly.

While weaning is quite precisely accomplished, toilet training is very relaxed. It was noted above that women can often sense when an infant is about to urinate or defecate and they then hold the child away from them, so that a child may be trained by early childhood. No data were collected regarding specific ages, but it appears that most children are toilet trained by three or four years of age, and some considerably earlier. When infants can sit but not walk they are often seated balanced on the mother's extended legs and defecate on the floor or ground. This is easily cleaned up and not noted, positively or negatively, by others present. When children are able to walk (at about one year), they wear only little smocks and no pants at all in the summer, so that they urinate or defecate wherever they happen to be standing.

Again, no fuss is made, though they may be taken outside or to the toilet if they are noticed in time. When they are a little older, they learn to squat while defecating (as do adults), further simplifying the process. Whenever seen squatting, they are taken to the proper place and quickly learn the association.

During this period, the differential treatment of the sexes becomes much more apparent. The slight amount of extra attention that infant boys receive becomes marked in early childhood. The attention of fathers increases at this time; infants are not particularly interesting to them. Their attention is directed mainly at boys; girls are given little. Children of both sexes are hugged and told that they are pretty, but boys more so than girls. Small girls do not cry or demand attention to show they resent being slighted, but just sit quietly and observe.

Another aspect of differential treatment is that little boys are allowed and sometimes even encouraged to hit their older sisters, who are not allowed to retaliate. Little girls seldom strike anyone and are not encouraged to do so. Behavior that we would call "spoiled" (such as tantrums) is both exhibited more by boys and tolerated more with regard to them. While one seldom meets a spoiled little girl, spoiled youngest boys are the norm.

Moroccan children at this stage are much less sheltered than their American counterparts. They are allowed to roam freely about the house; there is no special concern to keep them away from the fire in the kitchen or to prevent them from falling down the stairs. It is not that the adults do not care; they are concerned when there is a reasonable danger, but they would see most American parents' behavior as overprotective. After a period of residence in Morocco, one comes to the conclusion that children are very durable and that they can assume a great deal of responsibility at an early age.

For example, one little girl was found toddling around on the roof where the rabbits were kept, ingesting their excrement. When the mother was informed, instead of rushing the child to the nearest clinic she merely smiled and remarked, "I guess she thinks those are vitamin pills." One local family used to laugh at the way I would nervously watch their five-year-old son whenever he rode his tricycle over to the top of a steep flight of cement stairs; he had not fallen down them yet and they felt it unlikely that he would. The same boy failed to come home for dinner about 8 p.m., and his sister said, "He must be at his aunt's house—or somewhere. He'll come home sooner or later." Most American mothers would have considered the possibility of his falling in the river, wandering out into the hills, and other grim occurrences. The only time a family appeared worried about a child (for reasons other than illness) was when a local six-year-old was missing overnight, and he was later found staying with relatives in the adjacent town.

While American preschoolers are playing and being sheltered from the hardships of life, Moroccan children are enjoying more independence and learning pragmatic skills. Girls especially begin helping their mothers at this time. While boys sometimes run errands, such practice is regarded as "cute" rather than as a contribution to running the household. Girls, however, begin running errands, washing dishes, sweeping, and caring for younger children at this age. It is not unusual to see a five-year-old carrying a one-year-old on her back.

Children of both sexes begin to hshim at this time. Hshim and the related concept of *'qel* (discussed below) are both very important in Moroccan child-rearing; once children have mastered both, they are grown up. Hshim means literally "Show some shame!" or "Behave!" when spoken as a command, and is related to *hshuma* (shame). To hshim is to behave properly and not to exhibit bad manners or morals. Since the behavior expected of boys and girls varies, so does the meaning of hshim as applied to each. For a small boy it means to sit quietly; for a girl it demands bodily modesty in addition to quietness. Three-year-old girls are encouraged to cover their legs with their dresses while seated, and strict parents do not even allow them to wear the short, French-style dresses. For a mother to say about her daughter *"Kathshim"* (she's well behaved) implies an element of shyness, since proper behavior for girls includes a demure aspect. Often these girls would stare at the ground and blush while their mothers spoke (appropriate behavior when one is being discussed), leading me initially to understand Kathshim to mean "she's shy or frightened." It should also be noted that hshim applies to observable behavior; it is more an external judgment by society of one's actions rather than something felt only internally and individually by a person. One can relate it to Western concepts of guilt and shame, where guilt is internalized self-punishment but shame is imposed on one by others. In Morocco shame (hshuma) is the most common means of control of behavior, whereas very little guilt appeared to occur. A child did not feel "bad" about stealing something because one should not steal, but felt "bad" only if he was caught, because then he would be publicly shamed. The effectiveness of shame as social control was revealed in a class of preschool children in the village. Because a child would not behave in response to directions or even slaps, the teacher stood him in the corner for a few minutes. That he then cried as if his heart were broken is not understandable unless one realizes the impact of being publicly shamed.

Another aspect of child training that begins during early childhood and persists throughout may be related to the prevalence of shame over guilt. There is a striking inconsistency in the way in which children are disciplined. The first time a little girl takes a large lump of sugar from the tea tray and begins to suck on it, she may be laughed at or even admired, especially if guests are present. The next time she does it she may be soundly spanked; corporal punishment, while not very harsh, is frequent. There seem to be no concentrated efforts to teach children precisely what is right or wrong, and they are punished or rewarded indiscriminately. The main variable seems to be the mood of the parent rather than the nature of the particular act. Thus one would hardly expect the child to develop an internal sense of what is right and wrong, since it all depends on an exterior factor, the parent. Such methods lead directly to feeling only shame, imposed from outside, when caught. One might also speculate that herein lies the origin of the almost uncanny ability of many Moroccans to "psych out" people; it is a talent they develop early, in self-defense against their parents' moods.

LATE CHILDHOOD

During late childhood further differentiation of the sexes occurs, with boys engaging in play and attending school while girls take on more and more responsibility at home. Probably partially as a consequence of their increased responsibility, girls begin to develop 'qel, or more mature behavior, but boys do not do so until much later. During this stage (and sometimes earlier) boys undergo circumcision, which may have a disturbing psychological effect. Perhaps the most outstanding characteristic of late childhood is the fact that the boys are literally terrors outside the household, and one marvels to think that somehow they will be socialized into very restrained and proper men like their fathers.

Between the ages of six and twelve, girls are of maximum usefulness to the household. Although they further refine their housekeeping skills during adolescence, they are then no longer allowed to go out freely because one becomes concerned about their honor. The institution of "little girl maids" (*mta‘llmat*) depends mostly on those in late childhood. Girls in this age category learn to do all the basic household tasks of washing, cleaning, cooking, and child care, and in addition run errands to buy food or deliver messages. More of these girls have been sent to public school recently, but many are too valuable as assistants for their mothers to spare them. One notes again the pragmatism of this training; it is difficult to imagine an American twelve-year-old as perfectly competent to run a household. These girls do play with peers, usually after dinner in the evening when all the work is done.

Boys, on the other hand, seem to spend most of their time playing. Most boys attend the public school for at least three or four years, but it must operate on split shifts because of crowding and thus occupies only a few hours of the day. The rest of the time is spent outside in unsupervised play; the only household task that might be asked of a boy is shopping or taking a message to his father, and that is infrequent. The most reserved or controlled game played by groups of boys is soccer, which is a great favorite. Another common game involves a gang of boys, each trying to kick one another in the pants. This seemed more typical of the play of these boys—very active and expressing a lot of aggression.

One wonders where all the aggression comes from, since girls do not seem to exhibit it at all. Is it related to the fact that small boys are spoiled but inevitably "dethroned" by the arrival of a new baby, whereas girls lack this experience? Yet girls receive less attention immediately after infancy than do boys, so that transition could be more difficult for them. Or perhaps it is related to the fact that girls' energy is channeled directly into household activities, whereas boys' energy lacks a productive or appreciated outlet. While all the above may be contributing factors, I suspect that the circumcision of boys between the ages of four and eight, with no prior warning or explanation to them, may also play an important role in explaining their aggression. There is no equivalent event for girls in Morocco.

For boys, however, circumcision (*tahar*) is a major event and the basis for a large celebration, to which friends and relatives are invited. In that regard, the circumcision is for boys what a wedding is for girls: the major ceremonial event to focus on them. Of course, the groom also celebrates his wedding, but the bride is the center of attention. Boys enjoy all the attention they receive at their circumcision, including wearing fancy clothing, parading through the streets on a white horse, and having musicians play in their honor. They also enjoy the feast, and at the men's party may be encouraged to smoke, drink wine, and dance with the dancing girls, revealing the initiatory aspect of the circumcision. Since most boys are still very young, their participation in the latter activities is more a charade than a reality.

However, all this celebration usually occurs before the actual circumcision. Mothers explain that it is wiser to wait, for if the child should fall ill as a result of the operation, the mother would have to attend to him and could not see to all her duties as hostess. It seems that boys are aware of the more glamorous aspects but are not told in advance what the actual operation will involve. By eight years of age or so, children may discuss it among themselves, but younger boys are not prepared by their families.

When one assumes the naivete of the boy, the actual circumcision must be quite frightening. After all the music, dancing, and eating are over, several women file into a house with the boy's mother. He is brought in by an uncle or other male relative (seldom by the father; one wonders whether he cannot bear it). The operation is usually performed by a barber-surgeon who specializes in it, although recently it has also begun to be available at health clinics. One village boy of five, waiting near the door as everyone filed in, showed a sense of what was impending when he said, "Well, I think I'll just wait here outside." But it was his circumcision and he had to go in. The male relative holds the child steady, the barber-surgeon removes the foreskin, and the women all sing loudly so that the mother will not hear the child cry.

After the operation, the child is placed on the back of his mother as if he were an infant, and she remains bent nearly double as she carries him to the room where he will recuperate for a few days. During this passage both mother and son are covered with a white sheet, one suspects as a defense against the evil eye. Friends and relatives then file in and each gives the child a little money and says something comforting. On one such occasion that I attended, the five-year-old boy cried heartbrokenly, a cry that suggested more than physical pain. He did not even pause when one of his visitors, an old midwife, said, "Don't worry, sonny; it'll grow back as big as this!" and displayed her forearm. One of my bigger regrets was that I did not interview this child in the next few days and ask him just what (he perceived) had happened; he was a very verbal child and would probably have had a lot to say. When I finally did ask him, about six months later, all he said was, "Wel-lit sghir" (I became small).

While boys seem to become wilder and less controllable during late childhood, girls have the opposite experience. Girls are allowed to laugh, run, and play in the streets (when they have time) as do their brothers. But as they approach adolescence, girls are encouraged to become quieter and more sedate. One little girl in particular comes to mind; at six she was almost as much a tease as her brother, with a twinkle in her eye and a ready laugh. But by ten she had become more restrained, and by twelve she was a "perfect little lady," seldom running or giggling, and the sparkle was replaced by a soberness and a sense of responsibility.

In fact, the greater responsibility borne by girls probably is one of the main factors in their development of ʿqel before the boys. ʿQel, or the more common dir lʿqel, means literally to "develop a mind." It refers to the development of a person into an intellectually capable, or socially responsible, person. Abdelwahed Radi, a professor at Mohammed V University in Rabat, suggests that ʿqel involves internalizing the values of one's elders. One sees here an interesting contrast with the American concept of child development. We tend to perceive a child's development as linear through time, beginning in infancy, with each successive stage building on the previous ones. Moroccans do not share the concept of linearity; a child exists for a time, and finally one day it is discovered to have developed ʿqel. Girls act quite sensibly by the end of childhood and during adolescence most are recognized as having "become responsible." One can leave them in charge of the household and expect everything to be functioning smoothly when one returns. If it is not, they are held responsible and punished.

For boys, however, the picture is different. The last thing one would expect of boys at this age is that they would have ʿqel. Rather, they behave irresponsibly, sometimes even destructively, but are not blamed. People used to warn us never to allow children in our house because "they have not yet 'become responsible' and might steal something." We assumed the warning applied to children under seven, as was in fact correct for girls; the boys they referred to were up to fifteen and evidently not yet held responsible for theft. These differences in the rate of assuming responsibility may be partly due to the fact that the realm of a woman lies inside the household and is fairly easily mastered when young, whereas that of a man involves many and varied interactions with the outside world that cannot be easily learned in the setting of the home, or at play, or in school.

ADOLESCENCE

During their teens girls exhibit relatively little change, except in the area of increased sexual modesty. Boys may begin to develop 'qel, especially if they must work to support themselves or their families, but they are also expected to sow some wild oats at this time.

Girls' socialization continues to be within the household, although they may also have friends in the neighborhood. With the onset of puberty girls begin to cover themselves more and are seen less frequently in the street. They quickly learn (most have already) that exchanging banter with boys or men is forbidden, and instead they pass by with eyes cast down. Most girls marry in late adolescence and are fully prepared to become wives and mothers.

Boys are still experimenting during this period, often with smoking, eating ham, drinking, and prostitutes. Obviously most of their socialization now occurs outside the home, with peer groups or with older males with whom they work. The son has a great deal of respect for the authority of his father, and the relations of the two are rather distant by this age. A son will not smoke in front of his father and would be very embarrassed to encounter him in a bar or a brothel. Thus the father is not responsible for much of the son's socialization, except as he represents a strong authority figure. The lack of dependable guidance for boys at this age probably contributes to their problems. Many perceive their fathers as old-fashioned and unsuccessful in the modern world. While I did not have enough contact with adolescent boys to be certain, it appeared that their main ideal was James Bond, but emulating him did not adequately prepare them to function in Moroccan society.

Mothers may threaten to tell fathers of a son's misbehavior, but in the final case the mother more frequently defends him to the father. Mothers hope their sons will love and respect them, and ultimately most do, but not until they are in their twenties. Teenage males often abuse both sisters and mothers, who are hurt but tolerate it. One young man of our acquaintance was very sharp with the female members of his family (he was brusque or silent with his father) and occasionally threw plates of food on the floor when he was especially irritated. Young men in Morocco today do face many problems, the main one being widespread unemployment. Given their position and lack of power in the society, women are the only available targets for their resentment. This particular young man was also very impatient with his six-year-old brother (who was otherwise the darling of the household), but one suspects it is less manly to pick on children than on women. All of this behavior worried his mother, but not because she saw her son as developing into a bad person—she knew how unhappy he was.

Boys manage to survive adolescence and are usually married in their early twenties. They develop ʿqel about the same time; few families would trust their daughter to an immature husband who had not yet developed ʿqel. The "socially responsible" couple then begin their own cycle of childrearing.

NOTE

1. Since the mid-1970s, when these data were collected, certain changes have taken place. The reader should be aware that by the mid-1980s (a) nearly all town children tried to finish primary school; (b) the age of marriage had increased by five to ten years; (c) the value of daughters relative to that of sons had increased (but had not become equal) as girls became more educated and many worked outside the home to help their families, while fewer adult sons lived with their parents.

Children and War

Louise Berdal

Since the end of World War II, practically every country in the Middle East has been involved in war or disturbances on some level: independence wars, civil wars, revolutions, foreign invasions, armed put-downs of strikes and demonstrations, coup d'etats and coup d'etat attempts. The Gulf war of 1990–1991 as well as other, more drawn-out conflicts, such as the Lebanese civil war, the Palestine-Israel conflict (and history of wars involving Israel and its neighbors), the Iran-Iraq war, and the Soviet presence in Afghanistan, have proved highly disruptive to Middle Eastern citizens. Although parts of life are put on hold, noncombatants work to conserve as much normal routine as possible. Children in countries such as Afghanistan and Lebanon, however, have known little else than war in their lives, and war itself thereby takes on aspects of normal routine. Louise Berdal nursed the many wounded—including children—with Doctors Without Borders in Lebanon during the Siege of Beirut in 1982 and for six months in Afghanistan in 1984. —Eds.

For me, the children are the saddest part of war. They have nothing to do with what is going on but are so often caught up in it. War, although it was very different in Beirut than in Afghanistan, is a game played with few rules. There is no black and no white. Anyone with his or her own reasons for doing whatever he or she did could be involved, and no one could say whether it was good or bad.

BEIRUT

Our unit of Doctors Without Borders was not attached to a hospital but largely did emergency work in bombed houses and flattened buildings throughout the city. After a bombing or street fighting we would rush to the scene, give emergency aid, and when the wounded were patched up enough to be transported, they were moved to a hospital for further treatment. So many of the wounded and killed were children.

In Beirut, war was a double game—more regularized than in Afghanistan. Although events seemed totally arbitrary on most days, the participants, including the children, realized that sometimes there was logic to what went on. You could always be shot if caught out in the street—as I was once—but the threat was mainly bombings, regular bombings announced by air raid sirens.

Much of life went on as usual. Students would study for about one-half hour, then evacuate to the bomb shelters. When the raid was over, they went back to classes. The Lebanese considered education vital, and the schools were kept open no matter what.

The little Lebanese girls stayed close to home, helping their mothers or tending the younger children. Compared with the image of Arab women we had in mind when we arrived, Palestinian and Lebanese girls and their mothers were liberated. The Palestinian women fought against the war by keeping everyday life moving. I saw them on the streets going to work, buying food. While they did not fight alongside with the men, they carried supplies and provisions. Many mothers believed that they fought for Palestine by educating their children to be revolutionaries.

The little boys were often in the streets, playing, running errands, off to sell something or to buy food when the bombing came. Often their mothers didn't know where they were. Of course, the boys were eager to participate in the fighting: to act as a messenger or to bring food to big brother at the checkpoint. Big brother, the fighter, might be fourteen or fifteen years old. Little brother, the junior messenger, would be eight or nine, champing at the bit to be part of the war. For some, it was a game they wanted to take part in; for them—as for their older brothers—glory lay in being at the front, and they shared in it if they could.

Then the bombing came. Children didn't have much defense against the bombing. They didn't know where to go, exactly what to do, and they panicked easily. I don't think it was real for them. It stopped being a game when they were hit or if someone died. If someone in the family was hit, at first some children would react as if it were a glorious occurrence. Then they realized that the person would not come home again, or would come home minus a leg or an arm. Then they knew that things had changed and would never be the same again.

You could see it in the children's eyes. They didn't play anymore; they didn't laugh, they didn't brag. They looked as if they were half-alive. They couldn't express their thoughts; they tried to find the words to talk about what was happening, but they couldn't. They had a way of looking at you as if you were the one who had set off the bomb—the one who was responsible for all this.

I saw more cluster bombs in Afghanistan than in Lebanon, but there were plenty in Beirut. They were vicious, especially dangerous for their main victims, the children, because they were purposefully made to look so innocent. The children thought they were rocks or colored toys and picked them up. When the bombs exploded, their hands were blown away, or their faces took the brunt of the explosion.

The bombing panicked everyone. The kids said they would listen for the whistling because, if it still whistled, the bomb had passed over you. You would hear the whistling, then a short moment of silence, then the explosion. Then everyone looked for the black smoke to see where the bomb had landed. If the bomb didn't whistle, then it had landed beside you or somewhere else close. If the bomb landed amidst tall buildings, the explosion was deeper, reverberating among the buildings. If it landed on a rooftop, then the explosion was deafening.

One day, a building in West Beirut was bombed. When we arrived we found total destruction—forty-one people dead in the wreckage. From what we could piece together, they must have been attending a meeting, since many were from outside the neighborhood. No adult survived, but the search dogs found a ten-month-old baby in the ruins, protected by the rafters which supported a few inches of roof above him. Despite serious wounds, he did not make a sound. As everyone was dead and none of the neighbors recognized him, we could never find his family. We believed that he was the child of someone attending the meeting, but we had no idea who or how to follow up. The rest of his family must have assumed he was dead. We were not even sure whether he was Palestinian or Lebanese. We left him with the social services; they named him Muhammad.

AFGHANISTAN

Afghanistan was different from Lebanon—a different type of society and a different type of war. In Beirut, we worked in the city; in Afghanistan, we were out in the fields, close to the mountains north of Kabul. We saw no street fighting but mainly experienced bombing, which was ofttimes nastier than the bombing in Beirut. The Soviets used gas bombs, cluster bombs, and napalm in remote areas, as well as a gas which contracts the muscles of the stomach and makes you look as though you are laughing although you are in extreme pain.

In Afghanistan war struck without warning. You could be bombed; you could be gassed. Life was never normal. No rebel children went to school. Afghani women and girls were practically invisible. They gathered food and took care of the children and household. Their environment was harsh, and housework took all of their time and energy.

Treating the wounded was trickier than in Beirut. Here we had no hospitals. We stayed in natural caves which were not noticeable from the air. We ran the electricity on generators, when they worked, and set up primitive operating rooms. We used to say that we were cutting off legs and putting band-aids on them.

There was a constant shortage of everything. Supplies were airlifted in from France and other parts of Europe, but they didn't always come in on time. Because the USSR bombed almost every flat surface in the country which could be used for agriculture, food was scarce. It was also extremely difficult for planes to land, and supplies were often parachuted in. In fact, my team and I were parachuted into Afghanistan. To make all the materials last as long as we could, we wouldn't use them unless there was a great need. We were always short of painkillers and anesthetics. The bottom line was that we would let people scream or use whiskey to get them drunk. We operated with whatever we had.

Children seemed to have the highest threshold of pain. One day, Mahmoud, an eight-year-old favorite of mine, brought me a flower. I saw him approaching about ten meters away, holding out a flower in his hand, his other hand reduced to a flap of flesh. I stood transfixed, not believing what I was seeing. He walked unhesitatingly toward me and tried to give me the flower. When I saw bone crushed in his damaged hand I knew it would have to be amputated. I thought he would panic to see his hand crushed, but he must have been totally in shock.

Another day, a nine-year-old was brought in; his foot had been blown up after he stepped on a bomb. If we had been in France or in the United States, we could have spent ten hours in surgery, worked gently with the fragments, and perhaps reassembled the foot. But here we were working against time and had no supplies. We had to amputate his foot. Luckily, we had electricity and were able to use the electric saw for the amputation. But we had no anesthesia left. I poured a half-bottle of whiskey down the little boy and then took some hashish from the old men who habitually smoked it and had him smoke a joint. When he was totally drunk we operated.

The boy came out of his drunk about a day later. His mother told him what had happened to his foot before he could see it. He took the news better than I expected. No reaction; he did not say one thing. Losing a limb seems to be accepted; so many have lost a leg or an arm. The children don't like it, but they don't take it as the tragedy a child or an adult in my country would.

Memoirs of a Street Tough

Yusuf Abu Haggag
Translated and Introduced by Everett K. Rowson

An important feature of urban society in Egypt until recent times was the institution of the fitiwwa, the neighborhood tough. At his best, the fitiwwa represented a form of local recourse and authority for the residents of the hara (urban quarter), accessible and sympathetic to the humblest of them in a way the official government was not. At his worst, he was a pestilential thug, extorting protection money from the hara and spending his time carousing and brawling with his rivals.

Westernization in the nineteenth century undermined the fitiwwa's more beneficent functions, and the institution declined. At the same time, as the urban elite became both more Europeanized and more nationalistic, the archetype of the "traditional Egyptian" came to be increasingly identified with various lower-class figures, including the fitiwwa. One of a series of accounts of lower-class life published in the 1920s is the volume excerpted here, the 1929 memoirs of Yusuf Abu Haggag, the fitiwwa of the Huseiniya quarter of Cairo. Unlike other works of this sort, Yusuf's reminiscences were not recast in standard literary Arabic, but rather transcribed directly from his own rough-spoken account. They thus constitute a rare example of oral history in Arabic.

Radical demographic and social change in Cairo has by now made the role of the traditional fitiwwa obsolete; the last to achieve wide notoriety were those of the 1930s and 1940s. Street brawlers have not disappeared from the city, however, and the kind of life described by Yusuf Abu Haggag is still pursued, although with little hope of achieving any real power or status within the wider society. In elite circles, as the past recedes, there has been another wave of interest in the traditional life of the hara, perhaps best typified by Naguib Mahfuz's 1978 novel on the fitiwwas' medieval predecessors, al-Harafish. —E. Rowson

Excerpted from al-Muʿallim Yusuf Abu Haggag, *Mudhakkirat Fitiwwa* [Memoirs of a Street Tough], transcribed by Husni Yusuf. Cairo: al-Matbaʿa al-ʿArabiyya bi-Miṣr, n.d. [1926].

I was born in Huseiniya Street, which is half in the precinct of Gamaliya and half in the precinct of Wayli. My father and mother lived in Harat al-Husr, which is in the precinct of Gamaliya. So you see I was raised among people who love bad language and hate book learning, and would rather learn about cleavers and whetstones. The fact is, most of the people in Huseiniya are butchers; they know how to slaughter and skin, but not, of course, how to read and write.

My father—may God have mercy on his dear soul—was a butcher, with a shop on the corner in Nuzha Street in Abbasiya. God had been good to him, and his business went well. He brought me up until I was seven, and had to put up with thirty fights a day from me, without letup. Then one day, after my mother's brother had a real fight and a half with my father, they ended up, after a lot of talk and bickering, sending me to the Quran school of Lady Sutuhiya, opposite Bab al-Futuh. I went every day, but only after a whipping from my uncle and a few pokes from my mother.

I would walk into the school with my loaf under my arm, and the monitor would meet me and reach out politely to take my loaf and put it in Master's cupboard. Then we would all sit down on the old mats and tattered rags, and off we would go with our alphabet: "*Alif*, with no dots; *ba*, one dot underneath; *ta*, two dots on top. . . . " After two or three hours of this we would write on our slates and do memory work. Then we would recite, and nobody would escape getting two or three lashes. Myself, I almost always ended up with my feet in the stocks.

At noon, His Lordship the monitor would go out, along with yours truly and two other boys, each of us carrying an enormous bowl. We would go to the pickle factory in Seedsellers' Lane, fill up the bowls, and come back to school. Then they would collect the lunch money we had got from our families, and we would sit and gobble down the pickles. When we finished, we would have a reading lesson.

How long did I keep this up? Three and a half long years, of torture and total misery, until God had pity on me and I left the damned school. I had just barely learned to work out the letters, write my name, and read a line in a newspaper in an hour—or maybe two. My father took me on at the shop, and I soon forgot even the little bit of reading I had learned. So in the end I just resigned myself to God's will in my miserable condition. The truth is, friends, that "a constant buzzing in the ears gets the message across better than magic," and my father—God rest his soul in heaven—used to go on and on to me with, "Why should I send you to school, my boy? No books, no bother! Am I going to get a civil servant out of you, or a lawyer? Are you going to 'catch me a rat by the tail'? We've got a few sheep, a couple of calves, and the shop, and with the good Lord's help. . . . " So you see, friends, my father was the reason for my failure and lack of education. I resigned my fate to God, took off the fez and put on the skullcap and scarf, traded in my shoes for peasant slippers, and became a real street kid, to put it politely.

Time went by, and I grew up in this environment. I started hanging around with a group of guys who were all trouble by the bushel, who only knew God as a friend of a friend. We would go around together every night, to the bars, or the hashish dens, or we would spend some time in the red light district. And the reason for all of this was my father. If he had been brought up right and educated, I would have turned out like him or even better. . . . Gradually I became a member of Urabi's gang. Not a wedding or circumcision procession would go by without us all getting up to pick a fight with them. We would ask for a tune, and if they agreed we would dance and they would get off safely; but if they didn't, there would be hell to pay.

One day I left the house and went to the cafe, and found the gang had decided to go have a look around the zoo. They asked me what I thought, and I said, "Fine with me. Let's go!" We started off at eleven and got to the zoo at noon; but when we started to go in, it turned out that it was Sunday and they were charging five piastres admission. That put us in a bad mood, so on the way back we stopped in Dokki for a few pipes of hashish, and cheered up. Then we took the tram as far as Ataba, and got off and walked on to the place behind the post office. We stopped there, and I said to the gang, "What do you say? I'd like to do a little stick fighting, and this is a good open place for it!" They said, "For sure," and so we set to it. People gathered around as if they had heard the call of the snake charmer. I beat two guys, and started with a third; but this guy wanted to show off in front of everyone, thinking he was such a big deal, and went too far and gave me a real hard well-placed whack. The people laughed at me, thinking he had beat me, and I lost my head and let the devil take over. I took my stick and started laying into everyone standing around, just to show them that I was ready for anything and didn't care how many I took on. Everyone ran, except a guy from Huseiniya, who came up to me and started cursing my ancestors up and down. I grabbed him by the neck and threw him on the ground; he bloodied his face and broke a few teeth.

Then the police arrived and formed a ring around poor little me, and off we went to the Muski police station. They took statements from me and the guy I beat up, worked up the official police report, and put me in a cell. In the evening they let me out on the recognizance of the shaykh of the hara. A few days later the summons came, and I went to the hearing at the Gamaliya police station, and stood before the judge. A word here, a word there, he saw I had no record, and found me innocent. This was, after all, my first job in my new career as a fitiwwa! I left the courtroom with my friends, and went home.

I got my usual ten piastres allowance from my mother, and went back out again to the cafe. We sat there for a while, then a friend of mine named Balha turned up and said to me, "Come talk to Master Urabi! He wants you about something important." I said, "Okay," and went off to the cafe he went to, taking Balha with me. I found Master Urabi sitting there with Hagg Muhammad the cook, the fishmonger, and the guy I had tangled with on the day of the stick fighting. Then I realized that they had set up an unofficial hearing of their own! "Good evening." "Good evening." "Welcome, please take a chair." Then came the coffee and the water pipe. Finally, when they had heard what both of us had to say, they judged unanimously in my favor and against my opponent, and decided that he owed me recompense. Now in the code of the fitiwwas, recompense means that the losing party has to throw a party and invite all the brothers to it. So on the next day we had a real first-class party. Al-Arabi sang, and all the fitiwwas and 'itras[1] came, and the evening ended nicely and peacefully.

I went home to bed, but then, just at the crack of dawn, I heard this guy Balha calling me. I opened the window and saw him, and he said, "Get down here fast!" I jumped into my slippers and threw my scarf over my shoulder, and went down without even washing my face. "Good morning!" I said. "What's up?" He said, "Good morning to you! Today there is a wedding in Bayn al-Aqdar, and we mustn't miss breaking it up!" I said, "Sure, whatever you say!" We went off to the cafe, where I washed my face, and we sat down and started the day off with a couple of pipes of hashish. Then we went off to have some beans for breakfast at Uncle Fal'us's, just at the end of Huseiniya Street, and came back again. We loafed around as usual, playing cards, until two in the afternoon. Then we went off for lunch at the offal shop, and came back to home base.

A couple of hours later we saw a wedding procession coming, and got up with our clubs in our hands. As the procession got closer, we saw a whole herd of men leading it, and I was put forward to pick the quarrel. I asked for a tune, and that guy Sirafi, the fitiwwa of Bayn al-Aqdar, came up to me and said (pardon my language), "Stuff it!" This word from him was like a knife in the neck of yours truly, and my friends and I started bashing them. The procession broke up and became a mob. The guards fled, the police came, whistles blew. By that time we had slipped away to Costi's Tavern, the one beside the public facilities in the street with the tram that goes to Abbasiya. We sat and tossed back whiskey, cognac, and wine until evening. Then we went off to Bayn al-Aqdar. We went in and the fight began immediately. Lanterns and chairs went crashing, and the attendants and guests fled. The guard of the hara ran off like a shot, blowing his whistle, and out of nowhere it seemed like the entire precinct was in the hara—not to say that they had had advance warning! They arrested me and Balha right away, took us off to the station, and wrote up a real mess of a police report on us.

After spending four months in prison, Yusuf decides he must take up a trade and becomes manager of a butcher shop. But his constant brawling and debauchery leads to a series of further jail terms, one as long as three years. When not in prison, he continues to work as a butcher, and finally resolves to go into business for himself:

I found a shop for rent in Sakakini Street, and took it. I opened it up, stocked some mutton, and started doing business. The customers came in droves, and God was good to me. "Trust in the Lord, and you will be safe from people's envy." I applied for a license, and a few days later His Worship the *ma'mur*[2] came by, bringing along a detective, the shaykh of the precinct, the shaykh of the hara, and, for good measure, a police officer with a black leather briefcase under his arm which he kept fussing with. The ma'mur came in and looked the shop over, left and right, as if he were the khedival architectural engineer. Then he looked at me and asked, "Why haven't you put some oil paint on the walls?" I said, "Listen, uncle, there's no question of 'oil'[3] here. What are we going to do with the place, hold parliament in it?" He said, "Shut up. I don't want any lip. I'm telling you: paint it." I shut up. Then he said, "This icebox won't do." I said, "For sure! But I'll lay you odds, by God, you won't find one as good in your house! Ha! You've left out a lot! You haven't said: Put red and white marble on the floor, install a faucet with a drain, bring in some Italian broad and sit her down on a chair and put a cash register in front of her, make price coupons like they do at Matossian's[4] and put them on the meat, fix up a glass display window and put mutton and veal kidneys in it, install electricity, and 'turn the sea into sesame paste'! Come on, go easy on me—'a dry twig breaks easily'!"

He said, "Mind your manners, boy!" I said, "Manners?! When you come in here bellowing and throwing your weight around and issuing orders right and left? And for what? Do you think you're giving me a license for free admission to heaven? The way you come in here with those guards of hell behind you, you'd think this was Judgment Day, or that we'd killed somebody, and you've come to do an interrogation! Isn't it the case, my dear sir, that you've been commissioned by the government only to inspect, not to shoot off orders all over the place? Let's get it over with, what do you say? I want to close up and go home and eat dinner, without all this hassle."

In the end he wrote down something or other and put it in the briefcase the policeman was carrying, and left, taking the whole crowd with him. I said, "Good-bye! 'The boat that takes away is better than the one that brings.' " With or without the license, I was going to keep working—I was there, and that was that! What kind of authoritarian crap is this, my friends? It seems like we never manage to use our wits when we really need them. Here we are, listening to what we don't want to hear, all for a butcher's license! By God, do you know why they feel they've got to make life hell for us? Because a butcher won't give them a pound of meat free of charge or a choice piece of brisket! They'd rather people opened shops to sell cocaine, heroin, morphine, hashish, *manzul*,[5] opium . . . all those illegal things whose sellers always have their hands in these guys' mouths and who they can always get a reward for hauling in and then go out on a spree and spend it all! But a *gada*[6] like me, who loves the Prophet and just wants to open a butcher shop—a respectable trade, needed by the pashas, beys, and effendis, and even those architectural experts—the whole kit and kaboodle of them—they walk all over him in the course of issuing him a license, hoping maybe something will fall out when they shake him or he'll let a word slip so the officer can claim that he insulted him or pulled off the buttons on his uniform—then you get the interrogation, the session in court, and the fine, which goes right into the safe, and "Good-bye!"

The next day I ran into that guy Balha, at the bend in the road in Sakakini, being beat up by four black guys. I lit into them, pow! bam! "Oh, my eye! You bastard!" One of them said that to me and I completely lost my head; I came down with a blow from my stick right in the middle of his ugly mug, and drew blood, and with the second he went down. His friends ran away, and next thing I knew here was this big hulk of a cop running up, blowing his whistle.

Without even thinking I grabbed Balha by the arm; there was a tram passing near by, and I went and jumped on it, bringing Balha with me. We got to one stop, and then another, and the whole time the cop kept running after us and yelling, until he was really panting. The conductor started to blow his whistle to stop the tram, but I grabbed the whistle out of his hand and said, "Shame on you! You shouldn't hold up all these nice people just because of something of no importance! You think that's a paying customer? He just wants to ride for free! Never mind about him; let him be!" The cop finally ran out of energy and gave it up. We got off the tram and went to Costi's Tavern for a few glasses, then sneaked out without paying and went to a hashish den for a few pipes. We fed our heads, and went back to Huseiniya, and each went home.

A few days later the shaykh of the hara came by with a piece of paper with my name, saying the ma'mur of the precinct wanted me. I thought, "Now you're in for it, you reprobate! One of those black guys must have recognized you, and something must have happened to the one you beat up." Anyway, I set off on a Soares cab[7] to the station. When I got there, I went upstairs and found the sergeant, Abdu, and asked him, "What does the ma'mur want me for?" He said, "By God, I don't know. Go in and ask the prefect." I went into the prefect's office, and he turned out to be a student type, about nineteen, sitting there on his chair like he owned the world. There were seven or eight guys in front of him who had apparently been hauled in for brawling, but he, bless his soul, just sat there joking and laughing with this effendi type in street clothes. I stood and waited with the latest arrivals. Then, bless his soul, he rang his bell, and in came a policeman dressed in a gallabiyya[8] and carrying a broom. He propped the broom up against the door and came in and stood in front of the prefect and threw him a real civilian's salute. The prefect said, "Bring the bey some coffee." He said, "Right away, sir," and disappeared. A moment later he was back with the coffee, and set it in front of them. The prefect took out a pack of cigarettes, handed one to his friend, and lit one himself. They just kept talking, while everyone standing in front of them was quiet, waiting for this bit of piecework to be done.

Finally, I got bored with waiting, and stepped up to the prefect and said, "Come on, sir, take care of our business; after all, we have our own work to see to, too." He replied, "What do you want? When did you get here?" I said, "I think you're old enough to remember that! You've just not been paying attention! Actually, I came here to see your ugly mug, sir!" He said, "Listen, here, you bastard!" I said, "Shut your mouth or I'll tear you to pieces! 'Not all birds have meat you can eat!' No, you'd better watch your step and make a real careful reckoning of this guy standing before you!" He said, "Who do you think you are? Urabi?" I said, "As good as!" Then the effendi sitting with him got up and said to him, "Ignore him. You don't have to have any truck with him. He's just a street kid, anyway." I said, "I may be a street kid, but I understand more than you ever will, you with the jacket and tie!" The prefect said, "Mind your manners, boy!" I said to him, "You'd best shut up! By the right of the one who made you a prefect and put that star on your shoulder, I'll take that police report in front of you and put it on your head—and your friend, too—and I'll mess up your face real good! Do you two think you're sitting here in a dance hall? You're sitting in a government office, you jerks! Get with it! Take care of these people here and let us go about our business!"

We started yelling back and forth at each other, and His Honor the ma'mur heard us. He sent for me, and also called in the prefect. When we went in, the ma'mur asked me what was going on, and I told him the whole story from beginning to end. May God prosper his house and raise his status. When he heard what I had to say, he scowled at the prefect and asked, "Who was that sitting with you?" He said, "Nobody." I said, "What do you mean, nobody? Let me go get him, ma'mur, sir!" I started out, but he said, "Wait, you!" and rang the bell. He said to the policeman who came to the door, "Fetch the effendi who is sitting in the prefect's office." The man went out, and came back in a moment and said, "I couldn't find him, sir." I said, "He must have slipped off when he saw how things were developing." The prefect said, "That man is a liar, ma'mur, sir!" But His Lordship the ma'mur was nobody's fool, and sent for the policeman who brings the coffee and asked him. He replied, "Yes, my Lord, there was an effendi with him, and he left just when Your Lordship asked for the prefect." Then the ma'mur turned to the prefect and said, "Well, then, Mahmud Effendi, are you the liar, or is he?" He said, "He's the liar, of course!" I said, "Come on, now, show a little fear of hell! Suppose I am a liar. And the policeman who brought the coffee is a liar, too. Who knows, maybe there's something between you two. Maybe he used to be a corporal and you've just ripped the two stripes off his sleeve—and here you come again to rip off my good sense and hoodwink His Lordship the ma'mur! What a bad 'un you are, my friend! Look here, we're the sons of good people just like you're the sons of good people!" Then the ma'mur turned to the prefect and said, "Go see to your work. The police station is a government institution, not a coffee shop for the officers and their friends." The prefect slunk out of the office so red that his neck would have made toast.

Then the ma'mur turned to me and said, "What's your name?" I said, "Yusuf Abu Haggag, at your service." He said, "A man named Murgan[9] from Sakakini Street has filed a complaint against you." I said, "Who is this Murgan, Your Lordship? That wouldn't be Murgan the son of Emerald, whose grandfather was the shaykh Ruby and whose brother is that boy Diamond?" He said, "What are you talking about, boy?" I said nothing. He said, "Answer me, boy! Why are you silent?" I said, "I'm thinking, Your Lordship, about a saying I heard from my grandfather—God be gracious and merciful to him!" The ma'mur asked, "What's that?" I said, "He used to say, 'If speech is silver, then silence is golden.' " He said, "Cut out this nonsense, boy! What do you have to say about this complaint which has been filed against you? It says here that you are a 'vicious, depraved delinquent.' " I said, "Great! A 'vicious, depraved delinquent.' So what about it?" He said, "I have to make out a police report." I said, "This warrants a police report? Well, all right, I'll welcome that with a hundred jasmine flowers, a thousand narcissus! I'm at your service, at your beck and call!"

He rang the bell and transferred me to the prefect. I went out and found that the prefect from before had gone off duty, and his replacement was a *gada*ʿ, a little dark brown guy who looked like a mongrel, with a father from Kordofan and a mother from Cairo. I went up to him, and he said, "Are you So-and-so?" I said, "I am him and he is me." He laughed, and I could tell he was a simple type, and I thought maybe a decent sort. He said, "What is your trade?" I said, "Butcher." He said, "Where do you live?" I said, "I live in the wellspring of *gad*ʿ*ana*[10] and the school for skirmishing." He said, "So you live in Huseiniya?" I said, "Give me your hand on that one! You're a sharp one, they can't deny that! What luck for me!" He said, "How old are you?" I said, "Ha! Whatever you think! Is this a recruitment center? I trust your judgment." He said, "I'd say thirty or thirty-five." I said, "In between." He said, "What, then?" I said, "Write thirty-two, and let the good Lord decide whether it's true."

The report completed, Yusuf is released on bail. Pessimistic about the outcome of his day in court, he bids farewell to his friend Balha:

"My brother, my parting advice to you is to do whatever you can to come keep me company during those lonely nights in jail. The first big lout that says a word to you, make a pancake of him and bury him alive!" He said, "By God, believe me, brother, I'll be lying in wait for them like the Angel of Death! And I'll mete out my mischief so each one gets his share!" I added, "And forget about things like mercy and humanity—not in these times! These times, when people say "Oh Lord, I want . . . " and nobody has any use for virtue! Read the Fatiha[11] and accept the advice of your good brother, a gadaʿ who can shake the deepest foundations of the prison, and who will

soon be director of the most prestigious cell in the place! Good-bye, Abu Ali!"
"Good-bye, brother!"

Once in court, however, Yusuf manages to goad the plaintiffs into insulting the judge and unexpectedly wins his case. Disillusioned with his disorderly life, he gives up drinking and brawling, marries a cousin, and settles down to the life of a respectable butcher.

NOTES

1. Particularly powerful fitiwwas.
2. The police captain of a precinct, who was assisted by the resident shaykh of the precinct. A precinct was subdivided into haras.
3. Bribery.
4. A tobacconist.
5. Name for several narcotic concoctions for eating, usually including hashish.
6. A manly, street-wise person.
7. A horsedrawn bus service.
8. Traditional men's garb, a shirt-like robe.
9. "Pearl," a typically Sudanese name.
10. The quality of being a *gada*ᶜ.
11. The first chapter of the Quran, recited to solemnize occasions.

"Of the Dust and the Wind": Arranged Marriage in Afghanistan

Margaret A. Mills

Courtship and weddings, among the most important events in the lives of Middle Easterners, are joyously anticipated as much for the parties and attendant excitement as for the marriage itself. Courtship entails many rituals which must be satisfactorily observed if the wedding is to go forward. Detailed negotiations over the bride's dowry, the furnishing of the house, and attendant matters can consume the attention of the families of the bride and groom for months. —Eds.

This is a story told by Abdul Wahed "Lang" ("the Lame," so called due to a spinal injury at birth which left him partially disabled), a day laborer, about fifty years old, illiterate, never married on account of his poverty, resident at the time of this performance in the household of a nephew in Tau Beriyan village, Herat Province, western Afghanistan, August 31, 1975. I recorded it while conducting research in Afghanistan from 1974 to 1976. Professor Sekandar Amanolahi of Shiraz University, Mr. Muhammad Zaher Siddiq, and Mr. Kazem Alami advised me on translation and dialect.

The title, "Xaki o Badi ("Of the Dust and the Wind"), is a colloquial term for illegitimate birth. In conversation after this tale was told, an elderly male member of the household where I was recording, who had listened to the story, corroborated its relevance to everyday experience with a reminiscence about an actual case of suspected illegitimacy in his village. The tale itself is considered fictional by its teller. For Western readers, it may be somewhat enigmatic in its integration of extremely accurate details of everyday life in Afghanistan and moments of comic absurdity. The storyteller, Wahed, mixes broad foolishness with exuberant enjoyment of performance opportunities (such as his street vendors' cries, very enthusiastically rendered, which cannot really be done justice in a written translation) and a wry wit concerning life's ironies.

In the story, one central irony concerns the power relationships between men and women, in which men make claims to social initiative and control but really are at the mercy of "women's tricks" (*makre zan*), the latter a common topic in men's humorous storytelling. Among Persian-speaking men with whom I have discussed this story, there is uncertainty about the hero's final attitude toward his wayward wife: whether he remains an innocent dupe, as he has shown himself to be at other moments in the story, or whether his acceptance of five illegitimate children represents a wry resignation toward circumstances which his poverty prevented him from controlling.

Wahed's abrupt switches of narrative voice, from third person to first and back, and finally back to first person again, may also leave an unfamiliar audience wondering how closely to identify with the hero. Wahed turns the entire story of Mir Lal Beg's travels into a personal-experience narrative, perhaps a familiar genre to him from the talk of returning migrant workers. When the hero arrives back in Kabul, he reverts to a third-person object, no longer a reporting subject, during the payoff scene with his father-in-law. Yet he regains his first-person voice as he reluctantly accepts the rationale of his erring wife. First-person narrative, inviting audience identification with the hero, thus correlates with the hero's periods of helplessness: as a poor man abroad, and at home with an unfaithful wife.

The hero's predicament, in which he must defer his marriage for several years in order to raise the required brideprice, was a real one for young men of ordinary means in Afghanistan even in recent years. Employment opportunities as guest workers in Iran or the Gulf states to some extent facilitated the accumulation of capital by working people in recent decades. The effect of the influx of foreign earnings on marriage patterns in Afghanistan since World War II has not, to my knowledge, been studied. In the early 1970s, Afghanistan still had one of the lowest per capita annual incomes in the world, estimated at $90 (U.S.).

Wahed evokes for us the Afghanistan of his own youth, or perhaps that of his father's youth, in references to the old monetary system and the lack of motorized transport, but the circumstances and worries attendant on finding a wife and traveling for work, leaving that wife to the supervision of others, were pertinent for young men in Herat in the mid-1970s as well. During the summers of 1975 and 1976 in the Herat area, informants estimated that 50 percent or more of the adult males in some villages were working abroad, in Iran and, to a lesser extent, in the Gulf states, leaving their families in the care of other relatives. The revolutions in Afghanistan and Iran in 1978 and 1979 have of course massively altered the circumstances of migration and work patterns. In the mid-1980s, there were an estimated 1.5 million Afghan refugees in Iran, and another 3 million in Pakistan.

Regional chauvinism and competing cultural claims between major cities such as Kabul, the present capital, and Herat in the west, which historically had much greater cultural and political importance than the modern capital, are also themes which figure in the consciousness and identity of contemporary Afghans. On one level, this is a Herati story making fun of the ostensibly less sophisticated Kabulis.

OF THE DUST AND THE WIND

Once there were two brothers in Kabul, and one had a wife and a house, and one had none. The one said to the other, "Brother, look, even though I don't have any money, I want to look around and find you a fiancee. You go find some work and get some money together, and we'll get you engaged."[1] He said, "Fine." The younger brother was called Lal Mir Khan, and the older was called Sadr Khan.[2] He said, "Brother, do you want So-and-so's daughter, or So-and-so's, or So-and-so's? Tell me who, and I'll go ask for her." He said, "Any girl you choose, and can get for me, would be fine." So he went and came back, and said, "Now, Brother, I went and asked for So-and-so's daughter, and they've given their answer. They want thirty thousand rupees from us."[3] He said, "Very good."

"There, now, I've brought your needle and thread."[4] He said, "Now, God willing, you can go off and raise the money, get yourself some kind of work, so you can come back and get married."

"Very good."

The next day, the younger brother went and asked his brother's wife, "Can you give me a few rupees to go visit my fiancee?" She said, "I don't have any cash, but go out to the field and gather yourself a shirttail full of the harvested corn, and take that for your courting." He went out to the pile of harvested ears and picked a shirttail full of grains off the cobs, but by the time he did that, it was getting dark. When he got to his father-in-law's dooryard, he saw that the gate was shut and locked. He walked all around the compound, and saw that everyone seemed to have gone to bed. He found a place in the wall where sparrows had dug holes for their nests, and tried to use the holes to climb up on top of the compound wall, but a handhold gave way and he fell back down, spilled his grain, and bruised himself all over. He gathered up all he could of the grain, then took a better grip, and crept up like a cat to the top of the wall.

He crept over the flat roof, and saw that his father-in-law was asleep to one side, his fiancee to the other, sound asleep. His fiancee had a veil spread over her, and he carefully lifted it off her and spread it out, and put the grain on it.[5] Then he bent his head to give her a kiss, and just as he was about to kiss her, she woke up and socked him in the jaw, so hard it knocked him aside like a cat. He said, "Now, fuck your father's soul! This is too bad—I came here, and what did you do? By the Quran, now I'm going, and I'm not coming back until I get all the money—if I can't bring every bit of the money for your father, I won't come back for you, till I die."[6]

He went back out, over the wall, went back home, and the next morning he said to his brother's wife, "Make me up a few pieces of bread—I'm going off to Herat to look for work." She sent him off to the corn pile again to get grain, and to bring her the hand mill for her to make the bread.[7] She made him five or six loaves, and he put them in a knapsack on his back and set off, saying, "God keep you! I'm off to Herat to work and make some money, so I can come back and get married."

As he came along the road, he saw a broken piece of melon lying there, and he picked it up and chewed it as he went along. As he walked along, chewing, he met a caravan coming from the direction of Herat, and they greeted him by name and asked him where he was going.[8]

He said, "I'm going to Herat for work—is there work there?" They told him, "Yes, there's plenty of work there, anybody who's willing to work can make themselves some money." He said (to the caravaneer), "Countryman, the road is long, and it's cold—would you give me your trousers so I won't get cold on the road?" Now those pants were so worn out that about all that was left of them was the waistband and the cuffs.[9]

When I [the narrator, Wahed, switches to first-person narration here] put them on, I saw that the seat was worn clear through, so I took that piece of dried-out melon skin and stitched it in to cover the hole. Then I set out, walking and walking, and as long as the melon rind was a little bit moist, it was OK and I went along easy. Once it got dry, I went along crackling and crunching.

Finally I got to a big rock, in the middle of nowhere, where I couldn't see either Kabul or Herat, one way or the other. I almost gave up right there. I sat down on that rock, sweating with worry, and ate some of my bread. But finally I got up again and, walking and resting, walking and resting, I came down out of the Hazarajat Mountains. Finally I came down into a town and asked the people, "Is this Herat?" They said, "No brother, they call this Pahlavan Piri." They were making mud bricks to build a qaleh.[10] I said, "Brothers, I'm looking for work, can you give me a share of this job?" They said, "It's late, come back tomorrow and we can give you a qeran,[11] and your bread as well." I said, "Fine."

So I worked all the next day, mixing mud for bricks, and they gave me my qeran, and my bread. I put the coin in a little purse, and tied it under my belt. The next day I said, "What about it brothers, do you want me to stay?" "It's early yet—today we'll give you two qeran, and your board." I said, "Fine," and I stayed that day.

Once I had three qeran in my pocket, I said, "Forget it. Which way is the city? I'm going to see the city." They said, "If you want to, take that road," and I did and arrived at the Kandahar Gate with all its shops. The shopkeepers all greeted me by name,[12] and I asked them what there was for work. I said, "Can you find me a shop to get started with?" They said, "Did you bring any money to start a shop?" I said, "Oh, yes,'" and got out my three qeran of cash. They said, "Oh—if you took this to the sheepshead-cooker it wouldn't buy you a pound of stew![13] And you want to open a shop—amazing!" There was one Kabuli among the merchants who felt sorry for me, and he said, "If you take this big road, you'll come to Kebabian village. You can buy a donkeyload of carrots there for three qeran. Bring them back and I'll help you find a scale and show you where to sell them. With God's help, maybe it will work out." "Good."

I went off to Kebabian, following the road, and asked around till I found a farmer who would let me help dig and wash the carrots and load them on his donkey, to make up part of the price, and I got a big donkeyload for three qeran. When I got back to the city with my load of carrots, my new friend found me a scale and some old stone weights. He showed me a place in the bazaar below the city fort to unload and told me how to call out, "Come on! Sweets of Kebabian! Come on, black carrots! Five sir (half-kilogram) for three cents, ten sir for six cents!"[14] I said, "OK." So I unloaded my sacks full of carrots and started in, hawking carrots till the afternoon prayer, and all the carrots were gone, and I saw that I'd doubled my money—six qeran! "Ah! May I be a sacrifice for my countryman's eyes! One qeran profit on every qeran!" So the next morning I went right back to Kebabian, and this time I got a donkeyload of carrots, and another load of turnips. I set up shop in the same spot in the market and started hollering again, hollered and hollered till afternoon prayer, and I was sweeping up—sold them all. And then I counted and counted—twelve qeran! "Ah, I'll be a sacrifice for my countryman's eyes! By God, and I, just for bread—I'm making a qeran for every qeran!"

The next day I went to Kebabian and bought a donkeyload each of carrots and turnips and squash, and I bought a bowl of snuff, too, and I came back and set up my stand, hollering, "Come on, fresh snuff! Come on, black carrots! Come on, turnips! Come on, squash—big squash! Come on, black carrots—sweets of Kebabian! There now—sweets of Kebabian, five sir three cents, ten sir six cents! Squash, one qeran! There, now, fresh snuff! Fresh snuff! Intoxicating snuff!" So I hollered and hollered, and by the afternoon prayer, I was ready to sweep up, and I saw I had forty qeran! Heaping praise and thanks on my countryman, I went off to Kebabian and got two donkeyloads of each of the vegetables, a bowl of snuff, and a big bowl of yogurt, and hawked all of that. Brother, the people all came crowding around, they bought their own bread from the baker, and I sold them yogurt, half a bowl for the price of a whole bowl.[15] That day I sold clean out, too, and after a while, I was able to get myself a shop, selling yogurt and snuff, brother, and every kind of vegetables, till my shop got to be a thriving business. To make a long story short, I stayed in Herat for seven years.

After seven years, one day a fat envelope arrived from Kabul, brought by some countrymen, and it said, "To Lal Mir Khan! May he be in health! Since he went away to Herat, his household and all his kids are close to starving!" I said, "Hey, now, brother, since when do I have a household full of kids?

What's going on? I'd better go to Kabul." I sold my shop and everything I had, and got all the cash together, but it was too much to carry, so I bought gold, and went to get myself a donkey for the trip. I found a good, big, white one with the packsaddle and all the trappings on it for seven hundred rupees. I said, "That's too expensive," but he said, "Baba, that's cheap—look what a good, big donkey it is, with all its gear." So I bought it, anyway—I was rich— and then I wanted a woven-carpet saddlebag. I saw a guy carrying one around, folded over his shoulder. I asked how much, and he said, "Five hundred rupees." I bought it from him. Then I saw a nomad with a sword, and I bought that for one thousand rupees.[16]

I brought all that back to the shop—I still had to clean up a few things in the shop, so I took the donkey and tied it in the caravanserai where I had a room, gave the donkey some hay, and went to the shop. The bowl of yogurt was still there, so I decided to test my new sword. I laid the sword's edge on the surface of the yogurt and saw that the yogurt sheared away cleanly below the sword. "Oh, boy, that's a good edge! It cuts yogurt without the slightest trouble!"

Around about dinnertime prayer, I went back to my room in the caravanserai, and decided to take the packsaddle off my donkey for the night. When I went to lift the saddle off, it wouldn't come off, and when I yanked it off by force, I saw that the donkey had so many saddle sores, under all the gear, it's like he's been plowed up from his mane to his tail, and the saddle and cinch had stuck to the wounds. But his belly was faultless as a flower. I thought, "If only you had looked at the donkey in the bazaar, taken the gear off to see! Look how you've been tricked—his back is all cut up! Now what? He'll never carry you like this! Well, I'll have to wait around and see if I can heal the sores—I'd better look at the saddlebag, to see if it's full of holes, too!" As soon as I looked it over I saw that it had such holes in it that if you dropped a seven-pound squash into the top it would go right out the bottom. "Oh, curses on his father, what do I do about this saddlebag?" I went off to the bazaar and bought myself about twenty pounds of horsehair thread and a big sack-sewing needle, and came back and sat in a corner of the serai, and there I stayed, putting salves on the donkey's back and feeding it and sewing up all the holes in the sack, for about three weeks, till the thread was all used up and the donkey's back was healed. Then I bought one qeran's worth of tea and one qeran of tea sweets, and filled up the two sides of the saddlebag with that, took up my sword, mounted, and rode off singing "Lady Laili," off toward Kabul.[17]

(In those days, brother, there were no cars—traveling day by day with a donkey, it was a month's travel.) We were on the road for a month, till we got to Kabul. I sent word that I'd arrived, and my old mother came out, with five kids clinging to her skirts and in her arms, saying, "There now, Lal Mir Khan, your papa, is back! Babies, there now, your papa's back, and welcome! There's your papa home safely!" She's talking like that, with me coming along the street. Oh, curses on her father, what's this? Whose kids are these? That she's carrying around and they're all clinging to her! Five of them following her, and she's saying, "Here's your papa!" I took the middle one out of my mother's arms, kissed it, and gave it back to her, and went on to the house, and there's this huge samovar set up, and my whole family got word, "Lal Mir Khan's back," and came to see me. Each one had to sit and drink tea and eat something, and three days passed that way. I opened the saddlebag, with the tea and sweets, and laid it all out. Then I said to my brother, "This gold—take it to my father-in-law, and ask him to prepare for the wedding."

[Wahed switches back to third person.] He changed the gold back into cash, and went off to his father-in-law's along with his brother. He said to him, "My brother went off to work, and now he's back and he asks permission to claim his wife." He said, "Very good. Did you bring the money?" "Yes." "Give it to me." They poured it all into his lap, to the last qeran. "Now, bring out your daughter, I'm taking her with me." "Fine."

He brought the girl out, and there was that same little boy, at their side, saying "Ohh, Mama, where are you going? Ohh, Mama, where are you going?" He thought, "Huh? This is a strange business!" As they came out of the house, here she came, with all five of these kids. He said, "Great, fine! Damn your father! Where did all these kids come from?" She said, "Ohh, where do you think they're from? One is from the time you climbed over the wall. When you passed over the roof to get to me, one is from then. One is from when you lifted the veil off me. One is from when you poured the corn into the veil. One is from when you leaned down to kiss me. Are there any extras? Curse your father! What do you mean, where did they all come from? Where else did I get them? Didn't you do these things?"

So [switches to first person] I thought it over. "Baba, it's true, you did those things. What a place this Kabul is, that you can get someone pregnant just by setting foot on a roof, or by lifting a veil off someone, or putting grain into the veil, or just leaning down to kiss her! If I had been here in Kabul the whole time, by now I would have five hundred kids!" So I said, "OK, now I've taken you from your father, and you bear that in mind—or I swear by the Quran, I'll cut you up one side and down the other!" "Fine, that's your choice, it's your authority." So then [switches to third person] he laid that woman down, and that was it, God had given him the five children, and after that they stayed there and I came here.[18]

NOTES

1. Marriage is a family project, usually initiated by the groom's family on his behalf. Either women or men may be the initial negotiators. Final negotiations are

conducted between elder male relatives of the prospective bride and groom (fathers or elder brothers by preference). Major items of negotiation are the bride price paid to the girl's father, as compensation for his expense in raising her, the amount of clothing and household goods which the groom and his family will settle on the bride herself, and the amount of divorce compensation to be settled on the bride if the marriage is terminated through no fault of her own. The two former amounts are actual outlays, the latter a form of deterrent, in a setting where no-fault divorce was and is extremely rare and much frowned upon.

It is quite normal still, in all but a minority of urban marriages, for the couple never to have met before their engagement. The groom is expected to visit the bride, with gifts, repeatedly during the period between engagement and marriage, as he attempts to do in this story. Traditionally, a form of bundling was practiced in the Herat area: engaged couples were put to bed together, fully dressed, for courting purposes. The couple was expected to abstain from sexual intercourse until the marriage was finalized.

2. "Khan" is an adult male title. Among nomads, it refers especially to tribal leaders, but settled people use it as a respectful designation for any adult male.

3. Thirty thousand rupees equaled U.S. $600 at the 1975 exchange rate, about six times the annual per capita income at the time. The storyteller mixes terms for two different currency systems—the present one and that prevailing up to approximately the 1920s. His simultaneous intention is to portray a bygone day, when money was worth more and harder to come by than it was in the 1970s, and to portray concerns and realities common to both periods, such as the expense of marriage and the hardship wreaked on prospective grooms by high bride prices.

4. A needle (often actually a decorative stickpin of gold) and thread, together with a silk scarf, are the first, formal gifts from the bride's family to the groom's, which signal agreement to the marriage offer.

5. The *chaderi*, the veil worn by married or engaged women outside their homes in Herat, is a full-length garment with many narrow pleats and an unpleated, knee-length face panel with an eyepiece of embroidery mesh. The cap over the head and the unpleated front panel are often decorated with fine embroidery, and the whole is dyed in one of several vivid colors. The precision of the pleating and the color and the fineness of the embroidery, along with the quality of lace which decorates the traditional white trousers whose hems show below the veil, are all taken by men as hints of the physical attractiveness and youth of the woman wearer. A large body of folklore concerns the flirtatious dimension of veiling. In the story, the girl was using a chaderi as a sheet to cover her in sleep. More typical would have been the use of a so-called *chader shau* ("night veil"), simply a large square of cloth used by village women as a full-length veil (a corner of which is pulled up to cover the face when in view of strangers) and for a variety of purposes, including covering for sleep, around the house.

6. According to tradition, once the engagement agreement is reached, the timing of the wedding is at the discretion of the groom's family, which pays for the wedding. The bride's family cannot abrogate the agreement, no matter how long the delay, unless formally released from it by the groom's family. This can work a hardship on the bride's family, which must continue to support the woman indefinitely, and in the worst case may find that her marriageability ends before the groom finally releases her. In an actual case of this kind, a woman I knew in Herat City was engaged in childhood, but the groom's family moved away and lost touch with hers. A member of the woman's family told me they had asked a *qazi* (religious judge) what they should do. He told them to hang the young girl's chaderi on the wall, and when it disintegrated and fell off the hook, she would be released to marry someone else.

When I knew her, she was about forty and had been married two or three years previously as second wife to a local merchant-land owner. The marriage was childless.

7. This laborious process is narrated in detail. It has been condensed here because of space constraints. Corn, regarded as inferior to wheat, the staple grain, is a poorer food for poor people.

8. The lively greetings and conversation, in Kabul dialect, are repeated verbatim, adding to the verisimilitude of the narrative. Persian-language narrative regularly quotes speech directly rather than indirectly. Wahed exploits these opportunities to enhance the sense of realism by using everyday speech and bits of personal detail.

9. These are woolen trousers (*pantlun*) as opposed to traditional, baggy cotton pants (*shalwar*). The humor here again veers toward hyperbole, as it did when the hero was sent out to pick grains of corn off the cobs to take to his fiancee's house, and when, in his poverty, he salvaged a broken bit of melon to chew on as he walked, but here the absurdity becomes more unambiguous. The hero is so naive that he does not recognize that the caravaneer's traveling pants are worn out.

10. A fortified private residence, built of unbaked mud brick with walls ten or more feet high, the standard architectural form of the countryside, where security from bandits and stock thieves is a concern.

11. The qeran was a currency unit predating today's afghani (known colloquially as a "rupee"); it was integrated into the new system as 1 qeran = 0.5 afs (= approx US $.01 in mid-1970s), but was worth much more in the old system—enough for two or three meals of rice and meat at a bazaar foodstand, for instance. The going price for such a meal in the mid-1970s was about US $.30. A day's pay for an unskilled worker was about 50 afs or US $1.

12. Lal Mir Khan is apparently happy with his earnings, not intending to leave his job permanently, but curious about the city. The merchants he meets are portrayed as having moved there from Kabul. There is an implicit claim for the cultural and commercial superiority of Herat over Kabul, both in this scene, in the hero's inability to distinguish the small town he first approaches from the real city, and in his curiosity. This scene includes a lively exchange of greetings, reported as direct speech, in the original.

13. The heads and feet of goats and sheep are bought from butchers by entrepreneurs who clean and stew them and sell the cooked product for either home or bazaar consumption. Regarded as poor people's food, "heads-and-feet" (*kaleh-pacheh*) are nonetheless humorously enjoyed by many people.

14. These carrots, actually a deep purple color, are very sweet and tender. One sir in Herat is now about 1/4 pound or 100 grams, with ten sir per kilogram. A "cent" (*paisa*) is the smallest currency unit; 100 paisa = 1 afghani (50 paisa = 1 qeran) in the present currency system. The storyteller loudly and enthusiastically repeated the street hawker's cries every time they occurred in the story.

15. The demand for his yogurt was so great that he was able to raise his price over the established rate. Prices of everyday commodities sold in the bazaar are usually very stable and known to regular customers, so that bargaining is minimal. Bread with yogurt and sweetened tea is a standard noon meal.

16. Perfect verisimilitude in the way things are sold here alternates with comic hyperbole. All these prices are greatly inflated and the hero is being fleeced repeatedly. There is a reference to regional stereotypes in this series of scenes. Heratis have a reputation for being sharp traders, ready to fool the unwary.

17. The tea sweets are *dashlameh*, a boiled candy which is a specialty of Herat, consumed in preference to sugar with tea. "Lady Laili" (literally, *Xanum Laili*) is a traditional song that was very popular several decades ago and is still well remembered.

18. The hero resorts to a vague threat to assert control over his wife, in place of his father-in-law, who has failed to control her properly in his absence. The use of the idiom "God gave (a child or children)" is normal in referring to any birth, but here it has an ironic twist. The final statement, "They stayed there and I came here," is a formulaic ending for fictional folktales.

The Son's Return

Driss Chraibi

Driss Chraibi, a French-educated chemist from Morocco, writes in this passage from his autobiographical novel, Heirs to the Past, *of the cleavage between generations which can result from exposure to the West. As traditionally educated parents realized the importance of equipping their children to deal with the technologically oriented West, newly independent nations adopted British and French education systems wholesale, and many talented students were sent to study in France and Great Britain. At times a by-product of this education was the alienation of a native from his or her own culture. Chraibi, like many other Moroccans, admired French culture and technology although he had a strong emotional attachment to his home. When given a chance to attain the gloss of Western civilization in France, he left his home and sought education and work abroad. —Eds.*

A seat away from me, in front, there was an Arab with a European woman. The man was young, outwardly at least, with black frizzy hair, all shiny, a moustache as thin as mending cotton, and an array of pens clipped to his breastpocket. He was talking in a loud voice, describing poetically the vast domain owned by his father; selecting an orange and peeling it with his thumbnail, he exclaimed, "O-la-la, these are sold by the heap in Morocco, practically given away. You'll see, my pet, you'll see." The woman was laughing. I heard the laugh, I could not see it. Behind her gold-rimmed spectacles her short-sighted eyes were timorous. She was what psychoanalysts call phobia-obsessed, like the kind of women I had known and loved during my long stay in Europe—a dread of people mocking at sex, a fear of change, a fear especially of death, taking all possible precautions against it. Orderly and methodical in their work as in their private life, conscientious and realistic,

Adapted from *Heirs to the Past*, trans. Len Ortzen. London: Heineman, 1972.

they were symbolic of the West which had brought me to manhood. She had hands which would have inspired a Rodin, breasts straining forward like a pair of greyhounds on the leash, and hair that was very long, falling over her shoulders, onto the seat and her husband's arm like a flow of molten bronze. The man was talking and she was laughing bleakly, without the slightest sign of merriment on her face. Just her hands, now and again, closed over and kneaded her husband's hand, while he looked at her with the face of a worshipper prepared to wipe out a whole tribe for love of a woman.

I was surprised to find myself smiling. Perhaps it was her that I was smiling at. Through the window and seen from thirty thousand feet up, when the clouds thinned out and became like watered silk full of holes, this country I had believed in and still did believe in, and which was slipping past under my feet at five hundred miles an hour, appeared as no more than a map with waterways and sprawls of green that my ancestors had dreamed about in the course of centuries.

The moment I stepped out of the plane I was almost blown over. It was a free, wild wind, straight from the desert. My lungs were suddenly filled almost to bursting with warmth, oxygen, and light. For more than twenty-four hours I had been dead to all feeling except that one—the call to life.

Slowly, and shivering all over, I went down the steps. And just then came the sound. The long-drawn-out call rose from behind the white barrier, crossing the airfield, and burst behind me like a grenade at the feet of the Arab and his wife, who were descending the steps. But it seemed to have come from the depths of the past.

"Ooohoo! Bouchaib. Ooohoo! My son!"

It was frightening to hear: a hymn to joy. And the man who had uttered it was even more frightening. He was an old peasant, dark and withered like a burnt stick, barefooted, bareheaded, wearing just a shirt, with muck up to his knees and the color of dust up to his eyes. He was not so much astride his mount as lying along its back—a little donkey that was the very image of its master: ragged and shorn, mouth open and tongue lolling, eyes starting out of its head, lifting all four legs at a time and spreading them in all directions, and galloping, galloping in the wind straight for the white barrier, as no other representative of its breed had ever galloped before, in the memory of donkey-man. And the old peasant was urging the animal on with kicks and blows, stroking its neck, shouting fond names, calling it little jewel, God's blessing, hell's motor-car. He was promising it a she-ass, a bale of hay, some green peapods—lovely green peapods, oh so good—the whole of his coming harvest of barley and oats, if only it would gallop faster, faster still. And the donkey shook its ears madly and seemed to leave the ground altogether. And the old peasant, welded to his mount, shaded his eyes with his hand, opened his toothless, cavernous mouth, and gave his long-drawn-out call of joy.

"Ooohoo! Bouchaib. Ooohoo! My son!"

We were standing there in our clothes of civilized men and probably with our problems of civilized men—passengers, policemen, customs officials, and loafers, all of us fascinated by this stampede of primitive man and beast—we had eyes for nothing else. The Arab with the thin moustache was standing among us in his expensive suit, which was flapping in the wind. He kept looking at his wife, and she stared back with scared eyes, as though afraid to understand. The wind was catching at her long copper-colored hair and making it stream round her head like a banner. She tried to hold it down, but her hands were trembling and the wind was stronger than any human sentiment.

She said, "What is it all about, darling?"

"If only I knew," he replied in a wary tone.

Then he shouted: "But-I-do-not-know!"

She took his arm and they began to walk on again. We who were there, we bestirred ourselves and set off too. She said, and it was only a murmur, yet even amid the roaring of the wind and the shouting of the old peasant, we heard the murmur like an explosion, "But I'm sure there's something the matter, darling. Everyone's looking at us."

"Well," he shouted, "it's a confounded habit in this country!"

And he began to walk faster, as though the only hope was in flight, dragging his wife along on his arm.

And it came to pass: the donkey could not stop its headlong flight and crashed into the barrier, the old peasant toppled to the ground, picked himself up and prepared to jump the obstacle. We who were watching, we all saw him and can bear witness: it was a man overcome with joy who was trying to take a leap, a man whose trembling hands were stretched out to the person he kept calling his in the voice of the damned; an old man with a face as small as a child's, and so wrinkled as to appear seamed, a dog-like face bathed in tears. When the policeman caught hold of him and said, "Hey, granddad, where d'you think you're off to? Keep away from this barrier," the old man answered in a voice that trembled as much as his hands: "But that's my son!"

"All right, all right," said the policeman. "That's your son, I'm not saying he isn't, but keep away from this barrier."

"Very well, sir," said the old man politely, "But you see, that's my son. His name is Bouchaib."

"Bouchaib," repeated the policeman. "Bouchaib. All right, I'm not saying it isn't, but keep away from this barrier."

"But do you see, sir? I've been waiting for him for five years. That's my son, my son Bouchaib. That's him, over there. I'd know him with my eyes shut."

He started calling again. "Ooohoo! Bouchaib! Ooohoo! My son!"

"Take it easy, granddad," said the policeman. "Don't do anything silly. I'm a peaceful sort, I am, and I shouldn't like you to spend the night in the cells at your age. So stay quiet and keep off this barrier."

The old man seemed to understand; he calmed down, contenting himself with blowing a kiss to his son over the policeman's shoulder and calling to him: "I'll wait for you. I'm here. I shan't budge. You've only to go round the customs shed and you'll find me here. I shan't go away. Just tell them that you're my son and they'll let you through first. They all know I've been waiting for you a long time."

He explained to the policeman: "That's my son. He's just come back from France. He's highly educated. I say, sir, when you come off duty this evening, will you be one of our guests? There are couscous, a roasted calf, and honey cakes."

"This evening, you say? With pleasure, dad. There'll be a roast, you say?"

"Oh, only a little calf. Not very big, but I'm not rich. I've sold every-thing—"

"Ah, yes, that's the way of things. With pleasure, uncle, but keep away from this barrier. . . . "

We were still walking across the airfield toward the customs shed when I heard the young woman ask her husband: "Do you know him, dear?"

"Know who?"

"Why, that man, of course! Anyone would think you were blind!"

"What man?"

There was a short silence between them. I saw her slow down, on the point of stopping, and all of us who were following prepared to come to a halt too.

"I don't understand Arabic," she said, "but that man seems to me to have been calling to you for some time. Everyone has noticed it except you. Are you trying to tell me that it's not you whose attention he's been trying desper-ately to catch?"

He turned round, and it was as though he was seeing his father for the first time—the first time in his life. I was watching him, and I can bear out that his face became distorted with rage. Then he looked at his wife, and it was as though he was seeing her for the first time, too. But his face had fallen, all the muscles were sagging.

"Yes, you're right," he said. "It's an old servant." And he added quickly, "An old servant who has known me since I was born. I really hadn't recog-nized him. Of course, it's five years since I last saw him."

And he gave a friendly little wave to the old servant. She let go of his arm and looked him straight in the face. There was nothing of the phobia-obsessed about her now. She was no longer bothering about her hair stream-ing in the wind, and one would have said that we who were there mattered no more than a swarm of flies.

"But he recognized you straightaway," she cried in a shrill voice. "He's over there, weeping and calling you by your name. I may not know Arabic, but I don't need anyone to translate for me. I know how you pronounce your name."

"What do you want me to do?" he exclaimed, exasperated. "Go and throw my arms round his neck?"

"And why not? If he'd been able to, he would have come and thrown his arms round the plane."

"Now look, my pet, you don't know what you're saying."

"I may not know what I'm saying, but I know what I'm feeling. And it's my impression that you're hiding something from me."

"Look, dear." His voice had gone all tender. "You don't know anything about this country. . . . "

"He seemed to swoop down from the sky," she said vehemently. "If he'd had a car, he would have stamped on the accelerator to get here long before us. But all he had was his donkey, and if you didn't see that donkey galloping, then you didn't want to see anything. He's come a long way, just to meet you. Look at him, he's covered in mud, he was so afraid of being late. I wish I were like that old servant."

"All right," said the man wearily. "Wait for me here."

When the old peasant saw his son coming, he made no attempt to break away from the policeman. He merely said: "There you are, sir, you see? I told you he's my son. I haven't led you into error."

"All right, granddad, all right. I'm very glad, I'm sure. But keep off that barrier. I don't want to see you trying to jump it again, d'you hear?"

"He's my son, and he's been away for such a long time. He's the only one I've got now. I thought I'd lost him forever. Ohoo! Bouchaib! Ohoo! My son!"

"Quiet, I tell you. Calm down. Otherwise, I'll be obliged to deal severely with you, and I don't like tackling old men. So be sensible."

"Now I can die in peace," said the old man. "I didn't want to die before he came back."

"You seem to me like one of those wholemeal loaves that aren't made any more," said the policeman. "But do, please, keep off that barrier. If it gets broken, I shall have to take you to the station, and I'd much rather help you eat that roast this evening."

"Bouchaib!" yelled the old peasant. And when at last he was able to grasp his son's hand and raise it to his lips, he stood there kissing the fingers one by one and saying over and over again, "Bouchaib, Bouchaib, Bouchaib."

"Steady, steady now," the policeman was saying. "Don't get excited. Be philosophical. Breaking barriers and spending the night at the station isn't at all the thing for a man of your age. Steady, I tell you!"

"Are you all right, son?" the old peasant was saying. "Are you eating well? You're not ill? Is that your wife? Why didn't she come and speak to me? Ah yes, of course, she's shy. But she mustn't be shy, I'll do all I can to make her feel at home. Tell her that in her own language. Your old mother has been busy beating up the couscous since dawn, and she hasn't been to bed all night. You know her; she always does what she pleases."

And he started laughing, but his laugh was assuredly a sob.

"Go back to your village," said Bouchaib, "and wait till I come. It may be tomorrow or the day after. I have to get my wife settled in a hotel. Good-bye."

I was so close to Bouchaib's wife that I could have touched her. She was watching the scene intently, aching to understand what was being said. For a moment I was tempted to translate her father-in-law's words into French for her, and the answer her husband had just given. But I refrained, and it was a relief to me. It was up to her to discover the truth in her own way. All I did was to raise my right hand and clap her on the shoulder. She must have cried out, but I couldn't hear very well as I was laughing into the wind. I went on my way, and when I met Bouchaib he did not even glance at me and I said nothing to him; I was still laughing. It was only when I had almost reached the barrier that I stopped and my laughter stopped, strangled in my throat—the old peasant had tossed the policeman over his shoulder like a sack of logs and had started to break the slats of the barrier. He was just breaking off the tops, giving each one a sharp little pull, steadily and unhurriedly, as though he had plenty of time and was counting them as he went. And he threw them over his shoulder, one after the other, with a leisurely, casual gesture, as if nothing mattered any more. As he did so, he intoned a kind of litany that I had difficulty in catching, not because his voice was soft (it rose above the wind), but because he rattled it off at great speed.

"In the name of God, the Compassionate, the Merciful, I sold my father's field, amen. And my brother's field, amen. And the one I robbed my neighbor of, my neighbor of, my neighbor of. The sheep, the billy goats and the nanny goat, the hens, the mattress, the army rifle, all sold. Amen. Thy will be done, O Lord, in this century of science, decolonization and independence. Money order, sixty money orders, plus the postage. So that he might be worthy of my unworthiness. And three of my sons have died at their work, wretched are we, and turned to dust shall we be, amen. And now he is ashamed of his father. The road is long, so very long, back to the village, and I am weary, so very weary, Lord, I no longer even wish to die, I no longer wish for anything."

"And now, come along with me," said the policeman, getting to his feet. He spoke gently, as though to a sick child; but he was looking surly. "Come on, I'm taking you to the station. I told you to keep away from that barrier. Come on, granddad, come on."

Just then the donkey appeared, seemingly from nowhere. It finished chewing a blade of grass and then raised its old man's head to the sky and started to bray.

The Funeral

Driss Chraibi

Muslim burials are conducted as soon after death as is feasible. The deceased is washed, wrapped in a shroud, and carried to a cemetery. A coffin may or may not be used. The body is placed in the grave with the face oriented toward Mecca. Either at the deathbed or at the grave, the shahada (witness to God's oneness) is whispered in the ear of the deceased. The funeral prayer may be said at graveside, in the home of the deceased, or in a mosque. The memorial service held forty days after the death is as important as the funeral. Friends and relatives gather to mourn the deceased. Below, Driss Chraibi describes the chanting of the Quran at his father's grave. —Eds.

The wind had changed and was now coming off the sea, a fresh, soft breeze that was bringing a flight of coppery clouds. Whether it was a yew or a cypress, whether young or old, I could not say, but a tree stood there that was so covered with dust from the graves that it had assumed the color of death and of time. Somewhere in the tree, a bird was singing—a canary. Except for its trilling note, nothing could be heard, nothing beyond the pickaxe digging into the rocky ground.

Those who were sitting there, those who had found places on the flat tombstones or on the walls, and were bunched along the paths, had probably been there since dawn. When the funeral procession came through the cemetery gates, there they were, their arms folded across their knees, with lifeless eyes, as though they had no other abode on earth. The only clear space was the main path, and when we had reached the gravedigger, when he had said "In the name of Almighty God" and spat on his hands and lifted his pickaxe to start digging his hole before us all, and when, bent beneath his burden, Nagib had placed it on the ground (he had carried it himself, across his shoul-

Adapted from *Heirs to the Past*, trans. Len Ortzen. London: Heineman, 1972.

ders, and the idea of offering to help had occurred to no one), when he had straightened up, sweat streaming from his armpits, his body, and his brow—I turned round and saw . . . that the main path had never existed and that someone had shut the gates from which traditional gnomes were hanging.

All the time the gravedigger dug and shoveled up soil, the bird sang. And when the grave was long and deep, when the man who had dug it climbed out, himself the color of the earth, flung away his tools, and announced in a solemn voice, "Wretched are we, and turned to dust shall we be"—then the bird fell silent. It seemed to have flown off to another cemetery. A tidal wave of voices repeated, "Wretched are we, and turned to dust shall we be."

Then a man stood up. He had been sitting in front of me, his hands on the stretcher made of poles on which my father was lying. The man was of medium height, with no distinctive features, clad in a grey overall and wearing sandals. He got up and began to chant.

What he chanted was of no importance. It was not the words nor the meaning, nor even the symbolism, which moved our hearts, the men, women, and children who were there. We forgot why we were there the moment he began to chant. It was the incantation, and the end of our woes and miserable little problems, the aching and yet serene longing for that other life which is ours and to which we are all destined to return, the victors and the defeated, the fully developed and those still at the larva stage, the faithful and the atheists, through God's great compassion. There was all of that in the voice of the man who stood chanting in the sun, and we were in his voice, I was in his voice despite the vast legacy of incredulity that I had received from the West. When he reached the end of a verse, he paused, and so it came about—an outburst of fervor. And while he chanted it was like a man in the wilderness chanting his faith. And the voice rose and swelled, changed in tone, became tragic, soared, and then floated down on our heads like a seagull gliding gently and softly, little more than a whisper. And so—never, never again will I go in search of intellectuals, of written truths, synthetic truths, of collections of hybrid ideas which are nothing but ideas. Never again will I travel the world in search of a shadow of justice, fairness, progress, or schemes calculated to change mankind. I was weary and I was returning to my clan. That man who was not even aware of his voice of his faith was alive and held the secret of life—a man who could not even have been a dustman in this world of founts of knowledge and of civilization. Peace and everlasting truth were in him and in his voice, while all was crumbling around him and on the continents.

* * *

He stopped and sat down under a deluge. The clouds swept in by the wind had come to a standstill above the cemetery, thick, gray, and lowering, just over the tree where the bird had been singing, and they were sending down an autumnal rain on our bare heads. I had only just become aware of it.

But not one of us moved. Long after the man had sat down, we remained as we were. The rain fell in torrents, and we let it fall.

It was Nagib who lowered the body into the grave. He jumped down, then stretched out his arms and quickly drew it toward him. Someone tried to help, but Nagib bared his teeth. I heard a moan, and knew that my mother had just fainted. Then Madini came forward and took me by the hand. He walked with his shoulders hunched and his head drooping. When we were at the edge of the gaping hole, when Nagib climbed out and nodded, Madini went and picked up the gravedigger's spade, then held it out to me.

"This was his last wish too," he murmured.

I took the spade and gazed at it. The handle was quite short and the blade was wide. It was the kind that he had used for sinking his wells, going off all by himself with that and a pick, a bucket, and a rope ladder. He did not just dig where there would have been the best chance of coming upon water. He used to say: "Sometimes God causes water to fall from the sky—and a few ideas. And people wait for all that to germinate. And that's the downfall of individuals and nations." He would stand on a small hillock, look slowly all round him from horizon to horizon, and say, "There, there, and over there." Then he took his tools and went off to dig for days or weeks, in clay, stony or rocky ground. And he never gave up. I never saw him give anything up. And therein lay his strength, the source of his authority.

A bride in Iran. *Photo Mary Hegland*

A professional singer entertains guests at a wedding celebration in the courtyard of a private home in Marrakesh, Morocco. *Photo Dorothy Andrake*

A stepmother and stepdaughter chat in a courtyard in Iran. *Photo Mary Hegland*

Egyptian mother and son beneath a prayer rug depicting the Ka'ba at Mecca. *Photo Evelyn A. Early*

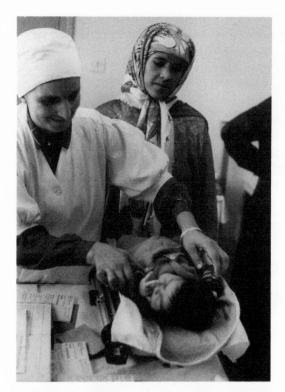

A mother-child clinic in Morocco.
Photo Evelyn A. Early

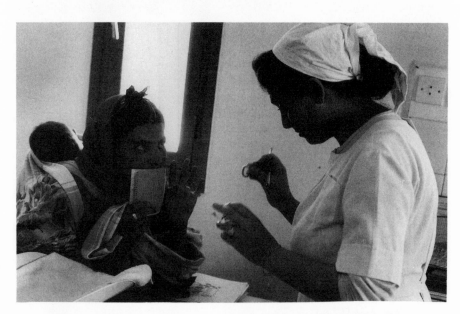

A nurse in a Moroccan family-planning clinic explains the use of a condom. *Photo Evelyn A. Early*

A child cares for a younger sibling in Meknes, Morocco. *Photo Dorothy Andrake*

A woman washes dishes at a communal spigot in Aliabad in southwestern Iran.
Photo Mary Hegland

Women wash laundry in an irrigation ditch in Menoufiyya, Egypt. *Photo Evelyn A. Early*

Women and children in a village in Iran. *Photo Mary Hegland*

A young man visits a relative in a village near Shiraz, Iran. *Photo Mary Hegland*

Preparing the midday meal in Marrakesh, Morocco. *Photo Dorothy Andrake*

Children play on a homemade swing in Asni, a mountain village in Morocco. *Photo Dorothy Andrake*

Handicapped girls learn to draw at a special school in Marrakesh, Morocco. *Photo Dorothy Andrake*

Baathist youth festival, Syria. *Photo Evelyn A. Early*

Moroccan boys listen to a tape-recorded musical performance.
Photo Dorothy Andrake

A Berber girl from a Saharan village near Zagora, Morocco.
Photo Dorothy Andrake

PART TWO

Gender Relations

INTRODUCTION

Middle Eastern gender roles have traditionally been governed by a patriarchal kinship system that was well entrenched in pre-Islamic bedouin tribal society and also in the Middle Eastern regions to which Islam spread. While men may move freely, women's actions have been more carefully delineated. Muslims note that Islam improved the plight of women in the seventh century by prohibiting female infanticide, limiting the extent of polygamy, and restricting men from unlimited right to divorce.

Islam considers women to be believers with full religious duties, including pilgrimage to Mecca. While Islamic laws prescribe gender-specific rights in areas such as divorce and inheritance, ultimately women's status varies from locale to locale—depending on the implementation of Islamic law and on local traditions and social customs, which are often more powerful forces than the letter of the religious law.

Men are expected to provide for their families; women, to bear and raise children; children, to honor and respect their parents and grow up to fulfill their adult roles. Sons are to become educated, to marry, and to assume steady employment; daughters are to become mothers and increasingly—given economic hardships—to work outside the home as well. Actions, whether honorable or shameful, do not reflect upon the individual alone; they reflect on the entire family.

Clear gender roles mean less confusion about social expectations. A woman's traditional role is domestic—to bear children and to raise them, to maintain the home, to cook, in the country to work in the fields, and in the city perhaps to run a sewing or vending business. A childless woman, as well as one who never marries, is somewhat socially marginal. Nevertheless, as Donna Lee Bowen demonstrates in her article on pragmatic morality in Islam, Muslim theologians have not taken a rigid position against birth control, but rather call for attention to the woman, the family, and other human considerations in the equation.

Women's special status is reflected in the term for women of the household, *harim*, which is derived from *harama*, to forbid. The weight of proper behavior falls heavily upon female shoulders. An unmarried woman avoids sitting in a room alone or being seen in public with a nonrelated male. She frets if she is accidentally thrown into the company of strange men, for she knows the consequence of improper behavior, no matter how innocent it may be.

Honor, an important cultural theme, is maintained through social decorum, keeping one's word, and providing for one's family. Honor can be a collective status, as when a woman's improper behavior stains a family's honor. In the past, such a woman might have been killed to wipe out the blot, and one can still sometimes read of honor killings. While honor killings today are rare, isolated incidents, chastity remains a critical question that, as Nawal al-Saadawi recounts below, can cause both psychological and social damage to an innocent young woman.

Islam accords men a higher status ("Men have a degree above them [women]," Quran 2:228), but men also bear an obligation to care for the women and children dependent upon them. For a man, being married or not, a father, or childless is not so important as it is for a woman. A man's improper conduct blackens his reputation and reflects on his family, but he cannot disgrace his family in the way that a woman can. There is more room for the peccadillos of male youth than for those of females.

Women are simultaneously cherished and seen as dangerous—beings who must be protected, but also possessors of strange powers which stem from their fertility. This thinking resembles the Western dichotomy of virgin and vixen. Evelyn A. Early examines traditional Egyptian beliefs which suggest that rituals surrounding charged life events such as birth, circumcision, and death are interrelated within a symbolic complex of blood and infertility. Folk tales similarly reflect the ambivalence about women's powers. The following proverb from the Aures mountains in Algeria suggests that women's demonic tendencies increase throughout life while men steadily become more righteous.

> The child of male sex comes to the world with sixty *jnoun* (spirits) in his body; the child of the female sex is born pure; but every year, the boy gets purified of a jinn, whereas the girl acquires one; and this is the reason that old women, sixty years and with sixty jnoun, are sorcerers more malignant than the devil himself. Blind she sews more material, lame she jumps over more rocks, and deaf she knows all the news. (Nelson 1973:52)

Fatima Mernissi, a Moroccan sociologist, has suggested that Islam is responsible for restrictions on women because Islam defines women as emotionally dangerous. It is woman, in Mernissi's interpretation of Islam, who is "the embodiment of destruction, the symbol of disorder. She is *fitna*, the polarization of the uncontrollable, a living representative of the dangers of sexuality and its rampant disruptive potential" (Mernissi 1975:13). This viewpoint suggests that women must be restricted to minimize their destructive potential and that local standards for decorum and Islamic restrictions on women's behavior have been developed to contain women.

Whatever may have been the respective contributions of Islam and local custom, it is clear that the majority of social restrictions on Middle Eastern women originate in cultural traditions such as patriarchy and honor, which are not in the tenets of Islam. A case in point is veiling, which literally means covering the face, although it is often used as a gloss for conservative dress or for seclusion. Islamic law does not mandate veiling but only requests that women dress modestly. Historically, in nineteenth-century Egypt, veiling and physical seclusion of women signaled the upward mobility of agriculturalists who moved to town and no longer needed women's labor. In the twentieth century, the veil has assumed political and social meanings. Muslim women of Algeria concealed bombs under their robes in the 1950s, and those of Iran used the veil to demonstrate revolutionary fervor and support for the Ayatollah Khomeini in 1978. More recently, modest Islamic dress has become an individual statement about piety and about society. Elizabeth W. Fernea analyzes meanings of veiling—traditional understandings as well as new manifestations rooted in Islamic activism.

Islamic law discriminates between genders on such matters as inheritance law, which limits a woman's share to roughly half that of a man. However, since in Middle Eastern society the male is expected to provide for his female relatives, the difference in inheritance is somewhat mitigated. A peasant woman in Egypt who was the senior daughter-in-law in an extended family household was quite secure in her position. Nevertheless, in the back of her mind she knew that her natal family would shelter her should she ever be divorced. Her family of birth assumed a mythic status as her potential refuge: "My brother Abdul Monaim has an extremely productive farm with six feddan and forty goats. He also raises water buffalo for investors. The grounds are green and succulent. If I went to my family, they would lift me up and care for me. . . . There is much goodness there with my brother."

The option of ending a marriage through divorce, which has traditionally been reserved for men, is now a possibility for women throughout most of the Middle East. Reforms in Islamic law (which differ by country) accord women the right to divorce in specified circumstances, but a woman must show just cause and contend with a sometimes unsympathetic justice system. Carolyn Fluehr-Lobban discusses the complexity of reconciling women's status in Islamic law with the realities of life in Sudan.

Even though gender roles are strictly defined, new forms of association, such as coeducation, have created ambiguous situations. Traditional mores prohibited male-female contact before marriage. However, when students began to attend coeducational secondary schools or universities, the prohibition began to break down. Writing on adolescence in Morocco, Douglas A. Davis and Susan Schaefer Davis show that lack of rules for informal social interaction often causes confusion for young men and women. Among more progressive Middle Eastern families, young men and women can mix so long as they are in a group. However, most families forbid dating as a single couple. A brother, sister, or friend chaperons the couple until they are engaged.

Although informal mixing may cause problems, Middle Eastern professional women experience little difficulty in their associations with men in the public realm. In essence, they become gender-neutral and are seen as "engineers" or "physicians" rather than as "women." Even among more traditional Middle Eastern women, interaction with non-kin males in the course of work is acceptable. Agriculturalists almost never secluded women historically; then and today women worked in the fields, marketed in the villages, and even hitched rides to market with men who happened to pass with a horse and cart.

In considering the selections below, we must ask what these examples from such divergent geographic regions tell us about gender relations. Do we learn, for instance, that courtship is not always a simple traditional act, or that women's legal status is greatly affected both by local custom and by specific judicial actions? How do Middle Eastern Muslims accommodate modern ideas of dating and virginity with local traditions and family planning decisions with religion? When we de-exoticize veiled women and the *harim*, can we see Middle Eastern Muslim gender relations in a more realistic light?

REFERENCES

Mernissi, Fatima. 1975. *Beyond the Veil,* Boston: Schenkman Publishing Co.
Nelson, Cynthia. 1973. *The Desert and the Sown.* Institute of International Studies, University of California, Berkeley.

Women and Sex

Nawal El Saadawi
Translated by Donna Lee Bowen

Middle Eastern women are expected to be virgins at marriage. There are many ways to produce the proof of virginity—a spot of blood on the marriage sheets. Chicken blood may be used as a creative substitute, and physicians routinely repair women who have lost their "virginity" riding a bicycle or otherwise. Nevertheless, the cultural expectation of virginity remains, and whether or not the woman's virtue is proved by a display of blood, her purity is a direct reflection upon her family and its status. Here the Egyptian physician and feminist Nawal El Saadawi recounts the personal crisis which afflicts a woman who may be socially chaste but biologically not a virgin. —Eds.

Although it has been ten years or more since I saw her, I still remember that young girl. I was a young doctor and had begun a practice in Maidan Giza. A doctor can see a great deal if he allows himself to go beyond the limits of traditional medicine and allows his own strength of character to overcome the shallow style of practicing medicine which we learned in school—a style which causes the sick person to lose his humanity and his individuality, and divides him into unconnected parts, isolated from the soul and separate from society.

In those days I used to contemplate the question of health care in Egypt from the safety of my clinic. I had recently completed five years studying and practicing medicine both in Egypt and abroad, and I had developed a belief that the majority of my patients were not ill; rather, the abysmal conditions in which they lived caused them continually to feel ill. Most illnesses, in any case, cured themselves by natural means and by the force of the human will.

The day the girl entered my office, I was sitting in my clinic contemplating

From *Women and Sex* [al-Marā'h wa al-Jins]. Cairo: Dar al-Sha'b, 1972.

these questions. Her terrified gaze drew my eyes to hers, and her anxious eyes sought help from mine. With the passing of years I have forgotten her features, but the look in her eyes engraved itself in my mind and has become a part of me.

She was not alone. A man was with her.

He said in an angry, upset voice, "Doctor, please examine her."

I directed my questions to the girl. "What symptoms do you complain of?"

She bowed her head and did not answer.

The man spoke for her roughly with increasing anger. "We were married yesterday, and I discovered that she was not a virgin."

I asked him, "How did you find that out?"

He said angrily, "It's obvious. I saw no blood."

The girl tried to open her mouth to say something. But he cut her off. "She claims that she is innocent, so I have brought her here for you to examine her."

The examination proved conclusively that the wife was still a virgin. Her hymen was of the kind that is termed medically to be elastic—in other words, it expands and contracts with penetration but does not tear, therefore producing no blood.

I explained the matter in detail to the husband. He was an educated man who had studied in Europe, and it seemed to me that he would understand and be satisfied with my explanation. The bride relaxed as though she were able to breathe again after a long siege.

The matter, however, was not to be solved so easily. After a few days the girl returned by herself. Her face was no longer the face of the eighteen-year-old whom I had seen earlier that week. It was the face of an old woman, aged before her time. Sorrow had sketched lines of pain on her face which made her resemble the faces of the dead—of whom I had seen too many in the shadow of the medical profession.

Her voice cracked, "He divorced me, and it almost became a scandal even though my father suppressed the matter."

I asked her, "Does your father understand?"

She shook her head, and her reddened eyes clouded over. I could see the signs of tears that flowed and dried and flowed and dried until they could flow no more.

"Oh, doctor," she sighed, "you are the only one who knows that I am innocent. Now I live in fear of the vengeance of my father and brother."

I went with her to her father's house and explained the situation to him. I told him that his daughter was a virgin still, and that her hymen was elastic and would not tear until she delivered her first child. The father was astonished when he listened to this technical account. He hit one fist against the other and cried out in anger, "This means that my daughter was wronged."

"Yes."

"Who is responsible for this injustice?"

"You all are, her husband and her family."

He said angrily, "Oh no. You doctors are responsible. You are the ones who have mastered the technical knowledge and hide it from the people. If it were not for this incident which happened to my daughter by chance, I would not have known anything about this subject. Why don't you explain this to everyone? In fact, it is your first duty—to communicate this to others in order that more innocent women are not harmed!"

I decided that day to return to my office and write on this subject, but I saw immediately that it needed attention from various perspectives. It was not purely medical, but involved social, economic, and moral concerns. Medicine only represented one side of the question.

Years went by and other stories of other problems passed in front of my eyes, and numerous tragedies made young girls, women, and children sacrifices to public ignorance and prevailing customs. Some of them died during abortions or circumcisions or childbirth in adverse circumstances or were targets of death or assault because of the lack of the proof of virginal blood. Some of them died psychological or social deaths after a tragedy for one reason or another. How many are the forces which confronted women in our society causing them to die psychologically or to make their lives a living death, except that death itself would have been more merciful in most cases.

My numerous travels to most countries of the world helped me to grasp the position of women in different societies—advanced and backward, capitalist and socialist. As a result of my readings in sciences other than medicine and in history and literature, I was able to comprehend how and why chains had been imposed upon women. This as well as my own experiences as a woman provided me with true knowledge of the deepest feelings and emotions of a woman. The world needs sound information about women, to change mistaken perceptions which prevail, to correct conventional wisdom which is circulated about women in the world, and which is generally written by men. For this reason, this material is not a commentary on the essence of women, but it represents the viewpoint of men toward women, and what a big difference there is between just a point of view and the truth. . . .

Cairo, December 1971

Dilemmas of Adolescence:
Courtship, Sex, and Marriage
in a Moroccan Town

Douglas A. Davis and Susan Schaefer Davis

*In any society, a gap exists between cultural ideals and reality.
The double standard of sexual mores which has always existed in
the United States is more pronounced in the Middle East, as we
shall see in this article on courtship in a Moroccan town. Of
course, there are Middle Eastern societies such as Saudi Arabia
where local custom dictates an even more conservative role for
women, as there are also some urban areas in the Middle East
where women's actions are less strictly monitored. In a Moroccan
town, a young man expects to experiment sexually with women
outside his kin group but to marry a virgin within his kin group.
He fights any advances to his sister, and women's behavior is
strictly defined. The introduction of modern sexual mores to adolescent society results in countless contradictions. —Eds.*

The boy [*ghulam*] is named on the seventh day, and taught manners at the
sixth year. When he is nine years old he should have a separate bed. When he
is thirteen years old he should be punished if he is not praying. At the age of
sixteen his father will marry him [to someone]. Then his father will take his
hand and say, "I've named you, taught you manners, educated you, and
found you a wife. Now I take refuge in God, if you sin in this world or are
punished in the next."

    —Hadith of the Prophet Muhammad, recounted by Annas (Bukhari)

    All human societies impose rules on the form and expression of sexual
behavior, and all societies have institutionalized to some degree the circumstances under which individuals are expected to mate and produce offspring.
While such rules are likely to be embedded in early childrearing practices,
they are especially important during the years after puberty, when increased

sexual drive may lead the individual to confront societal restrictions. At a time when most customary "Third World" societies are in rapid transition to postcolonial states in which traditional attitudes and practices are challenged by exposure (through migration, education, and telecommunications) to alien ideologies and new economic pressures, understanding the form and likely outcomes of such confrontations becomes vitally important. In many societies (including our own) recent decades have witnessed increased tension between traditional expectations of parental or other kin influence on marriage and the individual's desire to make decisions regarding marriage. In the following discussion, interviews with individual young men and women (recorded in Morocco in 1982 and 1984 as part of a Harvard University cross-cultural comparative study of adolescence) illustrate the general observations we make about changing sexual, courtship, and marriage patterns in Morocco.

COURTSHIP AND SEXUALITY IN THE MIDDLE EAST AND NORTH AFRICA

A capsule depiction of the significant markers in the socialization process for the male Muslim is contained in the *hadith* (authenticated saying of the Prophet Muhammad) quoted in the epigraph above. The reader will note (a) that Muslim tradition possesses a well-articulated conception of the stages of development, at least for males; (b) that fathers (hence the kinship network) play a central role in preparing the individual for membership in the social group; (c) that religious training is linked both to physical maturation and to punishment; and (d) that arranged marriage (with, the Muslim understands, a kinperson acceptable to the family) is the cultural norm. These generalizations would of course apply to most traditional Muslim societies of the Middle East. With respect to Morocco, however, several additional generalizations may help the reader form a picture of the cultural background against which the changing behaviors described below may be viewed.

Precolonial Moroccan values and practices have been described extensively in a classic anthropological work, E. A. Westermarck's *Marriage Ceremonies in Morocco* (1914). Three points must be briefly noted regarding courtship and marriage patterns in traditional Morocco: premarital seclusion largely prevented contact between unmarried females of good family and potential male suitors or lovers; arranged marriage was the norm, with the designated partner being a member of the same kinship group (and the preferred mate the son or daughter of a father's brother); and the community expected proof of the bride's virginity on the wedding night. These three cultural practices have changed in the last two generations in Morocco, but as we shall see they continue to set the terms on which many individuals evaluate their own behavior.

ZAWIYA

The ethnographic data presented here were collected in a large, traditional, semirural community of about 12,000 citizens in north central Morocco, only a few miles from a small city built during French colonialism. We returned to "Zawiya" during ten months of 1982 as one of the field teams of the Harvard Adolescence Project. We had lived in the same neighborhood a decade before. The focus of our ethnographic interviewing, testing, and observation was roughly 50 families living in one neighborhood of Zawiya, in particular their 150 children between the ages of 9 and 21 at the time of the study. In addition, a number of residents of the neighborhood whom we have known for many years assisted in the research and were interviewed at length about a variety of sensitive topics, among them the details of local sexual practices. Several unmarried male and female informants in their twenties provided much of the data concerning the details of sexual activities to which we refer below.

The general sense we have of the relationship of actual sexual behavior in this community to the traditional norms of propriety is that most individuals continue to cite and apparently value the norms even when these do not seem to fully determine the individual's behavior. Thus, the majority of unmarried males in the community hope to achieve sexual intimacy with the unmarried females they meet in school, on the job, or in the course of running errands; but these same males are appalled at the thought that their own sisters would so behave. The obvious double standard implied in such behavior is of course well known from our own society, but it has become an especially important issue for young Moroccans in recent years. At the level of major "ritual" attention to the proper preparation of the male or female member of the society—in this case circumcision of males at about the age of five and the virginity test at the time of a female's first marriage—traditional forms are still considered necessary. At the level of individual adolescent premarital behavior, the situation is one of substantial and rapid change. Males engage in a variety of premarital behaviors which are condemned by their religion and about which they feel shame, and in premarital flirtations females increasingly risk the honor which they continue to assert is an important aspect of the bridal trousseau.

EXAMPLES OF MALE AND FEMALE SEXUAL BEHAVIOR

Since Moroccan society has traditionally maintained a high degree of seclusion of unmarried females from nonfamily males, we expected that sexual alternatives to premarital heterosexual "dating" relationships would be pursued by adolescent males. Despite wide differences in history, religion, and social circumstances, the distribution of available sexual outlets for male Moroccan adolescents in this community is very similar to that of the rural United States after World War II, as documented by Alfred Kinsey's research (Kinsey et al. 1948). These include fairly prevalent male homoerotic play about the time of puberty, contact with prostitutes, and masturbation. Sexual play with other males occurs fairly frequently in small group settings. These activities are most common in early adolescence and usually decrease as heterosexual outlets become available. Exclusive or postadolescent homosexuality is considered shameful in this community, and is probably rare.

While social conditions have changed substantially during past decades, the rules governing the sexual behavior of adolescents in this community are still quite deeply embedded in traditional Moroccan and Muslim values. Both sexes experience new opportunities for romantic and sexual involvement in the context of schooling or employment, and tensions may result between traditional values concerning premarital female chastity and increasing contemporary interest in dating. Adolescent and young adult males described a variety of conflicts resulting from their desire to have sexual relationships with young women who were not prostitutes. These included jealousy and fear that the young woman who was intimate with them might also have been intimate with other males (that is, a double standard), attempts to engage in heavy petting without penetration of the girl's maidenhead or risk of pregnancy, and conflict over whether marriage was desirable with a girl who had become dishonored by sexual experience.

For the sexually active couple who do marry, the wedding night presents special problems. The guests at the traditional wedding party (which is still the preferred observance of marriage in this community) expect to remain until the bride and bridegroom have retired to a nearby room and consummated the marriage, and the bride's undergarments or bedclothes stained with hymenal blood are publicly displayed. One young man, whom we shall call Ahmad, described the attempts made to avoid pregnancy and loss of virginity, and possible scenarios on the wedding night. The following is excerpted from Douglas A. Davis's 1982 field notes:

Couples often approach premarital intercourse but attempt to prevent penetration. Many couples have vaginal intercourse, however; hence many marriages do not involve virgins. Several variations on the traditional Moroccan marriage appear to result. In some cases, the male has himself taken his fiancee's virginity, loves her, and wants to marry without embarrassment, so he either cuts himself on the wedding night to bloody the undergarments, collaborates with the girl in some other bloodlike deception, or foregoes a formal wedding, with the couple undertaking only the legal engagement (*khutba*) phase of the wedding ceremony rather than the traditional family celebration. In a second, more "traditional," and seemingly less common scenario the bride is not a virgin, and her brothers know this and stay close to the bridal chamber to calm or threaten the unsuspecting groom so that no scandal occurs. The rarest situation for the generation now reaching maturity in Zawiya is the one attributed to precolonial Moroccan society, in which the groom or the brothers have not known the bride is not a virgin, and the groom or the brothers berate, beat, or perhaps kill the bride. Ahmad claimed to know of many local cases in which the bride's nonvirginity was well known before the ceremony and either "bloody" undergarments were produced or there was in any case no outcry, but could produce no instance of real scandal as a result of the groom's ignorance of the bride's lack of virginity. He also repeated the belief that doctors can now re-create apparent virginity, and claimed that many girls have sex quite freely and then avail themselves of medical assistance. Some couples claim to be sexually abstinent even after the papers which are the legal proof of marriage have been signed, though Ahmad was skeptical that many of these in fact avoided intercourse.

There appears to be tension between strong traditional sanctions enforcing premarital female chastity and changing behavior in Zawiya. The complexity of individual behavior and feelings is often concealed behind public obeisance to traditional norms. With respect to contrasting standards for male and for female pre- and extramarital sexual behavior, today's Zawiya adolescents seem to live a clear double standard: the male attempts to engage unmarried females in sexual behavior which he would not tolerate in a female blood relative and which he is likely to take as indicative of immorality in a fiancee. That is, he may decide not to marry a girl because she has given in to his sexual advances, despite the fact that he promised marriage as part of the process of persuading her to become intimate.

Despite strong traditional censure of the unwed mother, premarital pregnancies do occur in this community. It is difficult to generalize about the outcome. We heard several reports of young women who left the community before giving birth, but there have also been recent instances of a young woman's giving birth at home to a child who is then raised by her or her parents. Abortion is illegal but has become widely available in recent years through private doctors in larger towns, and some unmarried young women are reported to have had several abortions.

For the many unmarried young women who become involved with males, a relationship will go through a number of stages of increasing intimacy. Among the settings where unmarried females are likely to meet males are the seven taps where the community of 12,000 obtains water. Girls between the ages of ten and twenty are the main water carriers, and they gather at the tap, waiting their turn, while young men between roughly fourteen and twenty years of age lounge against the walls of the surrounding houses, talking and watching the girls. A boy who finds a particular girl attractive may ask her for a drink of water, toss a joke or compliment her way, or try to talk with her on her way home.

Once a couple have become acquainted in this way and decide they want to see more of each other, they arrange to meet in dark corners while the girl is out on errands for her family. During these meetings, they may talk about their feelings for each other, and perhaps kiss. If the couple wish to pursue the relationship, they arrange to meet outside the town, in a place where their activities will not be so closely observed. This may be the nearby town of Kabar, where they can walk together and window-shop; the girl may suggest the boy buy her a gift. They may go to an empty house, or to the fields adjoining the smaller town, and engage in heavy petting, but the girl will attempt to preserve her virginity. Not only will an unmarried female's discovery in a sexually compromising situation (that is, any setting in which sexual behavior might occur) involve shame and the possibility of scandal; we heard of occasions also on which a couple discovered alone on the outskirts of town were assaulted by the young men finding them. Premarital intimacy is thus fraught with potential danger for the unmarried female in this community, and her needs to be both sexually attractive and perceived as chaste are frequently in conflict.

The conflicting attitudes of the unmarried female in Zawiya toward premarital flirtation and sexual intimacy, as opposed to preserving one's honor, are nicely illustrated by the following edited excerpt from a taped interview conducted in 1984 by Susan Schaefer Davis. The speaker in this case is an unmarried woman in her late twenties who has been asked to describe something that had happened to her that was not right or was unfair:

> About this matter of marriage. There's a boy—you trust him and he trusts you. He tells you, "I care for you. . . . If I don't see you, I'll go crazy; if you're away from me for only half a day, it feels like a year to me." And at that time he has feelings. He cares for you. Truly. Powerfully. But he doesn't have any money, and you just keep taking risks with him, talking to him, laughing with him. . . . And you lose your value—and your family's. Even though people see you together, you say, "They don't matter to me. Because even if I'm standing with him, he'll marry me, God willing."
>
> And finally, he doesn't marry you—how do you feel? It feels like you've been cheated, like a "psychological complex" [sic]. You feel angry at home, and you're always mad, because you don't trust . . . even your parents. When you risked yourself with that boy, you talked to him even out in the street. And finally . . . he marries someone else when he gets a good job and he's well off. He marries someone else; how do you imagine that would be? . . . It's that that doesn't allow the girl who's become responsible to trust a boy. She doesn't trust boys—never.

The premarital sexual behaviors we have described for Zawiya are in some ways quite reminiscent of the guilty experimentation, the concern over avoiding pregnancy, and the prevalence of a double standard which have been so frequently described in American society. As we have seen, the actual premarital behavior of adolescents in this Moroccan community is both quite varied and quite at variance with the norms described earlier. Americans take it for granted that learning emotional and physical responsiveness to a lover is a major challenge of early adulthood, and are forced to acknowledge that most relationships fail to meet such goals. Young Moroccans often experience conflict between traditional norms and their increasing desire for heterosexual intimacy.

It is important for the reader to realize that the individuals whose descriptions of their own and others' behavior we have mentioned here are aware that something of a double standard prevails in their society today, both as regards the relative sanctions imposed on males' and on females' premarital behavior and as regards the female's need to be sexually attractive to prospective suitors and at the same time to preserve her honor. These young adults, like young adults in many other parts of the world, are trying to come to personal terms with a rapidly changing and often conflict-producing social reality.

REFERENCES

Kinsey, A. C., Pomeroy, W. B., and Martin, C. E. *Sexual Behavior in the Human Male.* Philadelphia: Saunders, 1948.

Kinsey, A. C., Pomeroy, W. B., and Martin, C. E. *Sexual Behavior in the Human Female.* Philadelphia: Saunders, 1953.

Westermarck, E. A. *Marriage Ceremonies in Morocco.* London: Macmillan, 1914.

Pragmatic Morality: Islam and Family Planning in Morocco

Donna Lee Bowen

No questions challenge the status quo as much as those concerning the family. In Muslim nations from Indonesia to Morocco, religious scholars, ordinarily quiet on political matters, have been mustered to counter proposed government-sponsored changes to laws and practices which touch on traditional family order. Conservative Muslim reformers and activists have been particularly adamant that government-sponsored family planning programs are contrary to Islamic doctrine. They hold that, rather than to limit population, what is needed is to extend the knowledge and skills for developing agriculture and making the desert bloom. —Eds.

The birth of children, like many other things in this life, can sometimes be too much of a good thing. Over the millennium and one-half of their history, Muslims have struggled to increase the size of their families and community, fighting pestilence and disease to keep their children alive. In the latter half of the twentieth century, however, control over disease and better sanitation brought higher life expectancy, and populations rose dramatically. This increase in population has for the first time brought under scrutiny by the formulators of public policy aspects of Muslim family life that previously had been left to the guidance of Muslim community leaders.

Traditionally, Muslims have been exhorted by religious and community teachings to bear large families and thereby increase the size and strength of the Muslim community. However, the rise in population growth rates in Muslim nations, as in much of the developing world, has put pressure on limited economies. The resulting economic constraints have led technocrats to call for a limit on population growth in order to relieve the resource crunch. This in turn has resulted in psychological dissonance among Muslims who have been consistently taught that large families are valued socially and religiously. In fact, contraception threatens the traditional family order.

Two fundamental questions arise: Given the combination of religious pronouncements and Middle Eastern social emphasis on family life, does Islam say anything about birth control? What is the Muslim position on limiting family size? These questions have particular import for the Muslim nations with high population growth rates. A good example is the case of Morocco, where traditional Muslim values combine with a fast-growing population and a strong tradition of Islamic scholarship.

People tend to take cues from what is religiously sanctioned. Sources which delineate Islamic positions include the Quran, the *sunna* and *hadith* (words and actions of the Prophet Muhammad), and to a lesser extent the volumes of jurisprudence texts and commentaries which discuss all of the previously mentioned sources. The revelations of the Quran and the words and example of the Prophet Muhammad all point to the key position of family in society. Family, from the prescriptive point of view of Islam, is the means of organizing the Muslim community, the institution which regulates human behavior and puts the chaos of unordered sexual conduct at bay.

According to the Quran, marriage is highly recommended.[1] As Omar (the second caliph of Islam) said, "Only old age and sinfulness can stop one from marriage."

> By another sign He gave you wives from among yourselves that you
> might live in joy with them, and planted love and kindness in your hearts.
> Surely there are signs in this for thinking men. (30:21)

Family order, as based on revelation, assumes a patriarchal form, with husbands taking the lead in aspects of family law: marriage, divorce (repudiation), inheritance. Present-day religious scholars sum up the relationship of family members as one in which men provide the wherewithal for the family, women bear and raise the children, and children obey their parents. The Quran states:

> Grant unto us wives and offspring who will be the comfort of our eyes
> and give us (the grace) to lead the righteous. (25:74)

Marriage is not obligatory, for one basic reason—its cost. Before men marry, they are expected to have the means to support a wife and a family if they choose to have children.

> But he shall bear the cost of their food and clothing on equitable terms.
> No soul shall have a burden lain on it greater than it can bear. (2:233)

So a man marries when God grants the means to do so; women marry when God provides the husband. It is then her duty to follow his lead, for "men have a degree above women" (2:228).

The best woman is she who delights her husband and obeys him when he commands her, and, in his absence, looks after his wealth and dignity. (Prophetic hadith)

The importance of marriage and children to both society and individuals has not changed, but demographic changes have brought about a need for rethinking how a solid family can be maintained despite limited assets.

Islam has no organized clergy and has no hierarchy of leadership. Country by country, Muslim scholars (singular, ʿalim; plural, ʿulama) speak authoritatively for their national constituency, just as in the early days of the community, those men[2] who were scholars of Islamic texts—the Quran, the hadith and sunna, legal commentaries—contributed to the formulation of legal positions on questions undecided by the Quran, the first and most decisive source of Islamic law. The only Quranic mention of an issue related to family planning pertains to waʾd, a practice of exposing unwanted female children because they were seen as a nonproductive burden on a poor family. In condemning that practice, the Quran describes Judgment Day as "when the infant girl, buried alive, is asked for what crime she was slain" (81:7–8). Muslims interpreted this verse as an absolute prohibition of female infanticide. If the Quran is silent on a matter, the next recourse is to the sunna and hadith of the Prophet and his companions. Other matters are determined by the ʿulama drawing analogies to existing Quranic or hadith texts.

Following traditional roles delineated by centuries of precedent, religious scholars hold themselves responsible for correctly interpreting Islamic sources for the Muslim community. While Muslims are taught to "command good and set aside evil," realistic scholars fear that beyond the fact that humankind seems to lack continuous motivation to put aside evil, many well-intentioned Muslims are not sufficiently acquainted with the ins and outs of Islamic jurisprudence to work out difficult doctrines or practices. Therefore, the ʿulama serve as the custodians of the community and see themselves as keepers of the well-being of their people.

Knowledge of the Quran, the Prophet's statements and precedents, and the intricacies of the jurisprudence texts for their particular school of Islam (Morocco adheres to the Maliki school of jurisprudence) is not easily come by. A truly learned ʿalim has invested decades of study in Islamic sciences and Arabic language before taking on the legal texts themselves. Any study of the numerous volumes of early and medieval scholarship which constitute the framework of laws for Islamic society plunges one into a subtle world of revelation-based learning, precedent, and analogy. Scholars do not have total freedom; they must work with established sources of Islamic law. But within the constricts of these sources, they can formulate new interpretations best suited to community needs.

As the areas of law where ʿulama preside in Morocco (as in many nations where Islamic *shari'a* law is not the law of the state) have diminished over time and as more authority for legal matters has been vested in the state, the 'ulama have become particularly protective of their last preserves, family law and religious practice. In fact, given the dictates of the Quran on family law, they see the two as inextricably connected.

To ascertain Muslim positions on family matters, I conducted several years of research in Morocco during the late 1970s, including interviews with 'ulama, scholars of religion—professors, writers, officials of the Ministry of Islamic Affairs—and other religious leaders concerning Islam and family planning. Below I recount two representative interviews with Professors Zahraoui and al-Arhali, both of the College of Arabic Language Studies in Marrakesh, to give a sense of the questions asked regarding contraception as well as the scholar's responses.

Using the methods of analogy honed over decades of development of Islamic jurisprudence, all of the 'ulama interviewed drew implicit parallels to the contemporary situation from classical jurisprudence literature on contraception. Although the Quran is silent on this matter, representative jurisprudence texts record that use of *'azl* (*coitus interruptus*) is permissible with qualifications. If a husband intends to use 'azl with his wife, he can legally do so only with her consent, the logic being that as he wishes not to impregnate the woman, controls the method of contraception, and intends to employ it, her permission must be obtained as her rights (to children and sexual fulfillment) may be harmed by its use.

A point to be noted here is that the only practice the classical jurists examine is 'azl, the major method of contraception men can employ. Numerous medical texts dating from the eleventh and twelfth centuries list other contraceptive methods—the majority used by women. Since the theological discussion of controlling pregnancy is limited to 'azl, jurists did not concern themselves with, or were unaware of, contraceptive methods used by women such as infusions to take by mouth, suppositories, and magic. If they had taken methods which women employ into consideration, their reasoning would have had to extend to the husband's granting permission for their use. The omission of these contraceptive methods in the jurisprudence texts can be explained only by the unfamiliarity of male jurists with contraceptive methods employed by women.

INTERVIEW: PROFESSOR ZAHRAOUI

Professor Zahraoui and I met in his living room in a new villa in Marrakesh. A renowned scholar of Islam, he also taught comparative religions and referred throughout our discussion to comparisons to Christian doctrine and practices. According to Professor Zahraoui:

"If a female child were born to a family in pre-Islamic times, the family would be disappointed, and the infant's life often would be in peril. Once Islam was introduced, there was no religious value put on the sex of the infant. Various other traditions, however, have questioned this equal valuation of the sexes. In Paris in the Middle Ages, there was a question as to whether a woman were not half a person and half a devil.

"Recent economic development has changed the situation. Islam has traditionally advocated a division of labor between the male and the female. The duty of the wife is to work in the home and bring up the children. This entails taking care of their needs and teaching them proper morals and ethics as well as instructing them in everyday concerns. Well-trained children are the basis of a good society. If the mother is absent from the home, working or for other reasons, then who is to care for the children?

"Therefore, the woman has an economic role as important as that of the man. Each has half: he works outside while she cares for the house and the children. There is no place for unemployment in this system as both must work for the family unit to succeed.

"Marriage, although basic, is required in Islam only if certain conditions are met. At times it is required: if the man has money enough to support a family and desires marriage; also if he will commit socially disturbing acts if he remains single. At times marriage is forbidden: if the husband has no money and cannot support a wife and if he has no special desire for a wife. But marriage may also be optional: the man has a moderate desire for women, has enough money—if he wishes to marry or not to marry, either is permitted.

"A corollary to this is divorce. For the good of both the individuals concerned and society in general, spouses should not be forced to remain together contrary to their wishes. Under such constraint, one is likely to commit immoral actions. As couples are free to marry, they must also be free to divorce.

"This brings us to the question of contraception. Without question Europe is powerful materially. We in Morocco would like to be equally powerful, just as people aspire to emulate more successful people. Use of contraception is necessary to maintain that material success. The situation in eighteenth-century Britain illustrated this. Noting that British agricultural production would not be sufficient to keep up with a growing population, Malthus's studies warned of the danger of population growth. Contraception is a natural by-product of this concern. However, now there is no difference between East and West in this regard: we have followed their lead here.

"Application of contraception in Islam brings up various questions. One is that of fate (*qadar*). It is very difficult to understand the real effect of this concept in life and to determine the cause of actions. We cannot say that God has done all that is done. Also we cannot wait to see what God is going to do.

We must take action on our own behalf. One cannot say that 'Allah is the provider' (*al-Raziq*) or 'there is nothing on the earth but God provides for it' and then sit and wait for God to provide for you. One can say that God provides and then go out and find the means by which it can take place.

"Human power has its roots in economic production. It is better for us to confront the situation by increasing production, not decreasing our population. We need more production in the agricultural and industrial sectors. In Morocco we need total planning, more dams, water for irrigation, more animals.

"The question of personal contraceptive use is another matter to be considered separately from national policy. People practice 'azl. Mothers use it for health reasons, to prevent *ghayla*[3] when a child is small and she fears another pregnancy for his sake. When her health or a child's health is endangered, she should use 'azl.

"The Islamic principle of necessity being above the law takes precedence in these cases. When an outside factor forces disobedience to a law by necessity, then the law is not considered broken without just reason. For example, when faced with starvation or eating pork, eating pork is sanctioned. When one is paralyzed and thus cannot perform all the physical motions of prayer, one can do the movements with the eyes, and the validity of the prayer is still preserved. This establishment of reasonable limits gives Islamic practice a necessary flexibility. In the case of 'azl, it is to be used when its use will benefit people, not penalize them.

"'Azl is a means of preventing pregnancy. Other means analogous to 'azl are permissible under the same terms that 'azl is permissible. So birth control pills are permitted when their use is necessary. If they are unnecessary, then their use is forbidden. Included as valid reasons for contraceptive use are financial problems. Islam considers lack of money and the inability to bring up more children properly to be valid reasons to employ contraceptives.

"Abortion is another matter. Some schools believe that abortion is legal before 120 days of pregnancy have elapsed. Only after this time does the spirit enter the fetus, causing it to be formally created.

"Religiously, for Muslims, abortion is forbidden. However, exceptions can be made for health reasons. Even if the mother's life or that of the unborn child lies in the balance, two factors must be weighed in making the decision. It is a question of choice, and abortion in this case, although not forbidden, is not a good thing to do."

INTERVIEW: AL-ARHALI AL-FARUQ

I met with Professor al-Arhali at the College for Arabic Language Studies in Marrakesh. As it was a nice day, he suggested that we sit outside on the lawn of the courtyard to have our discussion. Students passing by saluted Professor al-Arhali as they went about their business. Two of his senior students who served as his research assistants joined us. As I formulated my basic questions, Professor al-Arhali sat back, then threw his arms out wide and stated in an authoritative voice, "The trouble is that no one in Marrakesh has any morals." Students within hearing range exchanged startled glances and walked faster in the opposite direction. He then went on. According to Professor al-Arhali:

"The world is filled with problems, but as each disease has a medicine to treat it, each problem has a solution if only it can be found.

"The world today is plagued by wars and the works of Satan. There are two major areas of concern: first is the problem of morals. People are increasingly seeking greater freedom in their moral standards, abandoning what was understood for centuries as traditional behavior. Second, underlying the first problem, people don't understand either the problems or each other, which keeps them from coming to grips with the problem. Without proper respect for others it is impossible to have good morals, so the morals they espouse are increasingly corrupt.

"Now, as pertains to family planning, we must first understand that the family is the world, and all else (in terms of morals) proceeds from that basis.

"If the family were taught well, everything else in the world would be all right as well. Therefore teachings and knowledge are necessary in order to know the necessities and the way of life. We must know what are our obligations to perform, and from performing them good will come. The world is based on these principles. If good is taught, good will come of it; if evil is taught, evil will result. This is only reasonable, and reason is the natural basis of our religion.

"Family planning refers to the way the parents bring up their families. Birth control separates a man and a woman, restricting them from having children. Islam approves of family planning, because Islam is all about teaching children well so that they can distinguish between good and evil by degrees.

"Birth control in the sense of limitation is not consistent with the tenets of Islam. First of all, we are taught by Muhammad to 'Marry, have children, and multiply so that I will be pleased with you on Judgment Day.' Thus marriage is institutionalized in Islam.

"Traditionally woman is characterized as being pleasant and chaste; man is stronger, being intended for grasping power and fighting wars. The combination of the two is needed. By cooperation between a husband and a wife—some help from inside the home given, some help from outside the home—they can work to make all strong and well in their life together. The husband works outside the home to provide the economic well-being as opposed to the woman who works inside the house and is specially concerned with teaching the children. The arrangement of the household points up the differences between man and woman.

"Adultery, which is practiced openly everywhere but in Islam, is a great challenge to marriage and good morals. Currently many women don't have children, negating the purpose of marriage. Each says that she has the freedom to do what she wants (which implies doing immoral things). The correct path is to bear children, an act neither the husband nor wife can perform alone. There true Islam would return to marriage.

"As far as use of birth control to limit a family goes, as long as the husband and wife are agreed on its use, then there is no problem. This is true even if they wish not to have children. They have the right not to have any at all.

"However, being a parent is better than not being a parent. As we look at life, we see that it fits into a pattern. Working to provide for economic necessity is necessary so that all the pieces can fit well together. Work is necessary in Islam.

"Abortion is prohibited, for it constitutes killing the fetus. Even if the husband and wife are agreed on the abortion, it is still forbidden. Abortion is forbidden whatever the advising doctor says, even if the woman is sick and will die."

When the interview ended, al-Arhali's two assistants asked me to remain with them after the professor's departure so that they could further discuss the questions I had raised. They made two major points:

"Marriage is necessary so that social order will be preserved and adultery will not take place. A man before marrying should make sure that he has some money to take care of his family. If he has no money to provide for others as well as himself, then he should postpone marriage and wait and fast until he has sufficient means.

"Birth control comes to Islam from the large nations and is forbidden. However, if the husband and wife are agreed in its practice, they can do as they please. Contraceptive use is forbidden if one partner doesn't wish to use it and the other tries to force its use."

Contradictions are evident in the interviews above. Some reflect the nature of discussion where points for consideration are thrown out as part of the major thought process. Other statements are rhetorical. Still others, such as the declaration by the assistants that birth control is forbidden, followed by a statement that it is permitted if both partners agree to its use, can be attributed partially to rhetoric and partially to technical language. The ʿulama set the term "birth control," or "contraception," in opposition to "family planning." In the classical texts, preventing a pregnancy would be a reprehensible action (although not forbidden; the assistants exaggerate). If the husband asks the wife's permission and she consents, then the reprehensibility is lifted and the action becomes free from condemnation.

Zahraoui and al-Arhali make five points worth investigating. First, both scholars assert, al-Arhali more adamantly, the importance of family as the basis of society and the bulwark of community morals and order. The integrity of the family must be preserved at all costs. They refer to social problems which have become more pressing with time. Their arguments seem to indicate that although the sanctity of the family unit must not be violated, certain adjustments in line with contemporary pressures may be considered.

Something already in the process of readjustment—although this is not reflected in their arguments—is the highly traditional division of labor between men and women: wives remain at home with the children and husbands support the household. Although this division is still the rule in Morocco, given the high incidence of unemployment—about 30 percent in Morocco—women often find themselves more employable than their husbands and venture into the workplace as domestic servants or other low-paid labor to support the family. Widowed, divorced, or deserted women heads of households become the primary wage earners. Despite the woman's work outside the home, she will still be primarily responsible for the household as well. Generally, any help she receives will come from female relatives.

A second point to which both scholars referred is the question of birth control. The term in Arabic (*tahdid al-nasl*) is translated as "limitation," or "restriction" of progeny. All the ʿulama I interviewed, as well as many other men and women, reacted negatively to this phrasing—at times likening it to genocide imposed from outside. "Family planning" (*tanzim al-usra* or *takhtit al-ʿaʾili*)—with the meaning of ordering, arranging resources for one's family—was far more acceptable. It did not imply a circumscription of family size, but rather the sense of best determining how to accomplish a goal.

Planning a family could include spacing pregnancies, having a limited number of children because of financial pressures, deciding to avoid future pregnancies because of the wife's health, even—according to Zahraoui—having an abortion performed if the physician indicates that the mother's life is endangered. These measures, both scholars emphasized, are to be undertaken after the husband and wife counsel with each other and resolve to cooperate to achieve their family goals.

Third, both emphasized that contraception itself is not a recommended practice; ideally Muslims would pursue large families. Reality, however, requires compromises. Zahraoui referred to the doctrine of necessity being above the law. This doctrine is used to reconcile questionable, even illicit, practices with reality. The context of a situation may impel a good Muslim to practices that when isolated are not permitted. In these cases—and he made family planning an analogous case—a practice which may not be necessarily good in itself, especially when extrapolated for all of society, may be beneficial in a particular context. Thus, even abortion, although he called it religiously prohibited,[4] may be permitted. Another situation which surfaced in interviews was the question of sterilization of the woman or the man. All ʿulama interviewed agreed that sterilization is unlawful and argued that it is prohibited because it is an unnatural practice, negating what God has created.

Fourth, any use of contraception is contingent upon the consent of both parties, the husband and the wife. As in the classical jurisprudence texts, which state that the consent of the wife is necessary for the husband to employ ʿazl, given the variety of contraceptive measures used today, a general guideline that both must agree covers any eventuality of contraceptive use. Since the wife would herself monitor use of birth control pills, IUDs, contraceptive injections, or (rarely) diaphragms and the husband would control use of ʿazl or prophylactics, the ʿulama simply caution the couple that to protect the rights of each partner, both must agree on contraceptive use.

Fifth, given the pattern in Muslim family law of the male having "a degree above" the female, the ʿulama's insistence—as voiced by al-Arhali—on each having the right to approve any contraceptive use is a significant voicing of the equal rights of both partners in regard to producing progeny. This is totally consistent with the majority of classical opinions on the subject (Bowen 1981). I should add here that each ʿalim interviewed, without regard to whether he viewed family planning negatively, stated that contraception is permissible religiously so long as both the husband and the wife agree to its use. This puts the husband and the wife on an equal footing in the matter; so far as the religious authorities are concerned, if either refuses, contraceptive practice becomes illicit.

Another way to look at this issue focuses on responsibility. The ʿulama have publicly cautioned husbands and wives as to the critical nature of family composition and family stability. Beyond that, it is up to each family unit to govern itself in light of its particular needs and situation. The responsibility for the health of their family devolves upon the husband and the wife. This emphasis may signal slight movement toward a more egalitarian view of family responsibility. It is echoed by government policy makers. In the early 1970s, the physician who headed the Moroccan Family Planning Office announced at a national meeting that he considered it his duty as a Moroccan to ensure that no Moroccan male ever received a vasectomy. In May 1990, a banner stretched above the largest cafe in Marrakesh. It read: "Family planning is also the responsibility of the male." To an outside observer it appears that government programs are beginning to catch up with the ʿulama's reasoning. In this one case of permitting contraception, women have equal status with men.

NOTES

1. Islam divides all actions into five categories: obligatory, recommended (an action better to commit than to omit), neutral, reprehensible (an action better to avoid),

and forbidden. Marriage, although highly recommended, is not obligatory, as are prayer and tithes. 'Azl, though not forbidden, is labeled by the classical jurists as reprehensible, unless the wife gives her permission.

2. The ranks of 'ulama are overwhelmingly, if not totally, male. While women may be privately educated in Islamic sciences, they are not invited to take positions which would expose them to public eyes as learned Muslim scholars. Only one woman, an Egyptian, held a position in the area of religious science at University Muhammad V in Rabat.

3. *Ghayla* (the small assassination) is the situation when a nursing mother with an infant becomes pregnant again. Nutrients which would ordinarily go solely to the fetus go into the production of milk, depriving the fetus of normal growth. This situation, which is condemned in the legal texts, is commonly discussed even among village women, and they seek to avoid it.

4. Two religious opinions are current on abortion. The first, as Zahraoui stated, rules it religiously prohibited. The only exception is when it is ordered by a physician in a life-threatening situation. The second stance, which permits abortion up until the beginning of the fifth month, uses as a source the following Quranic verse:

> We created man of a quintessence of clay. Then we placed him as semen in a firm receptacle. Then we formed the semen into a bloodlike clot; then we formed the clot into a lump of flesh; then we formed out of that lump bones and clothed the bones with flesh; then we made him another creation. So blessed be God the best Creator. (23:12–14)

Interpreters of the Quran hold that the semen, the blood clot, and the bones and flesh constitute three stages in the development of the fetus. Each stage is assigned 40 days. After the three stages, the fetus is created and implicitly the spirit enters the fetus. Thus, after 120 days the spirit has entered the fetus and abortion is not permissible. Before that, abortion is permitted.

REFERENCE

Bowen, Donna Lee. 1981. "Muslim Juridical Opinions concerning the Status of Women as Demonstrated by the Case of 'Azl. *Journal of Near Eastern Studies* 40, no. 4.

Fertility and Fate: Medical Practices among *Baladi* Women of Cairo

Evelyn A. Early

Since a Middle Eastern woman's status is inextricable from that of her family, both infertility and threats to her children's health prompt her to pull out all the stops to cope with crises. Husbands and fathers provide silent support and will also participate in major clinic visits. However, they leave the folk (here used in the sense of "local," "popular") Islam of shrines and vows to women.

Being an astute consumer, a woman calculates which medical remedy from the available folk, herbal, and modern cosmopolitan alternatives meets her needs. She asks which is cheaper, which is more accessible, which matches the seriousness of the symptoms. In this selection, traditional women of Cairo, Egypt, piece together folk and clinical medicine with the ritual power of shrines and vows to deal with their health problems. —Eds.

We arrived on Friday morning at the mosque of Siddi Qubba on the outskirts of Cairo while the pre-noon-prayer Quran readings still boomed over the loud speaker, and joined the women on a mat outside the mosque. With us were two young women who wished to become pregnant and had attempted several home remedies without success. As time for the call to prayer approached, women who sought to become married or pregnant began to gather around a four-foot-high slanted concrete post next to the mosque. When the noon call to prayer began, we all (they assumed I wanted to marry) put our left hand on the pillar and began to circumambulate counterclockwise—all clutching seven stones and throwing one over our shoulder at every turn. We recited "Siddi Qubba will solve (*yafuk*) my problem, and when he does I will bring chicken or turkey or any other demand." (Some people had bought chickens to the mosque today.) A mosque attendant waited to take money and tie it in a woman's scarf and untie (yafuk) it at the end of the service—as a further aid to solving a woman's problem.

The ritual at Siddi Qubba is an interesting mix of Quranic Islamic practice and local folk beliefs. It occurs next to a mosque and the burial site of a saint. The auspicious time is that of the main prayer of the week—Friday noon. The circumambulation around the pillar seven times is reminiscent of the circumambulation around the Ka'ba in Mecca at the time of the yearly pilgrimage. The symbol of untying a knot to solve a problem or to dispel a curse is criticized as magic in the Quran: "I take refuge with the Lord . . . from the evil of women who blow on knots." People visiting shrines commonly knot pieces of ribbon around posts, to represent their unsolved—yet to be untied—problems. This ritual is only part of the participants' search for a solution to their unmarried status or a cure for their infertility. It and other folk practices cannot be understood if they are treated as exoticisms and explained piecemeal. I want to interpret cultural themes of fate and envy in the context of a woman's everyday life and her concern with fertility.

In Middle Eastern studies a common distinction between male-public and female-private spheres of power assumes the following: "Women's power is in the 'informal' interstices of information (gossip) control" or "Women escape to the 'unreal' world of 'folk' beliefs where they are imbued with power unavailable to them in the 'real' world." I suggest that so-called folk beliefs integrate events in a woman's "real" life rather than offer her an escape from that life. "Folk" practices are especially popular in medicine. I look here at the articulation of childrearing and fertility behavior among *baladi* (traditional) Egyptian women with the broader social, cultural, and economic arenas of their lives. I use the term "fertility behavior" to refer to all matters associated with conception and children. I have picked this topic for two reasons:

(1) It demonstrates an important facet of women's resource management. Fertility allows a woman power over men. She may withhold it through birth control—threatening the family's existence or her husband's desire for more children (or for more male children). Or she may produce large numbers of children—providing her a claim to support and making divorce or her husband's marriage to another wife less financially viable. Fertility is critical in validating a woman's status in a society concerned with patrilineal continuity. Threats to her control of fertility are (a) physiological problems, most notably infertility and infant morbidity; (b) economic constraints on nutrition or medical care; and (c) accidents, calamities, or other traumatic experiences dramatically exposing a woman to death or to loss of control over health and fertility.

(2) Curative treatment within this area is more prone to require both medical and nonmedical, or folk, cures. Because family well-being is susceptible to invidious perceptions by others, women incorporate into the healing process nonmedical cures to ward off social dangers. Differences of abundance of children, bumper crops, and so on, are noticed and thought to be transformed into the social danger of envy, which, whether real, suspected, or anticipated, must nevertheless be countered.

Traditional Egyptian women divide afflictions into two categories: (1) "illness treatable by medicine (*dawwa*)," including cosmopolitan medicine and the remedies of indigenous herbal pharmacists; and (2) "illnesses whose treatment requires other agents—such as spellbreaking and petition of saints through vows," including consultation with specialists in *Tibb Rawhani* (spiritual medicine) or treatment of supernatural diseases by divination, amulets, manipulation of Quranic verses, and sponsorship of a *zar* (exorcism).

A wife and mother bears ultimate responsibility for producing a family and keeping them healthy; she is viewed as deficient in her role if she does not exert enough effort to produce and cure children. Children need someone to protect them; one frequently hears "The child is innocent, why should he have to suffer?" Almost every day of her life a married woman is preoccupied with conceiving or avoiding conception, inducing or avoiding miscarriage, retaining health during pregnancy and lactation, undergoing safe delivery, protecting her infant's health, nursing, curing her infants' colds and diarrhea, and so on.

The ambiguity of illness makes diagnosis a matter of trial and error, of experimenting until results are obtained; thus a woman may simultaneously pursue several tactics to "cover all possible bets," intensively probing both medical and nonmedical alternatives to ensure that no possibilities are bypassed. She diagnoses the problem not only to suggest relevant cures but also to justify her actions subsequently. Continually reevaluating, she develops a finely woven web of rationales as she approaches her problem (for example, delayed conception, a persistently weak child) via different curing strategies.

A WOMAN'S LIFE SITUATION AND FERTILITY BEHAVIOR

A woman's motivation to pursue health care aggressively is strongest where children are concerned. She seeks a more authoritative opinion by consulting several specialists. She may fill more than one prescription and administer all, assuming the more medicine, the better. She sees no contradiction in combining medical and nonmedical cures; she may take her child to the clinic and proceed from there to a shaykh to obtain an amulet. Explanations of what is happening in an illness's progression are constantly generated—whether in mundane forms ("There is no money for a private doctor") or in more coded forms ("She cannot conceive because she has been afflicted by a state of *mushahara* [infertility, insufficient lactation]" or "What God wills will happen: we will do what we can and the rest is up to him"). The first signals a desperate economic situation; the second implies an etiology (mushahara, fate) beyond the actor's power to influence. These explanations are spontaneously and continually offered in illness narratives in the open society of a traditional urban quarter where events are easily observed by neighbors, visitors, and passersby.

Encoded in such illness narratives are ultimate explanatory devices of success (for example, *Al-baraka kan fi idu*—"His [the doctor's] hands were blessed" or "The saving grace was in the doctor's hands") or failure (for example, *miyadu maktub*—"It was written as the time for him to die"). Death is not a catastrophe (infant death is not rare), but intercalated with the rhythm of diagnosis, duty, cure, and chance. It is fixed, but not by humans; it is referred to as "the appointed time" or as "written." However, such explanations do not provide a reason for inaction, but an *a posteriori* explanation. If a mother has not tried hard, she is still guilty of irresponsibility (*ihmal*), but if she has done her part and the child dies, it is God's will.

The mother is the facilitator—a crucial role, as evidenced by criticisms of irresponsibility leveled at women who do not act vigorously enough to pursue cures. *Causality* is determined only after the fact. That the cause is beyond the woman's reach may mean that the cure is also "beyond" her, but the road between the two must be well traveled. She does not take ultimate credit or blame, but she has ultimate responsibility as facilitator.

Mushahara is a pervasive cultural theme in Egyptian baladi culture, where much thought is given to avoiding it and to its cure if one is afflicted by it. This is understandable given the criticalness of fertility. Briefly, the condition of mushahara is caused by juxtapositions of a vulnerable woman (one newly married or delivered) with other people considered potent (and dangerous) because they are going through life-crisis rites (for example, circumcision or a funeral) or because of their condition (for example, recently shaven, having just weaned a baby, or carrying an object, such as an eggplant or a piece of raw meat). It is a socially induced situation resulting from a potent person's carelessness (if not malicious intention) in relating to a vulnerable woman.

Mushahara is a condition of infertility or of insufficient lactation, but it is also an idiom used by a woman to express her desire for fertility when she speculates that she is afflicted by either condition and deflects the explanation of a "slow" pregnancy from herself to others. Mushahara can also be invoked idiomatically by a woman who desires infertility. The following story was told by Sakkina after she had delivered twin boys, the last of eight, and wanted no more children. She suggested that a recently excised girl could afflict her with mushahara if she moved improperly (that is, turned in front of her).

One of my sons was fighting with a boy and I went out to stop him. The boy's sister Megda was there and they told me she had just been excised. After she (Megda) had already gone upstairs, I called up to her: "Did you turn around in front of me? Never mind if I don't get pregnant again, but I beg you not to dry up my milk." Then I reconsidered the possibilities of getting pregnant and went upstairs and dragged Megda from the couch and made her turn around and around in front of me. I always said, "Oh, I wish

I would deliver in a hospital and they would take everything out," but after
the twins I never became pregnant again.

Medical cures for mushahara abound. Gynecologists may be consulted,
lab tests run, vitamins and antibiotics prescribed. Midwives can provide special vaginal suppositories (*sufa*) or cups to absorb the "cold" of an infertile
womb. These cures seek to influence the affected organ, the womb. They may
fail either because of natural infertility or because someone has rendered the
woman infertile. (Of course, the husband may be infertile, but men will not
always agree to examination.)

Nonmedical cures resonate with the social causes of mushahara. For example, the afflicted woman may urinate over the other's (the "afflictor's")
urine or take the other's milk and rub it over her own breasts. Other cures
rely on some substance which is potent because of its role in a life-crisis rite
(not necessarily that of the potent person)—such as a vaginal suppository
soaked in circumcision blood or in the virginal blood of the afflicted woman's
wedding night. Special mushahara rings can be worn on the fingers to coun-
teract dangerous influences. Some of the women with us at the shrine of
Siddi Qubba were there to reverse what they perceived as a condition of
mushahara.

There are other "nonmedical" rituals like that of Siddi Qubba to which
women resort when they desire communal ritual sharing of a plight or when
other cures fail. Another folk ritual is that of Sitt Sukkariyya, who is buried at
the bottom of a precipice among the shrines on the outskirts of Cairo. After
circling a cliff seven times, throwing stones each time, a woman sticks her
head through an opening in the rock seven times, promising to bring candles,
henna, sugar, and candies on the third visit. A more dramatic cure is the *zar*, a
ritual of spirit exorcism conducted by a female spiritual specialist (*shaykha*)
and musicians representing various Sudanese groups. A woman responds by
dance and trance only to her rhythm. She sacrifices for the spirit, who may
also demand clothes and jewelry.

THE INTERSECTION OF MEDICAL AND NONMEDICAL TECHNIQUES

Because they are susceptible to physical and social causes, fertility and childrearing problems lie at the intersection of medical and nonmedical curative
treatments. One does not invoke folk cures to escape life or responsibility, but
to confront them. While exploring all possible paths, one suspects that children become ill, pregnancies fail, and healthy mothers wither because of
others' maliciousness or because one has flaunted one's good luck in others'
faces. But one only believes it *a posteriori*.

Zainab is a Cairene woman who fears God and who admires modern medicine. Having undergone several surgical operations, she lectures friends on the virtues of operations and cosmopolitan medicine. One of her daughters died during emergency abdominal surgery while still a young bride. Zainab thinks that her daughter had some "trouble with her organs," but one day she elaborated on this physiological information to provide a social context for the event:

> You know, I think that my daughter actually died from envy when she was a bride. I haven't told you before. She had an easy life because her mother-in-law lived with her, and the woman next door envied her that and her youth. This woman came in when my daughter was sleeping and told her to get up. My daughter said she was tired. The woman said, "Why? You have become pretty; your stomach is round; you must be pregnant." She put her hand on my daughter's stomach and from that moment my daughter started having pains. A week later she was dead.

This explanation helps to make sense of a family disaster. Zainab believes her daughter held a coveted position and uses envy in retrospect as a comforting explanation for the young woman's death. For Sakkina and Zainab, explanations encoding fate and envy do not blind them to reality but rather incorporate the tensions and uncertainties of their immediate environment into their understanding of what took place.

Nonmedical and medical practices often complement each other to ensure that a woman has "covered all bets." A pregnant woman with a history of miscarriages who is physically weak and who is taking antibiotics and vitamins may vow to pay money to a shrine if she delivers safely. The vow does not mean that she doubts that medicine will do the trick. Rather, her life situation is a biological history of miscarriage, a cultural milieu stressing fertility, and a social set of neighbors who may not have been as lucky as she (and who may thus "envy" her). If she makes a vow she can displace her problem from her shoulders onto those of the wider community who have had similar experiences. She may join women at shrines known to cure mushahara. She knows stirring tales of the success of vows and rituals, as she knows of times that they have been ineffective. She has not provided herself an invisible shield. Rather, she has joined a framework of trial and error and has entered a "community of believers."

She has not substituted religion or "folk" medicine for medical solutions. Rather, she has mobilized a repertoire of beliefs shared by her society to deal with the vagaries and the harshness of everyday life. Her fertility problem is an existential problem which hopefully places her only temporarily outside the normal structure of procreation. Infertility makes her for the time socially marginal. A truly barren woman is outside of, and in an inferior position to, the normal structure of procreation.

If the woman's vow is fulfilled and the case is dramatically solved (for example, ten years of sterility reversed; a child pronounced near death by doctors cured), her story becomes a stirring illness narrative. If her vow fails, she has not been betrayed. She has admitted beforehand that this may happen; as in religion one expresses one's human fallibility before a supernatural power, so she in her system has expressed her vulnerability in the face of repeated daily tragedies. She has joined the ranks of those who succeed and fail; she has generalized the blame for medical failure so that it is not specific to her, but falls at the doors of universal causality (*nasib*, or fate).

A baladi Egyptian woman picks eclectically from systems of action which for her form a coherent whole and help to integrate social, economic, medical, and cultural dimensions of her life. Such cultural themes as envy and mushahara help to validate her position within the family when her resources (children, fertility) are threatened or questioned. They legitimate her request for money for such ritual uses as hiring a shaykka for a zar or keeping a religious vow. Her ritual and curative activities link her to a society which provides community support for her choices. It is this society and her cultural practices which help her maintain some control over her fertility in all its forms, including progeny. Thus, such concepts as envy, fate, and mushahara are more than folk beliefs; they are part of a social and cultural system which helps a woman to control her life.

Personal Status Law in Sudan

Carolyn Fluehr-Lobban

Family status laws, which delineate the social character of Islamic society, have been the most resistant to modernization of all Islamic law. While other types of law have been either secularized along Western models—criminal law, constitutional law, commercial law—or relegated to the realms of personal worship, family law has remained virtually unchanged.

Islamic family law defines a kin-based patrilineal society which assumes that a woman's blood relatives support her if her husband or his family mistreats her. With increasing migration and dissolution of kin groups, however, many women are left isolated and unprotected. While some more secular states have given the wife the right to initiate divorce in certain circumstances, women remain basically unprotected when the traditional family ties dissolve. —Eds.

Sudan is both African and Arab, heterogeneous, multilingual, and multiethnic. More than 300 distinct languages and cultures are found within the borders of this African giant, which, with 1 million square miles, is the largest country on the continent. Although Arabic is the first language of only 40 percent of Sudan's 22 million people, it is the national language. Islam is the predominant religion, comprising approximately 70 percent of the population. Established Islam is characteristically an urban phenomenon, and a variety of folk and sufist expressions of Islam can be found throughout the rural northern Sudan. Southern Sudan is predominantly animist, with a small percentage of Christians. It is noteworthy that a historical and contemporary antagonism between the northern and the southern regions has taken on a religious dimension. Most recently the imposition of the *Shariʿa* (Islamic law) as state law in 1983 has been a major point of controversy between the regions, and indeed the harsh application of the Shariʿa weakened support in the north for an Islamic state based on religious law.

As his regime floundered, Jaafar Numieri attempted to rally support among the Muslims of the north, to the detriment of the animist and Christian citizens of the south, by implementing a policy of Islamization. A major element of this policy was the extension of Shariʿa law to all Sudanese citizens in the September laws of 1983. Before Islamization, Shariʿa law involved only personal status issues (and was applied only to the Muslim citizens). In 1985 Sudanese law further stipulated that the *hudud* penalties of Shariʿa law (for example, amputation of the hand for theft) would replace the Western-influenced code for punishing criminal actions. Numieri was overthrown in a bloodless coup in April 1985, but the subsequent years of democratic rule failed to return some balance of civil and religious law that would check the excesses of Numieri's application of Shariʿa law, which included numerous amputations and floggings meted out in the now infamous "Courts of Prompt Justice." During the democratic period (1985–1989) under the leadership of Prime Minister Sadiq al-Mahdi, little formal change in the Shariʿa occurred and it remained the sole law in force, although the application of the hudud penalties, including amputations, stopped. In June 1989 a new military government was installed, led by General Omar al-Beshir and backed by the National Islamic Front (NIF), which insisted on the absolute retention of Shariʿa as state law in Sudan.

SCOPE OF THE SHARIʿA COURTS IN PERSONAL
STATUS MATTERS

Prior to 1980 the Shariʿa courts constituted a separate division of the Sudanese judiciary with a separate system of courts and a separate court of appeals. The Islamic courts were presided over by the Grand Qadi, who headed the High Court of Judges and rendered final decisions on appeal. I had the honor to study the Shariʿa in 1979 with the last of the Sudanese Grand Qadis, Sheikh Muhammad el-Gizouli.

In 1980 the civil and the Shariʿa divisions of the judiciary were combined. The unified court system meant that judges applied both civil and Shariʿa law within the same court under a single system of appeals. Basically the Shariʿa retained its unique status as a personal law for Muslims, until the period of Islamization beginning in September 1983 and continuing to the present.

The issue of the Shariʿa as state law has become one of the most divisive in the nation at large, and it is a major factor in the continuation of the civil war between northern and southern Sudan. Southern movements have demanded the revocation of the Shariʿa as the national law, while northern governments have refused to revoke it since 1983. Islamization of the general laws of Sudan, however, has had little effect on the matters of personal status which are discussed below.

From the time of the organization of the "Muhammadan Law Courts" by the English colonialists in 1902, the primary jurisdiction of the Shariʿa encompassed Islamic dower, marriage and divorce, child custody, inheritance, and the transference of property and *waqf* (endowments; see discussion below). Historically, in the twentieth century, it is to this arena of personal status law that the Shariʿa has been tied.

By custom and tradition, Sudanese Muslims adhere to the Maliki school of Islamic jurisprudence, as do the majority of African Muslims. However, as a result of the Ottoman Turkish occupation in the nineteenth century, Hanafi law was imposed as the "official" school of interpretation, and this administrative decision was carried forward by the twentieth-century British colonial authorities. In 1902, the "Muhammadan Law Courts Ordinance," instituted by the colonial government, empowered the Grand Qadi of Sudan to issue judicial circulars which interpreted points of law to the Shariʿa judges. This unique Sudanese innovation allowed the Grand Qadi, in consultation with other ʿulama, to combine elements of Maliki and Hanafi law. This often meant a stated preference for Maliki over Hanafi law, and with respect to legal reform it opened the way for liberalization of the law regarding judicial divorce for women and the rights of women in child custody. Between 1902 and 1979, sixty-two judicial circulars were issued on topics dealing exclusively with matters of personal status law.[1] A concise history of the Shariʿa as applied in Sudan is contained within these circulars, and Islamic personal law can be understood through them in combination with a general appreciation of Maliki and Hanafi law.

MARRIAGE (*AL-ZUWAJ*)

A valid Muslim marriage in Sudan is contracted by two agents representing the bride and the groom, usually the fathers of each. The dower (*mahr*) is agreed upon and is customarily paid in both a prompt and a deferred payment. The contract of marriage, the *qassima*, is witnessed and signed in the presence of a *maʾazun* (registrar of marriages and divorces), and the beginning of the legal marriage takes place at this ʿaqid (contract signing) ceremony. Customarily in Sudan the ʿaqid celebration precedes by some months, or a year or more, actual cohabitation and consummation of the marriage. But the legal responsibilities of the husband and the legal rights of the wife begin at the contract signing. Sudanese wedding festivities occur at the time of the ʿeris, or *zuwaj*, celebration, which culminates in the consummation of the marriage. These festivities can extend over a three- to seven-day period.

An elaboration of Sudanese law has occurred in the area of consent in marriage (*wilaya fi zuwaj*). Differences in interpretation between the Hanafi and the Maliki schools become important in clarifying the woman's or the father's role in final consent to marriage. Hanafi law gives final consent in marriage to the woman alone, while Maliki law gives the father of the bride absolute authority in marriage affairs. A circular issued in 1933 stated that Maliki law on consent was the preferred interpretation over Hanafi law. The marriage guardian (*al-wali*) is usually the father, but failing him a set succession of close male relatives legally substitutes in marriage negotiations over the selection of spouse and amount of mahr. In some cases a Shari'a judge or any other upright Muslim male can act as a marriage guardian if the woman is without one. The guardian then speaks for the woman. There was sufficient resistance on this point by a growing body of organized Sudanese women, especially in the post–World War II period of intensified political activity, that in 1960 the Grand Qadi and the High Court reversed itself and reinstituted the Hanafi legal provision that the consent of the woman alone is final. However, Maliki traditions have reasserted themselves to a certain degree in the form of legislation in the early 1970s that clarifies that a woman's consent may be express or implied. Silence by the woman at the time of the marriage proposal means implied consent, as do cohabitation and the birth of children. The latter two points have arisen in response to a number of cases in which married women claimed lack of consent to a marriage which they had not opposed initially and to which children had been born. Thus Sudanese law recognizes Hanafi law and the importance of a woman's consent but does not require that consent be expressly or openly stated, as such behavior may undermine the authority of the father–marriage guardian.

Polygamy is, of course, permitted for up to four wives for a man; however, in practice only a very small percentage of men have a second wife. Polygamy has been challenged by some of the advocates of women's rights. I have seen some divorces granted in court to either wife if the husband has failed in any way to treat the wives equitably, and if such failure has been established with witnesses.

By contrast, Egypt has been through a recent period of dialogue and controversy regarding the subject of polygamy. In 1979, under the influence of Jihan el-Sadat, the wife of Anwar el-Sadat, legislation was instituted whereby the husband seeking to marry a second wife would need to inform the first wife and to have her permission. The same legislation gave the house or flat to the wife with children if the husband divorced her. In the extremely crowded living conditions of Cairo, with a chronic housing shortage, this law and indeed the entire legislative package became highly controversial. On the question of polygamy, the religious sheikhs at Al-Azhar University and many of the 'ulama said that any restriction of polygamy would be against the religion of Islam and must be opposed. In 1985 the law was rescinded on technical grounds and then reinstated in substance, so that the husband still needs to inform and to seek the permission of the first wife. The issue remains controversial in Egyptian society. In Sudan, the issue is raised as a subject in intellectual circles and within the Sudanese Women's Union, but so far it has not been subjected to legislative reform.

DIVORCE (*AL-TALAQ*)

It is a little-appreciated fact that Sudan was among the leaders in the Islamic world in the area of divorce reform. One of the early judicial circulars (Circular Number 17, issued in 1915 or 1916, date is uncertain), allowed the possibility of divorce for women on the grounds of nonsupport (lack of *nafaqa*); harm or cruelty (*darar*); and fear of temptation on the wife's part after her husband had deserted her for more than one year (*khuf al-fitna*). Such reform legislation was in process in Turkey during the last days of the Ottoman rule but was interrupted and ultimately transformed by the end of World War I and the more fundamental reforms of Attaturk. Thus Sudan appears to have been the first country to institute divorce reform, with Egypt following its lead in a modified version of the Sudanese law in 1920. Such reform in the divorce laws did not reach other Arab-Islamic regions until several decades after the initial steps taken in Sudan and Egypt.

The most consistent and well developed of the divorce law changes during the past six to seven decades has been in regard to divorce on the ground of cruelty, (*talaq al-darar*). Darar (literally, "harm"), originally intended to mean physical abuse of the wife, which when proven, would result in the judicial divorce of the couple, was gradually expanded to include mental harm as well. In a number of landmark cases the High Court has determined that the husband's repeated insulting behavior toward the wife or even a deep insult on a single occasion (such as the accusation that the wife was not a virgin at the time of their marriage) is mental harm and thus sufficient ground for divorce because of darar. I have seen cases in which the wife successfully argued her case for divorce on account of harm because the husband attempted to install a second wife in the same house as the first. Harm, physical or mental, when proven in court with witnesses, is the single most common type of judicial divorce in Sudan. Its prevalence stems from the fact that desertion and lack of support of the wife and children, which are common complaints in court, can also be interpreted as forms of harm to the wife. By extension, fear of temptation (khuf al-fitna) can also be viewed as a form of harm to the wife, who is not only denied support from the absent husband but is also denied the normal sexual life she has a right to enjoy in marriage.

The ground of harm as a basis for divorce is derived from the Maliki school of Islamic interpretation, which has deep roots in Sudan. It perhaps helps to explain why Sudan has elaborated this aspect of its divorce law beyond that which is found in Egypt, which follows more closely the Shafi'i school, except for the Nubian regions in upper Egypt, where the Maliki school dominates. Today in Egypt, talaq al-darar is also the most common ground for divorce used by women in court, but harm is more narrowly defined as physical abuse of the wife.

Building upon the tradition of harm as a ground for judicial divorce by women, in 1977 Sudan took the unusual step in legal thinking to develop the concept of *fidya* (ransom) in connection with divorce sought by women. In cases in which the woman has fled the marital home because of her fear of an abusive husband, she is in a state of legal disobedience (*nūshūz*) and therefore does not have the right to sue her husband for lack of support and is temporarily without rights to maintenance. If her absence from the marital home is alleged but not proven to be the result of cruelty, the wife may request in court that she be released, or "ransomed," out of the unwanted marriage by offering cash or valuables to the husband, or by relinquishing her rights in the marriage, such as the final payment of the dower. If the husband accepts the offer, the judge will divorce them on the spot; even if the husband rejects the offer, the judge may still order a legal separation so that the wife will not be trapped in a situation where she is denied access to her marital right of support and to divorce as well. Divorce using the fidya concept is but one example of the enlightened jurisprudential thinking that had characterized the development of the Shari'a until the laws of September 1983 ushered in a period of relatively harsh interpretation of Islamic law.

MARRIAGE ARBITRATION (*AL-TAHKIM*)

Marriage arbitration is a fundamental part of Islamic Shari'a that has been repeatedly emphasized in Sudanese applied law and is required by Islamic law. Prior to every judicial separation, the judge will ask that the couple submit to marriage arbitration, whereby a neutral party from the wife's side and one from the husband's attempt to find the cause of the marital discord and to see whether the problems can be resolved through negotiation. As a matter of court procedure, initially in divorce cases a judge can recommend marriage arbitration, appoint the arbitrators, and ask for a report in three months' time. If progress is made during that time, the judge will postpone the case again in the hope of a settlement of the conflict. If the arbitrators recommend divorce, the judge will follow their advice, but the fundamental approach in Islamic law is one of marital reconciliation rather than of separation.

CHILD CUSTODY (*AL-HADANA*)

Islamic law recognizes that the first right of custody rests with the mother— indeed, the Arabic word for the care and custody of children derives from the word for breast (*hidn*). However, owing to the strongly partrilineal character of Islamic society, the right of custody traditionally falls to the father and the patrilineal kin group at age seven for a boy and age nine for a girl, according to the Hanafi school. Maliki law, on the other hand, permits a woman to retain custody of her son until the age of puberty and of the girl until the consummation of her marriage. In 1932 the Grand Qadi issued Circular Number 34, which extended the period of custody for a woman if the court decides that doing so is in the best interests of the children. This decision accords with Maliki custom, which in Sudan is considered binding as law. A similar change in the Egyptian law did not occur until 1979, as part of the revision of the 1929 family legislation.

In Sudanese practice, custody of children after a divorce will automatically fall to the ex-husband at seven years and nine years for a boy and girl, respectively, unless the mother applies in court to retain custody. After ensuring that the custody suit will not adversely affect the welfare of the child (that is, by the father's stopping support payments to the mother), the court will begin its inquiry into settling the case in the best interests of the child. Here the Islamic court adopts much the same posture as Western courts in custody cases when it acts as an independent advocate for the child, legally a *guardian ad-litem*. Factors affecting a positive outcome for the mother include an irrevocable divorce made by the husband or a court divorce granted because of cruelty on the husband's part. A history of the husband's nonsupport of the ex-wife and children is also an important factor in the mother's behalf, but her personal situation and the nearness of the residential home to good schools or to grandparents are considered as well. Factors weighing against the mother include her remarriage (a favorable circumstance for the father) or work outside the home beyond the hours that the child is in school. I recall the case of an airline stewardess applying for custody of her two sons. Her work took her to London twice a month and she had subsequently remarried; these negative factors reduced her chances of winning the case. On the other hand, I have witnessed the religious courts award custody to a mother who had not remarried and who was schooling her sons in Comboni College, a Catholic secondary school in Khartoum; the critical factor was that the boys would be able to remain at that school, which is well known for its high academic standards.

To understand the applied law regarding child custody, it is important to recognize that the court departs from its normal role of impartiality and adopts an advocacy role with respect to the child, setting aside what may have been viewed in the past as paternal or maternal prerogatives in the matter of child custody. It is an enlightened development in the law, demonstrating the responsiveness of the Shari'a to changed social conditions.

INHERITANCE (*AL-WARITHA*)

The Islamic law of inheritance is the crowning gem of the Shari'a and its most complex expression of Muslim family life. Quranic shares of inheritance are fixed and are apportioned on the principles that lineal relations take precedence over collateral relations and that women generally inherit one-half that of men. This latter point of clear inequality for women is still best explained by the widespread economic dependence of women in Islamic societies. I have heard this legal point challenged only in Egypt, where land, housing, and other economic resources are scarce and where some women have been abandoned by husbands, thus making their economic need from their lineal kin more apparent.

In Sudan, changes in the applied law during the twentieth century have focused on strengthening the nuclear family in inheritance (over the patrilineal extended family, the male core referred to as the *'asaba*) and emphasized mutual inheritance between husband and wife. On the latter point, in 1925 Sudan made a remarkable break with established legal opinion among all four schools of Islamic jurisprudence when it entitled the wife or husband of a deceased spouse to the entirety of the estate if no other legal heirs were present. Up to that time the estate of a deceased spouse having no heirs gave a husband one-half portion and a wife one-quarter portion, with the remainder going to the Public Treasury (*bayt al-mal*). The reform placed the spouse relict on a par with the other heirs and was revolutionary in its time, evidenced by the fact that this particular innovation was not introduced in Egypt until almost twenty years later, in 1943.

Other reforms in inheritance law further strengthened the position of the nuclear family, reflecting its growing importance in a society undergoing transformation through colonialism and the introduction of a capitalist economy. The shares of full and half brothers and sisters were equalized (1939), and the share of the grandfather was equalized with that of full brothers (1943) so that the grandfather would not displace them in inheritance, as would have occurred in the unreformed law.

RELIGIOUS ENDOWMENT (*WAQF*)

Unlike other predominantly Muslim countries, Sudan has chosen to retain the essential features of both the *waqf* (endowment) made for public, charitable purposes as well as the family waqf (*al-ahli*).[2] Other Muslim regions have abolished both or have retained only the public waqf, traditionally used for the maintenance of schools, mosques, and hospitals. The family waqf has held potential for abuse insofar as it might be used to increase or decrease an heir's portion fixed by the Shari'a.

Sudan has opted to retain these *awqaf* (plural of *waqf*) in circulars, issued in 1970 and 1971, which apply certain restrictions to the nomination of a family waqf by a potential donor. Specifically the intention of the law is to subject family awqaf to a review process whereby the real intention and purpose of the endowment is clarified. Investigation by the court which would reveal that a proposed waqf deprives an heir of his or her share in inheritance, in effect precludes the potential donor's ability to make such a waqf. Likewise, beneficiaries to a waqf may have increased over time (awqaf are meant to be held in perpetuity) so that their number is unwieldy and the actual benefits are meager. In such cases, to end confusion or ill-feeling among themselves, the beneficiaries may make a collective application before the court to have the waqf canceled.

These precautionary measures on the part of the interpreters of the religious law have amounted, in effect, to the official discouragement of the family waqf without entirely abolishing its potential for genuine charity to relations in need. In practice I have seen the refusal of the court to accept a waqf which would have, for all practical purposes, disinherited two daughters in favor of a son at the time each took his or her portion according to the principles of Quranic inheritance. On the other hand, the courts will respond favorably to a family waqf donor who wants to endow a segment of his extended family, not fully protected as heirs, who have fallen on hard times and are in genuine need. Thus, with respect to waqf, Sudan has adopted a more conservative approach, one that intends to weed out harmful use of the institution while preserving its potential for good application.

Although Sudan has been through a difficult period when harsh application of the Shari'a has taken place within a highly politicized context (from 1983 to the present), the longer history of the Shari'a in the country is one of an enlightened and liberal interpretation of the personal status affairs it has governed.[3] In certain areas of divorce and inheritance, Sudan has been a leader in legal reform, anticipating innovations which were not introduced into other Muslim regions until years or even decades later. Sudan and Egypt were in the vanguard of many of the developments regarding family law, especially in the decades of the twenties, thirties, and forties of this century. In the period since independence in 1956, Sudan has elaborated its applied law especially in the areas of divorce because of cruelty, consent in marriage, and waqf nomination. The pattern of progress and enlightenment in marital affairs remains consistent even to the present time. Indeed, under the current Islamist regime, the new code of personal status ("the Muslim Personal Law of 1991") broadened the eligibility of men and women to marry by removing "pedigree" and "craft" as conditions for marriage. The former condition could eliminate a person with slavery in his or her background, while the latter fostered class endogamy. "Practice of religion" and "good morals" have become central in marriage selection.

The major question of the Sudanese political agenda is whether the Shari'a will remain as state law or whether it will return to its pre-1983 status as a personal status law only. There are strong secular and multicultural social and religious forces at work in Sudan that will urge a religious personal status law for Muslims and a secular, heterogenous state civil law as national law.

NOTES

1. The judicial circulars have been edited and translated and are published in C. Fluehr-Lobban with Hatim B. Hillawi, "Circulars of the *Shariʿa* Courts in Sudan (*Manshurat El-Mahakim El-Shariʿa fi Sudan*), 1902–79, *Journal of African Law* 27, no. 2 (1983): 79–140.

2. Waqf, a specialized subject in Islamic law, is an endowment in property, land, or cash which is normally made for charitable purposes, either public or familial.

3. See also the author's more general study on the Shariʿa in Sudan, *Islamic Law and Society in the Sudan* (London: Frank Cass, 1987).

The Veiled Revolution

Elizabeth W. Fernea

Since the early twentieth century, patterns of women's work and of dress have moved closer to the Western model. However, as Elizabeth W. Fernea shows, those patterns are beginning to shift again as young, educated women return to conservative "Islamic" dress, not for the reasons their grandmothers veiled, but to define their identity as Muslim women in a changing world. (This article was written to complement Fernea's film, The Veiled Revolution, *part of her film trilogy,* Reformers and Revolutionaries: Middle Eastern Women.*) —Eds.*

"The feminine veil has become a symbol: that of the slavery of one portion of humanity," wrote French ethnologist Germaine Tillion in 1966. That view of the veil appears again and again in the West, partly, of course, because the veil is indeed a dramatic visual symbol. It attracts us to a face that may not be seen and at the same time signifies a boundary that may not be crossed.

Such a barrier or boundary between men and women exists in some form in all societies. But the veil as a visible barrier calls up in the viewer a complex reaction. We tend to believe that those who look out (through the veil) suffer from the same exclusion as those of us who look at the veil and its hidden contents. However, we have no right to make such an assumption. Much depends on who makes the decision to veil—whether it is imposed or self-selected.

Until recently, veiling and conservative dress had been declining steadily in all parts of the Islamic world. Walking on the streets of Turkey, Lebanon, Iraq, Tunisia, Morocco, Algeria, Jordan, and Egypt, a visitor would find a veiled woman the expection rather than the rule. Yet veiling has continued to be the rule in Saudi Arabia, North Yemen, and some areas of Afghanistan and Pakistan. And now patterns are shifting again.

Western and Middle Eastern rejection of, or outrage against, the veil has been seen as rejection of, and outrage against, the values believed to be associated with the veil. These values include chastity, a prescribed role for women in the family, and, above all, unequal access to divorce, inheritance, and child custody. If these problems are reformed, many Middle Eastern women say, the use or nonuse of the veil will become unimportant.

But as the veil has been used over the centuries for political, religious, and social purposes, it is a symbol within the society itself that can find new uses, "an outward sign of a complex reality." The donning of modest dress or, as some women call it, "Islamic dress" is a personal statement in response to new and changing social conditions in Egypt.

The first thing that must be stressed, however, is that the contemporary use of conservative dress is a new phenomenon. Women are not "returning to the veil," for the garments they are designing for themselves and wearing on the streets of Cairo are not of the style worn since before the turn of the century—the *milaya*, the head scarf, the long, full black dress. The modest garments of today constitute a new style, developed only in the past ten years. The head scarf, the turban, the fitted long dress or the loose full dress are variations on an old theme—with new expressions and new implications.

The second point is that Islamic dress today is a middle- and upper-middle-class phenomenon, found mostly among educated working women. The majority of those taking up modest dress are young, in their early twenties, and many are in the universities and professional schools throughout Egypt. As a medical student at Tanta put it, "I think of Islamic dress as a kind of uniform. It means I am serious about myself and my religion but also about my studies. I can sit in class with men and there is no question of attraction and so on—we are all involved in the same business of learning, and these garments make that clear."

The young women who are wearing Islamic dress are often the daughters and granddaughters of women who wear Western dress. Some sociologists in Egypt suggest that the adoption of conservative dress is a form of rebellion, a rebuff to a parental generation whose efforts have not, as expected, improved conditions in Egypt. Economic conditions in Egypt are indeed better for a small percentage of the population, but for at least half of Egypt's people, the bright future promised in the 1950s has not materialized. In this sense, the new garb carries a political message: it is a dramatic, nonviolent protest against the establishment and its policies, as well as against the West.

But political statement, in Islamic countries, cannot be separated from religious statement. Egypt is a society which still considers itself a Muslim state, where religion and politics have never been separated. A small minority of Christians (Copts, Armenians, Nestorians, Eastern Orthodox Catholics, Roman Catholics) live in Egypt, but nearly 90 percent of the population is Muslim. The Quran is the basis for family law still, though some modifications have been made in recent years, and the criminal and civil codes are amalgams of European and Quranic laws. Thus religion is part of everyday life, and religious affiliation is part of one's social identity, whether or not one is a practicing Muslim or Christian.

Therefore, far from being a simple statement of religious affiliation, the wearing of Islamic dress is related to the very basis of social life in Egypt and in other Muslim countries, where the wearing of Islamic dress has also been observed (Jordan, Lebanon, and Libya are recent examples). The wearing of Islamic dress also relates to the individual's sense of belonging to a group, and to the individual's sense of her own identity. Although some men also wear a form of Islamic dress (a long, loose homespun shirt, a white skullcap, and beard), their numbers are not nearly so high as are found among women. Such apparel may even be politically risky these days because it suggests sympathy with Muslim "extremists," as their critics call them.

A third important point to be made, and one that women stress repeatedly, is that the choice to wear Islamic dress is one they make themselves, and it must come "from inner religious conviction." Although stories of organized Muslim groups paying women to wear Islamic dress are told by Westerners in Egypt, these seem generally to be unfounded. Women make their own choice, but of course they are influenced by their peers, and the decision is one hotly debated within families and among different groups of friends.

Finally, the wearing of Islamic dress has, in addition to the genuine religious motives avowed by many young women, many practical advantages. As one young woman put it, "My family trusts me implicitly, and now that I wear this dress, they are not worried if I stay out later than usual or mingle with friends they do not always approve of. In this dress, my reputation remains intact, for everyone knows that it is a respectable garment. People thus respect you if you wear it."

In crowded conditions, such as the streets of Cairo and the packed public buses, Islamic dress does offer some protection against importuning and aggressive sexual advances by men. Further, the new phenomenon of women working outside the home places many men and women in new situations—close to each other for long periods of the day—that place a strain on the traditional boundaries between men and women, and may also place strains on the public reputation of the young women. It is true that many of the outward signs of the older Egyptian society—veiling, seclusion of women, segregation of women from public work places, education institutions, and so on—have disappeared, but traditional attitudes are slower to change. The wearing of Islamic dress is a practical, simple way of stating publicly, "I am a respectable woman. Leave me alone."

A small number of women cover themselves completely. They take the Quranic injunction "and tell the believing women to draw their garments close around them" to its logical extreme and describe themselves as "devout, devoted to God and unwilling to enter the public workplace." The majority of women wearing Islamic dress do not seem to feel this way, however, but see themselves as making a statement or taking action that strengthens their own position within the society. They continue to attend colleges and universities, work outside the home, mingle with men in the classroom and on the streets. They also attend study groups in mosques and private homes to learn more about their own faith and law. Many have taken the "service" aspect of Islamic teaching seriously, and, under the direction of persons such as Dr. Zahira Abdine, director of the Giza Children's Hospital, do volunteer work among the poor. Two young medical students and one doctor spend one day a week at the Sayyida Zeinab mosque, where they have opened a people's free medical clinic. Others teach and offer services as social workers.

The veil, then, is a complex symbol that can have multiple implications and different impacts. Manipulated in one way, it can become a symbol for conservatism or for reaction against modernization; utilized in another way, it can become a symbol for an Islamic approach to the solutions of both old and new problems. However it is used, it means different things to different people within the society, and it means different things to Westerners than it does to Muslim Middle Easterners.

PART THREE

Home, Community, and Work

INTRODUCTION

Traditional institutions such as the family and the mosque teach the values and roles which preserve a cultural heritage and which ensure social stability. At the same time, a society must adapt to new institutions, such as secular education and corporate business. Each sphere affects the other. Traditional ties can dilute crisp, impersonal business dealings—benefiting interpersonal relations but sabotaging efficiency. Students who spurn tradition with their views or style of clothing may scandalize their grandparents. One thinks little about institutions unless they seem threatened; then there is great consternation and self-examination. Consumerism and obsession with material objects, widely criticized by Muslim activist movements, have been in highly visible conflict with traditional society.

The family, the sole most important traditional institution, filters the world to the child and conveys cultural values. As an adult one becomes involved in the everyday affairs of community and marketplace where individuals fashion their identities. Michael Gilsenan writes of young Lebanese men who define cultural modes of communication to create dazzling images for themselves during idle hours in village cafes.

In the past, religion reinforced the family as a vital institution of socialization. The Nasiriyya religious brotherhood described by James A. Miller and Donna Lee Bowen was originally the guiding moral force in the Moroccan Sahara: it governed the croplands and provided spiritual and social guidance as well as education for the community. With time, the government and the public schools weakened the brotherhood's jurisdiction. The Nasiriyya spiritual leader adapted to the times and still retains his position of moral authority in the community.

In many places today, village elders retain their influence, and the central government is hard pressed to implement programs they oppose. Tayib Salih's "The Doum Tree of Wad Hamid," the story of a Sudanese village, proposes the idea of institutional adaptation, whereby new technology need not destroy old social forms. The coexistence of old and new allows constructive change.

In a society undergoing rapid technological change, social rituals may help preserve family and community. Social ceremony enhances experience in the minds of social actors; activities as mundane as visiting or as dramatic as quarrels in the street depict social relations. Visiting or extending hospitality—as analyzed by Aida S. Kanafani—is not something one does to fill spare time. Mere visits are rare; rather, visiting is a social obligation which may also fulfill other functions. In the traditional households of the Emirates, one finds intricate visiting rituals and elaborate polite exchanges over tea and coffee. At the same time, however, family or social ties are reinforced, and information is passed and processed.

Education is the critical ingredient for modern careers today. Literacy in the Middle East averages 40 percent but is as low as 28 percent in some countries. Female literacy hovers at about 15 or 20 percent in many areas. The newly independent Middle Eastern nations have poured resources into facilities, teacher training, and rural education. Governments go to great lengths to train and retain teachers. In Iraq, for example, all school teachers were excused from the army in the late 1980s when every other able-bodied man was called to fight on the Iranian front. Given rapidly growing populations, however, limited school construction and teacher education cannot gain on the increasing number of children in any but the oil-rich states.

Education, seen as the most important key to social mobility, has been eagerly sought, and many families sacrifice enormously to educate at least one son. A peasant family in a mountainous area of Morocco is typical. The parents planned to educate as many of their sons as possible. The first son remained at home to work with his father in the family fields. The second son joined the army and began to contribute part of his salary to support brother number three in secondary school in the nearest provincial capital. Brother number four took a baccalaureate and became an air traffic controller with the military. Brother number five attended a university, then became a government bureaucrat. Brothers six and seven were expected to become engineers. The youngest two sons—numbers eight and nine—had the combined financial support of every older brother and groaned under the weight of family expectations.

In some countries, swelling university populations have created a huge, unemployable reserve of white-collar workers. Bishara Bahbah, as editor of the Jerusalem newspaper *al-Fajr*, exemplifies the personal conflicts in the growing professional class in the Middle East labor force. While white-collar jobs may bring prestige, skilled and unskilled labor are in higher demand and in many cases bring higher salaries than do positions as clerks, professionals, and bureaucrats.

The family was the locus of production of most needs in bedouin or agriculturalist societies where less was purchased. With industrialization and urbanization, a job or career became important to support a family. As some Middle Eastern nations experienced the oil boom, overpopulated, poorer nations furnished the oil-rich nations with skilled and unskilled workers. Rapid urbanization pushed housing, transportation, and service infrastructures past the breaking point. The oil-rich nations imported workers, but in labor-rich, capital-poor nations such as Egypt, Morocco, Algeria, and Tunisia seasonal unemployment totals more than 30 percent, and about 10 percent of the workforce works overseas.

With the Middle East's entry into a world economy dependent upon international market forces, Middle Eastern markets have changed and diversified. However, the essence of the merchant-customer or patron-client tie has not altered very much. Robert Fernea discusses how merchants establish themselves in marketplaces more through social rapport than through the sale of produce. Markets such as that of Marrakesh allow for compelling case studies of the place of traditional economies within the world economy. Side by side with traditional markets are the modern business sectors of the city, and the prominent families of the traditional markets are generally allied to the dominant business forces of the country. It is also in other modern sectors that many creative syntheses of the old and the new are wrought, as illustrated in Abdel-Salam Al Ujaili's short story about a country clinic where a Syrian physician practices modern medicine while salving the fears of clients still swayed by folk beliefs.

Nowhere is the collision between old and new, between the past and the present more pronounced than in questions of religion. The course of social modernization and religious change in the Middle East is a potentially explosive one. Some Middle Easterners, who perceive the West as materialist and nonreligious, have founded Islamic reform movements, while others have proclaimed the compatibility of new technology and traditional religion. Some reformers have pressed for Islam to adapt to new social needs and others have pleaded for Islam to return to basic family and community values in the face of a Western materialist onslaught. Hajj Brahim, in John Waterbury's sketch of a Moroccan merchant, presents a cogent synthesis of religion and business in a changing world.

The Middle Eastern community, then, is a scene with many contradictions. There are close-knit extended families and migrant laborers living alone. There are old-fashioned water wheels and modern electric pumps. There are mules and metros. But the real story is told in the lives of individuals who fashion a family and a career, who form a community. All the customs and ceremonies—greeting, visiting, eating, exchanging—are a means of getting through the daily grind of raising and educating a family and, quite simply, of surviving. As we see these everyday rituals unfold, we see also a melange of tradition and modernity.

Rites of Hospitality and Aesthetics

Aida S. Kanafani

Middle Easterners are renowned for their hospitality. The Arab code of generosity toward friends and strangers originated in the need to protect travelers from the hostile desert. Gulf Arabs evaluate aesthetic aspects of hospitality, such as the manner of offering food and the burning of incense, much as we might evaluate a play or a musical performance. One's social status in the United Arab Emirates is affected by how well one observes the social niceties. —Eds.

The example and recommendations of the Prophet Muhammad as found in the *Hadith* and cultural ideas of pollution and power are fundamental to an understanding and appreciation of aesthetic and hospitable behavior in the United Arab Emirates (UAE).

According to the *Hadith,* a woman should abstain from using perfumes when she goes out in public, where men will be present. A *hadith* states that as every eye is adulterous, the woman who perfumes herself and passes by an assembly of men (*majlis*) is an adulteress (al-Tirmidhi, Etiquette, 35). Insight into such reasoning is found in the distinction made between *tīb* (perfume, scent) for men and that for women: "Perfume for men is manifested in its smell and its color is concealed: perfume for women is manifested by its color and its smell is concealed" (al-Tirmidhi, Etiquette, 36). In other words, female perfumes are supposed to have subtle smell and odors are not to be detected from a distance but only on close contact. In practice, however, as women go out only to visit other women, strong scents are also used.

A man in the UAE may also wear perfume to please his wife, in accordance with the aesthetic norm prescribed in the *Hadith.* For example, a man came to see the Prophet, reeking of *khaluq,* a mixture of saffron and other

Adapted from Aida S. Kanafani, *Aesthetics and Ritual in the United Arab Emirates.* Beirut: American University of Beirut, 1983.

scents. When the Prophet asked him whether he was married the man said no. The Prophet then ordered him to wash off the scent (al-Nasa'i, v. 8, Adornment, 152–153).

Men also use perfumes before going to the mosque. As Prophet Muhammad said: "It is right (*haqq*) for every Muslim to wash, to get perfumed on Friday" (al-Tirmidhi, Friday, 381). The reason for the avoidance of unpleasant smells can be seen in the Prophet's sensitivity to unpleasant smells. An interesting hadith relates:

> A man asked him [the Prophet] about washing on Friday. "Is it a duty?"
> He said, "No, whoever wishes to wash may." People were needy and they
> wore wool, and they watered the palm trees from their backs and the
> mosque of the Prophet was narrow and low. People went there in their
> woolen clothes so they perspired and the minbar of the Prophet was short,
> it was three steps. People were perspiring in the wool. Their smell was the
> smell of the wool so the people were disturbed by each other till their smell
> reached the Prophet as he stood on the minbar. He said, "People, when you
> come to the mosque on Friday, wash; and use your best perfumes if you
> have any." (Ibn Hanbal 1:268–289)

In the UAE, avoiding pollution and being purified are related to the aesthetic symbolism expressed in food and body rituals. The aesthetic element is able to purify because it can be seen, smelled, and tasted, and is identified as conforming to the aesthetic patterns recommended by Islam. Perfumes, dyes, and spices are believed to be overt expressions of purification. For women in the UAE, beautiful smells and other cosmetic items are potent signs of cleanliness and purification (*nazafah* and *tahara*).

Two terms are used to refer to dirt: *khais* (dirt) and *adha* (that which is very dirty; literally, "harm"). Materials associated with khais are purifiable, and materials associated with adha are not. For example, blood in meat and body dirt such as sweat are referred to as khais and the impurity can be nullified, or at least reduced by the use of spices, oils, plants, and dyes which purify and make beautiful both food and parts of the body.

Materials associated with adha cannot be purified. For example, kitchens and bathrooms can be cleaned but not purified. Women in the UAE say that adha is very dirty. Adha is dirt characteristic of menstruation, post-delivery time, bathrooms, and kitchens. Although urine and feces can be washed off and the body cleaned with water and soap, the bathroom, which is the locale of these bodily excretions, can be cleaned with water, soap, and antiseptic but not purified.

A similar justification can be given for the impurity of the kitchen. The consumption of food is said to be polluting. Coffee drinking, perfume application, and censing are performed when the tray of consumed food is removed. As the perfumes which were on the visitors and the hostess are nullified, renewal of odors becomes necessary. The kitchen itself is not purifiable because it is the locale of permanent food preparation, and where food is prepared the pollution of ingredients lingers. The pollution of kitchens and bathrooms is permanent regardless of the number of times they are cleaned during the day, as adha is never purifiable.

This leads to the paradox that what seems to need purification most is not purified. This does not mean that a menstruating woman does not wash or that kitchens and bathrooms are not cleaned. A woman "who has blood" washes her private parts with soap and water but avoids using perfumes. She also abstains from prayer and sexual intercourse. She is in a temporary state of pollution and must not try to overcome it by applying things which belong to another status. *Wudu'* and *ghusl* are the main techniques for washing the body. The first refers to the ablutions for prayer and the second is performed after sexual intercourse and after menstruation. *Istinja'* and *istibra'* refer to the use of water after defecating and urinating.

A woman who is not menstruating and who has washed is clean and can be considered pure even if she does not use perfumes. Nevertheless, women in the UAE stress that perfumes reinforce the state of purity by their aesthetic quality and their having been recommended in Islam.

A menstruating woman is clean when she has washed with water. The kitchen and the bathroom are also clean when washed with water, soap, and antiseptic, but not pure, whereas other units of the house can be both clean and pure because no permanent dirt is associated with them. Any residual pollution from eating and the sexual activities performed in the sleeping units, which are also potential living rooms and places for receiving guests, can be easily removed with soap, antiseptic, water, and perfumes. But pollution of the bathroom and the kitchen is continuous; no matter how often they are cleaned they remain dirty, and their pollution remains highly potent.

Mention should be made of another aesthetic ritual which is also aimed at reducing pollution. Taking the shoes off at the threshold of a house keeps the dirt on the shoes out of the house. There is then a demarcation between the outdoors, which is subject to material pollution, and the indoors, which represents the sanctity of a dwelling. In addition to saying that the outdoors is polluted with trash, dung, mud, and so on, the people of the UAE also say that the custom of removing the shoes shows humility: "Greetings are to be said without wearing shoes." Moreover, it is considered a show of respect for the host or hostess who receives guests.

Visiting is an elaborate ritual designed not only to provide hospitality but also to deal with the outdoor-indoor space, polluted-pure dichotomy, and with the balance of power between host and guest. At the outset of the visit both host and guest have a certain amount of power which the visit triggers and develops. Part of the host's power originates from being in the host's own domain. But the guest has a certain amount of power over the host because the latter is required to behave in a specific way to fulfill expectations. To neutralize some of the guest's power, elements of personal power are removed from the guest, who is obliged to remove shoes, to sit on the floor, and to partake in the food and body rituals which are part of every visit.

Taking the shoes off not only symbolizes the removal of pollution but also represents an attempt by the host to nullify part of the guest's power *by making the guest similar* to the host. It is explicitly stated in the UAE that removing one's shoes at the entrance during a visit shows respect for the host. It is considered shameful (*'aib*) not to take them off; the greeting must be said inside the sacred space of a dwelling after the guest has removed his shoes. Similarly, the guest sits on the floor, as otherwise he "would be sitting on the head of the host." The host offers food, coffee, perfume, and incense, which the guest is expected to share. The host may be said to force the guest to eat food and to perform body rituals which are undertaken during the visit. Rejection of participation is an offense and an act with grave social repercussions (see Pitt-Rivers 1977:109). Hence, food, oils, and incense are status markers used by the host in an attempt to reduce the guest's power and are aimed at absorbing the guest by putting him in a subordinate and dependent position.

In general, the host is the provider of coffee, food, and perfumes. Cutting fruits, providing meat, circulating coffee and perfumes are also acts performed by the host. Such behavior aims at minimizing the social distance between the host and the guest, who is thus dependent on the host. As Pitt-Rivers has noted, a guest infringes the law of hospitality if "he usurps the role of his host by taking precedence, helping himself" (1977, 109). Choosing when the guest leaves is also up to the host, who determines the duration of the visit by bringing the perfume box. An interesting observation is that a high-status host shows his social distance from his guest(s) by delegating the role of provider to servants—for example, during the majlis held by prominent sheikhs and sheikhas (female members of the ruling family) when visitors come to pay their respects. In the majlis everything is performed by a servant. The coffee pourer is thus a servant or an armed guard (in the male majlis), who stands up holding four to five cups in his right hand and the coffeepot in his left. The first cup is offered to the host (unlike ordinary visits, when the host drinks last) unless he declines with a wave of the hand pointing to one of the guests out of respect for the guest's high status or age. Alternatively, the host may decide to offer it to the first person on his right. Usually the host accepts the first cup and the servant then proceeds to serve the person on the right. The servant has to wait until the last guest finishes before withdrawing. Similarly in a majlis, preparation of the *fu'ala* and replenishing plates are the work of a servant, not of the host. These differences in behavior suggest that the high-status host is eager to assert the social distance between himself and his guest by delegating his role of attending to guests to a servant. With individuals of similar status, absorption in a power relationship is possible because the host personally satisfies all the guest's needs, rendering him helpless to serve himself, to choose when to be served, or to choose when to terminate the visit.

The host, by fulfilling all his duties, is at the same time honoring his guest. Consequently, if the host violates expectations of proper conduct he is depriving his guest of honor and thus offending him overtly. It is within the power of the host to manipulate courtesy rituals and their performance. The guest is here powerless and must submit to the host's test: to honor him with the variety of food and body rituals or to offend him by the absence of part of these offerings, by limiting their quantity and variety, or by disregarding their quality. These rites seem then to be aimed at minimizing the guest's power, which also stems from various sources.

The guest is an individual with an ambiguous status. He comes from the outside, unordered world and must honor his host by being clean. If he is dirty, he overtly offends the host. A visiting woman who comes badly dressed and unscented offends her hostess. In response, the hostess would neglect to honor her with food and perfumes and only offer coffee, without a fu'ala. I was told that the hostess honors her guest because of the latter's decoration (*zina*). Cleanliness not only is associated with the use of perfumes, antimony, and other dyes, but also indicates that the person is pure.

In the UAE, as in other traditional Arab societies, the guest comes to visit at the times he or she pleases. Therefore, the host has to keep the house in a proper state to receive unexpected guests. The housewife usually incenses the guest area along with other potential visiting areas (that is, sleeping quarters) in the early morning: rooms must be kept clean and smelling nice. Recently, the UAE society has undergone several changes as a result of exposure to other Arabs and Westerners, and these days, especially in the cities, guests usually telephone before a visit. However, traditional visiting patterns are still followed in the desert and in the mountains, where contact with foreigners is less common.

It is interesting that through the lingering smell of perfume on a woman who was a guest the success of a visit and the performance of the hostess are evaluated in the absence of the latter. People who inquire about a visit have to ask about the food, but not about the perfumes, which are immediately perceived on the woman guest who returns home or makes another visit elsewhere. The nicer the smell, the higher the prestige accruing to the hostess, whose image is thus enhanced and broadened. Nuances or tones of the smells are easily detected by the women, who have developed a remarkable sensitivity to scents. Also, the more expensive the oil, mixture, or incense offered, the more prestige gained by the hostess. Skillful manipulation of expensive perfumes and incense further contributes to the prestige of the woman who makes and offers them, which her audience recognizes as coming from particular merchants who import good oils from India, Bengal, Pakistan, or Yemen. Every woman specializes in oil or incense mixtures that disclose her tastes, her expertise in blending the various ingredients, and her income.

In one instance, a woman left a gathering, angry and terribly upset because her perfume was not chosen as best. The context of this incident deserves relating. At a picnic in Himraniyah (in Ras al-Khaimah emirate), I was asked to choose between *mkhammariya* blends worn by two women behind their ears. Some of the mixture was passed to me. Perplexed, I chose. Furious, the woman whose perfume was not chosen left the company, and although the other women called to her as she walked away, no one, not even the man who organized the trip, could bring her back while she waited for a taxi to return her to Sharjah. Her refusal to obey the man was of course regarded as an offense, but she believed that the greater offense was made to her. A few days later, I was introduced to a woman. When she heard my name, she said: "Ah you are the one who decided on a scent." Embarrassed, I could only appreciate the insight into the importance of scents in the UAE that this incident gave me.

When individuals plan to visit, they usually wear their nicest garments and their nicest perfumes, which are to be evaluated by the hostess. If the image is satisfactory or flattering, credit is given to the guest as a person of fine descent (*asl*). Thus, when a woman enters a gathering, her clothes, jewelry, and scent are evaluated. If she has used expensive ingredients for her perfumes and mixed them in a skillful manner, she is regarded as a woman of prestige (*'izz*).

The renewal of scents at the end of a visit regulates the duration of a visit, ensures the prestige of the hostess, and returns the guest to a state of purity partly dependent on the aesthetic power of the hostess. When the guest enters, she brings her own aesthetic display; as she leaves, her smells are generously renewed by the hostess, who knows that she will be evaluated in turn on how she has restored her guest's beautiful smells.

Usually all hostesses perform their duties faithfully because the hostess one day will be the guest another. Thus it is rather infrequent that the rites of hospitality are broken. Moreover, unless the hostess fulfills all hospitality expectations, the guest may become an active agent of gossip.

There is no specific word for gossip in the UAE. The words *rams* and *solafah* are used both for conversation and for gossip. The people of the UAE dread being the subject of bad gossip. Violating the rites of hospitality would expose the host to the severest social disapproval. A hostess has to protect her role and status. When she is deprived of them, group integrity itself is jeopardized because of loss of face and of status. When the performance of appropriate rituals is suspended, the hostess is implicitly denying the status of her guest because group conventions are strict and specific about the proper treatment of a guest. Gossip is a potent reminder that irregular behavior offends and that the offense should be corrected. Group unity is also reinforced by the fear of gossip, thus protecting the status of all involved. The threat of group disapproval inhibits unilateral rule-breaking. That is why individuals seek to constantly reaffirm their roles and status through the rites of hospitality. Each guest evaluates the performance of the hostess, and if the hostess fails to meet the guest's expectations, gossip ensues (for example, "God forgive us, not even coffee was offered"). Whereas when the guest is satisfied, the hostess is praised to others (for example, "They honored me, they fulfilled their duty toward me"; "God protects this home, they honored us with the fu'ala and the *dukhun*"). However, there are extenuating circumstances so that if the hostess is in a difficult situation and the proper offerings are not made, formulas are used to waive the gossip threat (for example, "Forgive us. We have not accomplished our obligations").

It must be stressed that the association between gossip and the manipulation of power to maintain or to increase one's prestige means that the guest is not merely granted hospitality as most literature on the matter assumes but enforces it. The guest manipulates the hostess's prestige: she affirms, increases, weakens or destroys it according to the degree the various food and body rituals are fulfilled.

TABLE 1: **Power of Host(ess) and of Guest**

Power of the Host(ess)	Power of the Guest
Guest takes off shoes	Ambiguous status
Makes guest sit on floor	Imposes his presence
Obliges guest to eat food	Coerces the host with a series of expectations
Controls duration of visit	Gossip agent
Host is provider of food, coffee, and perfumes	Evil eye agent
Host reflects image of guest's status	
Host served first if wealthy	

Julian Pitt-Rivers (1977) has considered the status of the stranger as central to the hospitality. I propose that the host who receives a perfect stranger in his domain does not operate under as many constraints as he would have if the guest were from within the community. Moreover, the closer the guest is to the host, the more power he is endowed with. Close relatives and friends constitute the category of persons who are to be honored and treated with consideration to neutralize their potential power. . . . The stranger is more dangerous than powerful, and more power can be attributed to the guest from within the group. . . . The guest is (also) a powerful agent of evil eye, which may be defined as a force emanating from a person's envy which can cause harm with various degrees of intensity. . . .

The aesthetics of food and body rituals cannot be isolated from the social and cultural values of the UAE because they reflect the traditional aesthetic norms set by Islam in its present-day setting.

REFERENCES

Ibn Hanbal. N.d. *Musnad al-Imam Ahmad Ibn Hanbal*. Beirut: Dar Sadir and al-Maktab al-Islami.

Nasa'i. N.d. *Sunan al-Nasa'i*. Cairo: al-Matbaʿa al-Masriyya bil Azhar.

Pitt-Rivers, Julian. 1977. *The Fate of Schechem or the Politics of Sex: Essays in the Anthropology of the Mediterranean*. Cambridge: Cambridge University Press.

al-Tirmidhi, Ibn Isa Muhammad bin Isa bin Sawra. N.d. *al-Jamaʿ al-sahih wahuwa sunan al-Tirmidhi*. Cairo: Halabi and Sons.

The Doum Tree of Wad Hamid

Tayeb Salih

"The Doum Tree of Wad Hamid," by the Sudanese author Tayeb Salih, is a classic story of accommodation of the old and the new in a village. It offers lessons best heeded by developers, city dwellers, and national leaders. Although the story pits villagers against outsiders, the opposition is far from clear-cut. Wad Hamid is not a simple, stick-in-the-mud village; it is a place that will always endure. —Eds.

Were you to come to our village as a tourist, it is likely, my son, that you would not stay long. If it were in winter time, when the palm trees are pollinated, you would find that a dark cloud had descended over the village. This, my son, would not be dust, nor yet that mist which rises up after rainfall. It would be a swarm of those sand flies which obstruct all paths to those who wish to enter our village. Maybe you have seen this pest before, but I swear that you have never seen this particular species. Take this gauze netting, my son, and put it over your head. While it won't protect you against these devils, it will at least help you to bear them. I remember a friend of my son's, a fellow student at school, whom my son invited to stay with us a year ago at this time. His people come from the town. He stayed one night with us and got up next day, feverish, with a running nose and swollen face; he swore that he wouldn't spend another night with us.

If you were to come to us in summer you would find the horseflies with us—enormous flies the size of young sheep, as we say. In comparison with these, the sand flies are a thousand times more bearable. They are savage flies, my son: they bite, sting, buzz, and whirr. They have a special love for man and no sooner smell him out than attach themselves to him. Wave them off you, my son—God curse all sand flies.

Adapted from *Modern Arabic Short Stories.* Ed. and trans. Denys-Johnson Davies. London: Heinemann Press, 1967, 1976.

And were you to come at a time which was neither summer nor winter you would find nothing at all. No doubt, my son, you read the papers daily, listen to the radio, and go to the cinema once or twice a week. Should you become ill you have the right to be treated in a hospital, and if you have a son he is entitled to receive education at a school. I know, my son, that you hate dark streets and like to see electric light shining out into the night. I know, too, that you are not enamored of walking and that riding donkeys gives you a bruise on your backside. Oh, I wish, my son, I wish—the asphalted roads of the towns—the modern means of transport—the fine comfortable buses. We have none of all this—we are people who live on what God sees fit to give us.

Tomorrow you will depart from our village, of this I am sure, and you will be right to do so. What have you to do with such hardship? We are thick-skinned people and in this we differ from others. We have become used to this hard life, in fact we like it, but we ask no one to subject himself to the difficulties of our life. Tomorrow you will depart, my son—I know that. Before you leave, though, let me show you one thing—something which, in a manner of speaking, we are proud of. In the towns you have museums, places in which the local history and the great deeds of the past are preserved. This thing that I want to show you can be said to be a museum. It is one thing we insist our visitors see.

Once a preacher, sent by the government, came to us to stay for a month. He arrived at a time when the horseflies had never been fatter. On the very first day the man's face swelled up. He bore this manfully and joined us in evening prayers on the second night, and after prayers he talked to us of the delights of the primitive life. On the third day he was down with malaria, he contracted dysentery, and his eyes were completely gummed up. I visited him at noon and found him prostrate in bed, with a boy standing at his head waving away the flies.

"O Sheikh," I said to him, "there is nothing in our village to show you, though I would like you to see the doum tree of Wad Hamid." He didn't ask me what Wad Hamid's doum tree was, but I presumed that he had heard of it, for who has not? He raised his face, which was like the lung of a slaughtered cow; his eyes (as I said) were firmly closed, though I knew that behind the lashes lurked a certain bitterness. "By God," he said to me, "if this were the doum tree of Jandal, and you the Muslims who fought with Ali and Mu'awiya, and I the arbitrator between you, holding your fate in these two hands of mine, I would not stir an inch!" and he spat upon the ground as though to curse me and turned his face away. After that we heard that the Sheikh had cabled to those who had sent him, saying: "The horseflies have eaten into my neck, malaria has burnt up my skin, and dysentery has lodged itself in my bowels. Come to my rescue, may God bless you—these are people who are in no need of me or of any other preacher." And so the man departed and the government sent us no preacher after him.

But, my son, our village actually witnessed many great men of power and influence, people with names that rang through the country like drums, who we never even dreamed would ever come here—they came, by God, in droves.

We have arrived. Have patience, my son, in a little while there will be the noonday breeze to lighten the agony of this pest upon your face.

Here it is: the doum tree of Wad Hamid. Look how it holds its head aloft to the skies; look how its roots strike down into the earth; look at its full, sturdy trunk, like the form of a comely woman, at the branches on high resembling the mane of a frolicsome steed! In the afternoon, when the sun is low, the doum tree casts its shadow from this high mound right across the river so that someone sitting on the far bank can rest in its shade. At dawn, when the sun rises, the shadow of the tree stretches across the cultivated land and houses right up to the cemetery. Don't you think it is like some mythical eagle spreading its wings over the village and everyone in it? Once the government, wanting to put through an agricultural scheme, decided to cut it down: they said that the best place for setting up the pump was where the doum tree stood. As you can see, the people of our village are concerned solely with their everyday needs, and I cannot remember their ever having rebelled against anything. However, when they heard about cutting down the doum tree they all rose up as one man and barred the district commissioner's way. That was in the time of foreign rule. The flies assisted them too—the horseflies. The man was surrounded by the clamoring people shouting that if the doum tree were cut down they would fight the government to the last man, while the flies played havoc with the man's face. As his papers were scattered in the water we heard him cry out: "All right—doum tree stay—scheme no stay!" And so neither the pump nor the scheme came about and we kept our doum tree.

Let us go home, my son, for this is no time for talking in the open. This hour just before sunset is a time when the army of sand flies becomes particularly active before going to sleep. At such a time no one who isn't well accustomed to them and has become as thick-skinned as we are can bear their stings. Look at it, my son, look at the doum tree: lofty, proud, and haughty as though—as though it were some ancient idol. Wherever you happen to be in the village you can see it; in fact, you can even see it from four villages away.

Tomorrow you will depart from our village, of that there is no doubt, the mementos of the short walk we have taken visible upon your face, neck, and hands. But before you leave I shall finish the story of the tree, the doum tree of Wad Hamid. Come in, my son, treat this house as your own.

You ask who planted the doum tree?

No one planted it my son. Is the ground in which it grows arable land? Do you not see that it is stony and appreciably higher than the river bank, like the pedestal of a statue, while the river twists and turns below it like a sacred snake, one of the ancient gods of the Egyptians? My son, no one planted it. Drink your tea, for you must be in need of it after the trying experience you have undergone. Most probably it grew up by itself, though no one remembers having known it other than as you now find it. Our sons opened their eyes to find it commanding the village. And we, when we take ourselves back to childhood memories, to that dividing line beyond which you remember nothing, see in our minds a giant doum tree standing on a river bank; everything beyond it is as cryptic as talismans, like the boundary between day and night, like that fading light which is not the dawn but the light directly preceding the break of day. My son, do you find that you can follow what I say? Are you aware of this feeling I have within me but which I am powerless to express? Every new generation finds the doum tree as though it had been born at the time of their birth and would grow up with them. Go and sit with the people of this village and listen to them recounting their dreams. A man awakens from sleep and tells his neighbor how he found himself in a vast, sandy tract of land, the sand as white as pure silver; how his feet sank in as he walked so that he could only draw them out again with difficulty; how he walked and walked until he was overcome with thirst and stricken with hunger, while the sands stretched endlessly around him; how he climbed a hill and on reaching the top espied a dense forest of doum trees with a single tall tree in the center which in comparison with the others looked like a camel amid a herd of goats; how the man went down the hill to find that the earth seemed to be rolled up before him so that it was but a few steps before he found himself under the doum tree of Wad Hamid; how he then discovered a vessel containing milk, its surface still fresh with froth, and how the milk did not go down though he drank until he had quenched his thirst. At which his neighbor says to him: "Rejoice at release from your troubles."

You can also hear one of the women telling her friend: "It was as though I were in a boat sailing through a channel in the sea, so narrow that I could stretch out my hands and touch the shore on either side. I found myself on the crest of a mountainous wave which carried me upward till I was almost touching the clouds, then bore me down into a dark, fathomless pit. I began shouting in my fear, but my voice seemed to be trapped in my throat. Suddenly I found the channel opening out a little. I saw that on the two shores were black, leafless trees with thorns, the tips of which were like the heads of hawks. I saw the two shores closing in upon me and the trees seemed to be walking toward me. I was filled with terror and called out at the top of my voice, "O Wad Hamid!" As I looked I saw a man with a radiant face and a heavy white beard flowing down over his chest, dressed in spotless white and holding a string of amber prayer beads. Placing his hand on my brow, he said: "Be not afraid," and I was calmed. Then I found the shore opening up and the water flowing gently. I looked to my left and saw fields of ripe corn, waterwheels turning, and cattle grazing, and on the shore stood the doum tree of Wad Hamid. The boat came to rest under the tree and the man got out, tied up the boat, and stretched out his hand to me. He then struck me gently on the shoulder with the string of beads, picked up a doum fruit from the ground, and put it in my hand. When I turned around he was no longer there."

"That was Wad Hamid," her friend then says to her. "You will have an illness that will bring you to the brink of death, but you will recover. You must make an offering to Wad Hamid under the doum tree." So it is, my son, that there is not a man or woman, young or old, who dreams at night without seeing the doum tree of Wad Hamid at some point in the dream.

You ask me why it was called the doum tree of Wad Hamid and who Wad Hamid was. Be patient, my son—have another cup of tea.

At the beginning of home rule a civil servant came to inform us that the government was intending to set up a stopping place for the steamer. He told us that the national government wished to help us and to see us progress, and his face was radiant with enthusiasm as he talked. But he could see that the faces around him expressed no reaction. My son, we are not people who travel very much, and when we wish to do so for some important matter such as registering land, or seeking advice about a matter of divorce, we take a morning's ride on our donkeys and then board the steamer from the neighboring village. My son, we have grown accustomed to this; in fact, it is precisely for this reason that we breed donkeys. It is little wonder, then, that the government official could see nothing in the people's faces to indicate that they were pleased with the news. His enthusiasm waned and, being at his wit's end, he began to fumble for words.

"Where will the stopping place be?" someone asked him after a period of silence. The official replied that there was only one suitable place—where the doum tree stood. Had you that instant brought along a woman and had her stand among those men as naked as the day her mother bore her, they could not have been more astonished.

"The steamer usually passes here on a Wednesday," one of the men quickly replied. "If you made a stopping place, then it would be here on Wednesday afternoon." The official replied that the time fixed for the steamer to stop by their village would be four o'clock on Wednesday afternoon.

"But that is the time when we visit the tomb of Wad Hamid at the doum tree," answered the man. "When we take our women and children and make offerings. We do this every week." The official laughed. "Then change the day!" he replied. Had the official told these men at that moment that every one of them was a bastard, that would not have angered them more than this remark of his. They rose up as one man, bore down upon him, and would certainly have killed him if I had not intervened and snatched him from their clutches. I then put him on a donkey and told him to make good his escape.

And so it was that the steamer still does not stop here and that we still ride off on our donkeys for a whole morning and take the steamer from the neighboring village when circumstances require us to travel. We content ourselves with the thought that we visit the tomb of Wad Hamid with our women and children and that we make offerings there every Wednesday as our fathers and fathers' fathers did before us.

Excuse me, my son, while I perform the sunset prayer—it is said that the sunset prayer is "strange": if you don't catch it in time it eludes you. *God's pious servants—I declare that there is no god but God and I declare that Muhammad is His Servant and His Prophet—Peace be upon you and the mercy of God!*

Ah, ah. For a week this back of mine has been giving me pain. What do you think it is, my son? I know, though, it's just old age. Oh, to be young! In my young days I would breakfast off half a sheep, drink the milk of five cows for supper, and be able to lift a sack of dates with one hand. He lies who says he ever beat me at wrestling. They used to call me "the crocodile." Once I swam the river, using my chest to push a boat loaded with wheat to the other shore—at night! On the shore were some men at work at their waterwheels, who threw down their clothes in terror and fled when they saw me pushing the boat toward them.

"Oh, people," I shouted at them, "what's wrong, shame upon you! Don't you know me? I'm 'the crocodile.' By God, the devils themselves would be scared off by your ugly faces."

My son, have you asked me what we do when we're ill?

I laugh because I know what's going on in your head. You townsfolk hurry to the hospital on the slightest pretext. If one of you hurts his finger you dash off to the doctor, who puts a bandage on, and you carry it in a sling for days; and even then it doesn't get better. Once I was working in the fields and something bit my finger—this little finger of mine. I jumped to my feet and looked around in the grass, where I found a snake lurking. I swear to you it was longer than my arm. I took hold of it by the head and crushed it between two fingers, then bit into my finger, sucked out the blood, and took up a handful of dust and rubbed it on the bite.

But that was only a little thing. What do we do when faced with real illness?

This neighbor of ours, now. One day her neck swelled up and she was confined to bed for two months. One night she had a heavy fever, so at first dawn she rose from her bed and dragged herself along till she came—yes, my son, till she came to the doum tree of Wad Hamid. The woman told us what happened.

"I was under the doum tree," she said, "with hardly sufficient strength to stand up, and called out at the top of my voice: 'O Wad Hamid, I have come to you to seek refuge and protection—I shall sleep here at your tomb and under your doum tree. Either you let me die or you restore me to life; I shall not leave here until one of these two things happens.'

"And so I curled myself up in fear," the woman continued with her story, "and was soon overcome by sleep. While midway between wakefulness and sleep I suddenly heard sounds of recitation from the Koran and bright light, as sharp as a knife edge, radiated out, joining up the two river banks, and I saw the doum tree prostrating itself in worship. My heart throbbed so violently that I thought it would leap up through my mouth. I saw a venerable old man with a white beard and wearing a spotless white robe come up to me, a smile on his face. He struck me on the head with his string of prayer beads and called out: 'Arise.'

"I swear that I got up, I know not how, and went home, I know not how. I arrived back at dawn and woke up my husband, my son, and my daughters. I told my husband to light the fire and make tea. Then I ordered my daughters to give trilling cries of joy, and the whole village prostrated themselves before us. I swear that I have never again been afraid, nor yet ill."

Yes, my son, we are people who have no experience of hospitals. In small matters such as the bites of scorpions, fever, sprains, and fractures, we take to our beds until we are cured. When in serious trouble we go to the doum tree.

Shall I tell you the story of Wad Hamid, my son, or would you like to sleep? Townsfolk don't go to sleep till late at night—I know that of them. We, though, go to sleep directly the birds are silent, the flies stop harrying the cattle, the leaves of the trees settle down, the hens spread their wings over their chicks, and the goats turn on their sides to chew the cud. We and our animals are alike: we rise in the morning when they rise and go to sleep when they sleep, our breathing and theirs following one and the same pattern.

My father, reporting what my grandfather had told him, said: "Wad Hamid, in times gone by, used to be the slave of a wicked man. He was one of God's holy saints but kept his faith to himself, not daring to pray openly lest his wicked master kill him. When he could no longer bear his life with this infidel, he called upon God to deliver him, and a voice told him to spread his prayer mat on the water and that when it stopped by the shore he should descend. The prayer mat put him down at the place where the doum tree is now and which used to be wasteland. And there he stayed alone, praying the whole day. At nightfall a man came to him with dishes of food, so he ate and continued his worship till dawn."

All this happened before the village was built up. It is as though this village, with its inhabitants, its waterwheels and buildings, had become split off from the earth. Anyone who tells you he knows the history of its origin is a liar. Other places begin by being small and then grow larger, but this village of ours came into being at one bound. Its population neither increases nor decreases, while its appearance remains unchanged. And ever since our village has existed, so has the doum tree of Wad Hamid; and just as no one remembers how it originated and grew, so no one remembers how the doum tree came to grow in a patch of rocky ground by the river, standing above it like a sentinel.

When I took you to visit the tree, my son, do you remember the iron railing round it? Do you remember the marble plaque standing on a stone pedestal with "The doum tree of Wad Hamid" written on it? Do you remember the doum tree with the gilded crescents above the tomb? They are the only new things about the village since God first planted it here, and I shall now recount to you how they came into being.

When you leave us tomorrow—and you will certainly do so, swollen of face and inflamed of eye—it will be fitting if you do not curse us but rather think kindly of us and of the things that I have told you this night, for you may well find that your visit to us was not wholly bad.

You remember that some years ago we had Members of Parliament and political parties and a great deal of to-ing and fro-ing which we couldn't make head or tail of. The roads would sometimes cast down strangers at our very doors, just as the waves of the sea wash up strange weeds. Though not a single one of them prolonged his stay beyond one night, they would nevertheless bring us the news of the great fuss going on in the capital. One day they told us that the government which had driven out imperialism had been substituted by an even bigger and noisier government.

"And who has changed it?" we asked them, but received no answer. As for us, ever since we refused to allow the stopping place to be set up at the doum tree, no one has disturbed our tranquil existence. Two years passed without our knowing what form the government had taken, black or white. Its emissaries passed through our village without staying in it, while we thanked God that He had saved us the trouble of putting them up. So things went on till, four years ago, a new government came into power. As though this new authority wished to make us conscious of its presence, we awoke one day to find an official with an enormous hat and small head, in the company of two soldiers, measuring up and doing calculations at the doum tree. We asked them what it was about, to which they replied that the government wished to build a stopping place for the steamer under the doum tree.

"But we have already given you our answer about that," we told them. "What makes you think we'll accept it now?"

"The government which gave in to you was a weak one," they said, "but the position has now changed."

To cut a long story short, we took them by the scruffs of their necks, hurled them into the water, and went off to our work. It wasn't more than a week later when a group of soldiers came along, commanded by the small-headed official with the large hat, shouting: "Arrest that man, and that one, and that one," until they'd taken off twenty of us, I among them. We spent a month in prison. Then one day the very soldiers who had put us there opened the prison gates. We asked them what it was all about but no one said anything. Outside the prison we found a great gathering of people; no sooner had we been spotted than there were shouts and cheering and we were embraced by some cleanly dressed people, heavily scented and with gold watches gleaming on their wrists. They carried us off in a great procession, back to our own people. There we found an unbelievably immense gathering of people, carts, horses, and camels. We said to each other: "The din and flurry of the capital has caught up with us." They made us twenty men stand in a row, and the people passed along it shaking us by the hand: the Prime Minister—the President of the Parliament—the President of the Senate—the member for such-and-such constituency—the member for such-and-such other constituency.

We looked at each other without understanding a thing of what was going on around us except that our arms were aching with all the handshakes we had been receiving from those Presidents and Members of Parliament.

Then they took us off in a great mass to the place where the doum tree and the tomb stand. The Prime Minister laid the foundation stone for the monument you've seen, and for the dome you've seen, and for the railing you've seen. Like a tornado blowing up for a while and then passing over, so that mighty host disappeared as suddenly as it had come without spending a night in the village—no doubt because of the horseflies, which, that particular year, were as large and fat and buzzed and whirred as much as during the year the preacher came to to us.

One of those strangers who were occasionally cast upon us in the village later told us the story of all this fuss and bother.

"The people," he said, "hadn't been happy about this government since it had come to power, for they knew that it had got there by bribing a number of the Members of Parliament. They therefore bided their time and waited for the right opportunities to present themselves, while the opposition looked around for something to spark things off. When the doum tree incident occurred and they marched you all off and slung you into prison, the newspapers took this up and the leader of the government which had resigned made a fiery speech in Parliament in which he said:

" 'To such tyranny has this government come that it has begun to interfere in the beliefs of the people, in those holy things held most sacred by them.' Then taking a most imposing stance and in a voice choked with emotion, he said: 'Ask our worthy Prime Minister about the doum tree of Wad Hamid. Ask him how it was that he permitted himself to send his troops and henchmen to desecrate that pure and holy place!'

"The people took up the cry and throughout the country their hearts responded to the incident of the doum tree as to nothing before. Perhaps the reason is that in every village in this country there is some monument like the doum tree of Wad Hamid which people see in their dreams. After a month of fuss and shouting and inflamed feelings, fifty members of the government were forced to withdraw their support, their constituencies having warned them that unless they did so they would wash their hands of them. And so the government fell, the first government returned to power, and the leading paper in the country wrote: 'The doum tree of Wad Hamid has become the symbol of the nation's awakening.' "

Since that day we have been unaware of the existence of the new government, and not one of those great giants of men who visited us has put in an appearance; we thank God that He has spared us the trouble of having to shake them by the hand. Our life returned to what it had been: no water pump, no agricultural scheme, no stopping place for the steamer. But we kept our doum tree, which casts its shadow over the southern bank in the afternoon and, in the morning, spreads its shadow over the fields and houses right up to the cemetery, with the river flowing below it like some sacred legendary snake. And our village has acquired a marble monument, an iron railing, and a dome with gilded crescents.

When the man had finished what he had to say he looked at me with an enigmatic smile playing at the corners of his mouth like the faint flickerings of a lamp.

"And when," I asked, "will they set up the water pump, and put through the agricultural scheme and the stopping place for the steamer?"

He lowered his head and paused before answering me: "When people go to sleep and don't see the doum tree in their dreams."

"And when will that be?" I said.

"I mentioned to you that my son is in the town studying at school," he replied. "It wasn't I who put him there; he ran away and went there on his own, and it is my hope that he will stay where he is and not return. When my son's son passes out of school and the number of young men with souls foreign to our own increases, then perhaps the water pump will be set up and the agricultural scheme put into being—maybe then the steamer will stop at our village—under the doum tree of Wad Hamid."

"And do you think," I said to him, "that the doum tree will one day be cut down?" He looked at me for a long while as though wishing to project, through his tired, misty eyes, something which he was incapable of doing by word.

"There will not be the least necessity for cutting down the doum tree. There is not the slightest reason for the tomb to be removed. What all these people have overlooked is that there's plenty of room for all these things: the doum tree, the tomb, the water pump, and the steamer's stopping place."

When he had been silent for a time he gave me a look which I don't know how to describe, though it stirred within me a feeling of sadness, sadness for some obscure thing I was unable to define. Then he said: "Tomorrow, without doubt, you will be leaving us. When you arrive at your destination, think well of us and judge us not too harshly."

The Nasiriyya Brotherhood of Southern Morocco

James A. Miller and Donna Lee Bowen

The religious charisma (baraka) of a saint often was translated into forms of authority other than religious or theological. Basing allegiance and respect on the extraordinary power a saint can muster, local peoples turn to saintly lineages for guidance in disputes and in arbitration between tribes and villagers. If the descendants of a saint translated their baraka into other areas, such as education and commercial success, their position was further fortified. Some saintly families—the Safavids in Iran, the Alawis and the Dila'wiyyin in Morocco—used their local religious esteem to garner political power. The Safavids and the Alawis were successful. The Dila'iyya Brotherhood was destroyed by its political enemies. —Eds.

A *zawiya* (brotherhood or lodge) combines two dimensions: *baraka* (God-given grace), emanating from a person, and a place where the baraka takes on concrete form, such as a tomb. The resulting institution, resembling a Western lodge or brotherhood, derives authority from the sanctity of its founder, who is often referred to as a saint (*wali, marabit*).

Zawiyas may be large or small: from a small, domed mudbrick shrine covering the tomb of a local person renowned for his or her piety to a sophisticated urban compound occupying considerable space, owning a wealth of land, attracting membership from all over the country, and spawning affiliate branches in faraway cities and towns. The tomb of the saint is the focal point of any zawiya. Other physical components may include a school, a mosque, guest and caravan quarters, and agricultural land, as well as other properties offered as pious donations (*waqf, habous*).

Mysticism (*tasawwuf,* sufism) encompasses many areas of study and diverse forms of worship. All sufis trace their spiritual orientation to a sufi master and to a school of mysticism. A zawiya's worship practices reflect the teachings of a particular school of mysticism although the influence of a zawiya's founding leader is great. Some zawiyas reflect a highly spiritual bent, while others, like the Zawiya Nasiriyya, take a pragmatic approach to religion and emphasize addressing the temporal, as well as spiritual, needs of their adherents.

The case of the Zawiya Nasiriyya, located in Tamgrout, a small town in the far south of Morocco, illustrates the founding, history, and development of a zawiya as a local religious institution in which lines of history, geography, and spiritual belief converge.

THE ZAWIYA NASIRIYYA

As dusk fell on March 2, 1951, a long line of turbanned men wound through the two- and three-story adobe houses lining the narrow alleys of Tamgrout. They were led by a Frenchman in the uniform of a local administrator, the military governor of Zagora province, the furthest southern province beyond the Atlas and into the Moroccan Sahara. These community leaders—both French and Moroccan, representing tribal, government, and religious interests—knocked at the great main door of the Zawiya Nasiriyya, disturbing the family inside, which was deep in mourning at the death of its patriarch, Sidi Abdelsalem.

Once entered and seated on cushions in the long, narrow salon, the visitors requested the presence of Sidi Ahmed al-Dehbi al-Nasiri, one of Abdelsalem's thirty-three sons, a round-faced, black-eyed twenty-three-year-old. He had been educated both at the family zawiya and in the capital, Rabat, and had been his elderly father's lieutenant and constant support over the past few years. The French *caid* spoke first: "Sidi Dehbi, we have come to request that you accept the leadership of the zawiya and replace your father in carrying out his work." Sidi Dehbi protested, saying that he was too young; his elder brothers deserved precedence in the zawiya leadership. But the *caid* insisted, stating that Sidi Dehbi's personal maturity and stature in the family and surrounding community combined to make him the sole choice for zawiya leadership. This period of national unease as Moroccans agitated for independence from France was critical and required responsible leadership.

The court document which invested Sidi Dehbi as *khalifa* (head, or sheikh) of the zawiya sets out his obligations and responsibilities:

Judicial Court of Zagora
Act of Agreement

Before the undersigned *'adul* [notary], who has appeared,
   and
   the witnesses designated by name herewith,

who

have declared that Sidi Abdelsalem Ben Ahmed Nasiri, head of the
Nasiriyya Zawiyas, died during the night of Thursday to Friday 23,
Joumada I (March 2, 1951) in his homeland and was buried the same
Friday at 15 hours in the sanctuary of his ancestors;

and

had, while living, spoken many times of investing his son Sidi Ahmed
Dehbi with the title of Khalifa so as to succeed him as the head of their
zawiyas;

that

in effect, he had sent Sidi Ahmed Dehbi for several years in his place
and stead to represent him before the Sultan Sidi Muhammad V, the
Makhzen, and the Protectorate, to understand the situation of all the
faithful, to be unsparing in his counsel, and to be as concerned with
their state of things as of his brothers—uncles, cousins, *shurfa* [descen-
dants of the prophet Muhammad], *marabitiin* [saints or descendants of
saints], and inhabitants of the Zawiya be they Blacks or slaves—all of
whom wish by the grace of God that their voices be transmitted through
his son, Sidi Ahmed Dehbi, as their *naqib* (chief, an office subordinate to
the *khalifa*), with his mission to. . . .

Therefore

Sidi Ahmed Dehbi must fear God, present himself as a model, and act as
an example, knowing that he must apply himself, exercise all his efforts,
pray morning and night, consider all the people of the various localities
(of the Zawiya Nasiriyya) as brothers united, like the branches of a tree,
and to be the head to whom, from the farthest reaches of the country,
the faithful shall come, and to whom he will open the doors of his hospitable residence, where they shall consider themselves at home.

Thus

The witnesses are aware of these above-noted facts through kinship and
through their neighborly relations, the frequency and verification of
which they have established.

In witness thereof, their testimony has been entered at the request of the
petitioner.

Made and drawn up the evening of Saturday, 24 Jumada I 1370 and March
3, 1951.

[Signed by 144 witnesses.]

A TRADITIONAL INSTITUTION IN THE TWENTIETH CENTURY

In 1951 Sidi Dehbi took over an institution severely limited in scope from
what it had been in the past centuries. In the 1930s, French researchers estimated that the Zawiya Nasiriyya was the third largest Muslim brotherhood in
Morocco and was regarded by many as the wealthiest zawiya in the country.

Until the French completed the conquest of southern Morocco in the early 1930s, the Zawiya Nasiriyya was one of a handful of like institutions that governed the farflung areas of the south, beyond any effective authority of the central government. The zawiya school had historically served as a major center of Islamic learning for the south. In the eighteenth century it was regarded as one of three schools of university rank in the country, next to the Qarawiyyin in Fez and Ben Yusuf in Marrakesh. Scholars came from all over North Africa to study with the savants at the zawiya and to peruse their famous collection of thousands of manuscripts.

Today, thirty years since Moroccan independence, the Zawiya Nasiriyya survives as an important spiritual and cultural center in Northwest Africa, but vital elements of its past organization are gone. The zawiya lands were placed under the authority of the Ministry of Islamic Affairs; the rigorous education offered by the zawiya has declined to a handful of students and teachers. The slaves of the zawiya, personal property of the zawiya family, have been freed, but many continue in their traditional duties. As a symbol of Islamic learning and piety, its library is a point of interest for busloads of European tourists visiting the qasbahs of southern Morocco.

In the past, religion enfolded all dimensions of a Muslim's life: law, political authority, ritual worship, social and commercial interaction, spiritual values, education. As the religious arbiter in the Draa Valley, the zawiya traditionally served as the final authority in these areas. Over the course of the twentieth century, secularization has fragmented life into discreet sectors controlled either by the state, one's personal volition, or social pressure. Today, the zawiya's authority is recognized only in questions of religious ritual and spiritual values. Politics, land regulation, education, and legal questions have been delegated to civil and secular authorities in Tamgrout and elsewhere. State and religion have separated, and the state has appropriated most of the duties and responsibilities of the zawiya.

Two men in the Nasiri family played central roles in this process, each of them heading the zawiya at a crucial point in its history: in the twentieth century, Sidi Dehbi, who watched the central government take over many of the functions of the family zawiya; and Ben Nasir, who—having great spiritual baraka—founded the Zawiya Nasiriyya and led its growth to a preeminent institution in Morocco. Although both men were recognized at young ages as being exceptional, social and political circumstances ameliorated their direction of the family zawiya—for one, to build it; for another, to watch its dissolution.

ESTABLISHMENT OF THE ZAWIYA NASIRIYYA

In the early 1630s, Muhammad Ben Nasir arrived in Tamgrout to study at the Zawiya Sidi al-Nas under a regionally renowned sufi master and head of the well-established zawiya in Tamgrout, al-Ansari. Muhammad Ben Nasir came from a village a few miles north of Tamgrout where his father taught Islamic sciences as a *fqih* (local religious scholar). Zawiyas, sufi masters—some recognized as saints, some known as scholars—and their student followers populated the North African landscape during this period of turbulent regional politics. Itinerant students traveled from one zawiya school to another, drawn by the scholarly reputation and charismatic presence of different teachers. The young Ben Nasir was drawn to Zawiya Sidi al-Nas on the strength of several generations of steady propagation of the Shadili school of mysticism taught in the Tamgrout religious community. Here Ben Nasir pursued his developing strengths in Islamic studies. In turn, as Ben Nasir began to outshine his instructors, he set about formulating and disseminating his own theory and practice of religious doctrine.

Before al-Ansari died in 1635, he designated Ben Nasir as his successor. The zawiya soon felt the firm impress of Ben Nasir's style and, within a few years, the name of the zawiya was changed to Nasiriyya, reflecting the growing fame of Ben Nasir in Morocco and the western Sahara.

ATTRACTION OF NASIRIYYA DOCTRINE

Ben Nasir's appeal lay in spiritual consistency and moderation. His strengths were lodged in his own forceful personality. Nasiriyya doctrine, a distinctive interpretation of Islamic fundamentals, emphasized adherence to the Quran and *sunna* (the words and deeds of the Prophet Muhammad). Ben Nasir's message was aimed at avoiding practices contrary or unknown to those witnessed by the early Muslim community. He taught an Islam that prohibited popular ecstatic demonstrations (trancing, singing and dancing), discouraged worship diverging from strict observance of prayer and study, and aimed at improving everyday life through solving community problems. He cared little for money or material possessions and deeded all that he possessed to the zawiya.

Ben Nasir adamantly opposed all religious innovation. Dancing or use of musical instruments, such as tambourines or drums, which are widely used for music in the south, was prohibited. Ben Nasir enforced this edict with a blow of a sandal whenever he caught a miscreant indulging in popular music. He was equally opposed to tobacco in any form and prohibited its use in the zawiya: "All of that is forbidden! forbidden! forbidden! (*haram! haram! haram!*). Whoever smokes or takes snuff has nothing in common with us" (Bodin 1918:268). He led an ascetic life and devoted himself to education and prayer. His needs were simple, and he ate only a handful of dates a day plus some grain.

Ben Nasir's personal life and leadership of the zawiya compelled respect. By virtue of his community standing, it was he who came to arbitrate disputes between nomadic Ait Atta tribesmen and the threatened Draa villagers. He drew a strong line between politics and religion. Contrary to common practice, he refused to name the Moroccan sultan in the Friday prayers despite threats from the sultan. Ben Nasir replied, "You can only put an end to this mortal life" (Bodin 1918:269).

Ben Nasir's spiritual learning and altruistic life combined to make the zawiya in Tamgrout a major center of learning, increasingly identified with a specific spiritual message. Ben Nasir's message—simple, short, harking back to the basics of Islamic belief and practice—took root in a region removed from the mainstreams of Moroccan state and society. The appeal of the Nasiriyya doctrine brought scholars and pilgrims to Tamgrout, where basic doctrine could be learned and diffused outward.

The widely recognized baraka of the saint was the basis of the growing secular powers of the zawiya. Ben Nasir's sacred standing led Draa natives to hold his descendants in reverence and to regard the Nasiri family as community leaders who expressed the rights and needs of the river valley to the *makhzen* (the central government), on the one hand, and sheltered them from invading nomads, on the other. The Nasiriyya family emerged as social and political arbitrators in the Draa river valley, rendering verdicts on the wide variety of everyday problems: water rights, landownership, movement of caravans through the Draa. During Ben Nasir's long life, the zawiya became a focus for the full spectrum of Draa life: it was a religious, political, agricultural and commercial zone of encounter, converging on the zawiya itself.

Ben Nasir died in 1674. His imposing tomb was built near that of the Ansari founder of the original zawiya. Ahmad, Ben Nasir's son, assumed leadership of the zawiya and continued in his father's footsteps, extending Nasiri power and influence across Morocco. The second Nasiri generation married into prestigious religious lineages throughout the country. Ahmad was often invited to court to advise the sultan, Moulay Ismail. The high stature of the zawiya was confirmed when Ahmad, and his descendants after him, became the first of the ʿulama to proffer *bayʾa* (fealty) to the sultan in an annual ceremony.

THE SETTING OF THE ZAWIYA NASIRIYYA

Tamgrout lies at a strategic point in the caravan trade from Timbuktu to Marrakesh in the center of the vast Fazouata oasis of the River Draa. At first glance, Tamgrout is barely distinguishable from hundreds of other villages that form part of the landscape of date palm forest, almond trees, figs, and pomegranates lining the River Draa for nearly 150 miles through far southern Morocco. Below Tamgrout, rocky desert moonscapes extend far to the south into the Sahara Desert. The Draa has long supported a population of some thirty thousand people along its banks. Until very recently, it was the only source of water in the oasis. Like the Nile, the Draa defines a long, thin pattern of settlement, restricted by the ability of its residents to channel and impound its waters in times of sufficient flow.

The River Draa links the southern settlements with the fertile north of Morocco. Trade caravans moved from settlement to settlement along the river, confident of sufficient water and food, before branching off into the Sahara for the fifty-two-day trek to Timbuktu.

The major crop of the riverine oases, date palms, can withstand long periods of drought but must "drink to its thirst" at least twice a year to produce a good yield of fruit. The date crop guaranteed incomes to the Draa villages and formed the local basis of agricultural wealth of the zawiya.

THE SOCIAL AND POLITICAL CONTEXT
OF BEN NASIR'S PERIOD

Since the ninth century, when Islam was introduced to Morocco and subsequently was widely accepted by the Berber inhabitants, Moroccan politics have intertwined religious and political authority. Since the time Morocco became Muslim, power has been legitimized by devotion to an Islamic standard and by a pledge to maintain and advance the needs of the Muslim community. A succession of dynasties has claimed a right to rule based on either descent from the Prophet Muhammad (*sharif*; plural, *shurfa*) or reforming zeal directed against the corrupt standing regimes whose taste for pleasure outweighed their concern for Islamic correctness. On both the national and the local levels, religious authority, derived either from knowledge of religious sciences or descent from the family of the Prophet, commanded the respect of others and served as a type of currency to help build a power base.

In the sixteenth and seventeenth centuries, the collapse of strong national leadership encouraged the growth of regional centers of power, most of which were based in zawiyas—the powerful Dila'iyya of the Middle Atlas and the Alawis of the southern riverine oasis of Tafilalet (the present ruler of Morocco, King Hassan II, is the latest in the line of Alawi sharif kings)—each vying to capture and control the capitals of Morocco and to command the government. The period was one of great confusion as these forces battled Portuguese invaders, remnants of the previous ruling dynasties, and ultimately each other. In the attendant chaos the area controlled by the central government shrank and outlying parts of Morocco, often beyond the reach of the central government's armies and tax collectors, were left to their own devices.

Morocco south of the High Atlas mountains, although part of the Moroccan nation, nominally recognized the sultan's command, while supervising its own interests. The central government was seldom powerful enough to extend its control beyond the mountains. The major importance of the south lay in the three major trade routes to the Sahara Desert and beyond to West Africa: the seacoast route south from Agadir, Tafilalet south, and the River Draa. The caravan trade, which was of overwhelming economic import to the Kingdom of Morocco, depended upon safe transit through vast areas controlled by powerful and often hostile tribes. Safe passage demanded sufficient central control of the area to subdue or hold off tribal attacks on the caravans or, lacking that, some prestigious local institution powerful enough to guarantee or oversee caravan passage. In addition, vital aspects of everyday life—regulation of irrigation, land tenure, arbitration of disputes, maintenance of civil law—all required an entity capable of ordering local affairs in the absence of central government.

On the River Draa, far from the battles contesting control of the Moroccan monarchy, Ben Nasir built a zawiya which served as the local power the region had lacked. It did so by virtue of a number of factors: First, Ben Nasir's great baraka set him apart from other leaders and vested him with the most potent natural authority recognized in Morocco, proximity to the Divine. This charisma was demonstrated by his learning, piety, and saintly attributes and provided the basis for the growth of the zawiya. Second, the zawiya was located in an area devoid of central power but replete with activities whose success depended on monitoring by a recognized administrator—that is, overseeing the caravan routes and maintaining land and water rights. Third, the vacuum of political authority at that time enabled the Zawiya Nasiriyya to set itself up as the local authority without contest from more powerful institutions.

CONTEMPORARY TROUBLES OF THE ZAWIYA NASIRIYYA

In March 1958, the newly independent Moroccan government began the administrative consolidation of the enormous tracts of agricultural land and real estate owned and controlled by religious endowments (habous). The new government believed that the vast amount of accumulated habous land was deadening to the economy. In addition, many of the endowment properties had been mismanaged over the past centuries and needed new administration to restore their value.

As the Zawiya Nasiriyya held one of the largest endowments in Morocco and had little political clout, the Ministry of Habous and Religious Affairs began reordering the habous lands with the zawiya. In a decree, the king ordered the zawiya to turn its accounts over to the ministry to be administered by appointed officials. The Nasiris put up virtually no resistance to the decree. The zawiya had never possessed the power or influence necessary to resist or to mount a successful countercampaign in the capital.

To make the family situation more difficult, the family properties were mixed with zawiya properties. Ben Nasir had given his land and the considerable holdings of his wife, Hafsa, to the zawiya during his lifetime and the family had continued to administer zawiya property and family property together.

Since 1958, government bureaucrats have administered the properties of the Zawiya Nasiriyya. They have assumed duties formerly reserved for the head of the zawiya—the administrative duties enumerated in the court document which invested Sidi Dehbi as the khalifa of the zawiya. The *nadhirs* administer the agricultural lands, regulate date palm rental, collect monies, arrange for auction of the dates, account for the income of the properties, redistribute agricultural and rental earnings throughout the system of affiliate zawiyas. The Zawiya Nasiriyya, both the mother lodge at Tamgrout and the affiliate zawiyas, receive a stipend for operating expenses from the ministry.

The khalifa of the zawiya (now the eldest brother of Sidi Dehbi, Sidi Sheikh) performs largely symbolic religious and family tasks. He keeps an account of the family genealogy, welcomes and oversees visitors to the zawiya compound. Ben Nasir's tomb is a popular pilgrimage site, and the Tamgrout Nasiris extend considerable hospitality to visiting pilgrims. In addition, the khalifa manages family lands, overseeing the date palmeries and tenant farmers and dealing with the never-ending questions about irrigation. Long-standing disputes over landownership throw the khalifa into conflict with the government-appointed administrator of the zawiya lands. The khalifa is also the *de facto* head of the far-flung Nasiri family in regard to zawiya needs and interests.

The annual *mousem* (anniversary festival) is the largest display of zawiya hospitality. More than ten thousand family and local visitors visit the zawiya for two to three days of celebration, prayer and pilgrimage rituals, tea drinking and conversation. The property along the road leading into the zawiya fills with an impromptu market, and thousands of pilgrims mill around the vendors, buying sweets, drinking tea and making festive souvenir purchases. Most will finish their mousem visit with a pilgrimage to Ben Nasir's tomb to pay homage to the saint.

For the local people, especially for the poor of the area, the zawiya has more than a symbolic or festive function. Throughout the past centuries the Zawiya Nasiriyya has been ready to assist the poor, and today, although funds are severely limited, no request for help is turned away. Although the zawiya revenues include no budget for charity work, the khalifa of the zawiya considers charity a major duty of his office. To finance local charity he juggles his limited funds adroitly or turns to judicious use of credit.

The zawiya school lost both enrollment and quality of available education after the French occupied the area, but its decline accelerated after independence. It was eventually absorbed—along with other zawiya schools of sufficient size and quality—by the Ministry of Education and made a part of its

Islamic education system. Today it enrolls more than one hundred primary school students whose advanced age makes them inadmissable in the regular public system. The school is overseen by the Tamgrout primary school principal, and its curriculum is identical to that of other primary schools. The zawiya library has been dispersed. Most of the valuable manuscripts were moved to the Royal Library at the palace in Rabat; a collection of manuscript volumes remains in Tamgrout, where it is the focal point of the tourist visit to the zawiya.

The decline of the Zawiya Nasiriyya has been noted by few other than the Nasiri family in Tamgrout. Other members of the family had long pursued their fortunes in other cities in Morocco, and local needs were regulated by government authorities, but the reputation of the Nasiri zawiya for education and learning was sufficiently powerful that the inhabitants of the area retained their pride in the stature and learning of the zawiya. The fact that all but its religious operations are now defunct has not diminished the reputation of the zawiya—in fact, it seems to enhance it.

Since Sidi Dehbi's stint as sheikh of the zawiya, he has remained quietly in Tamgrout, rarely leaving his expansive house next to the mosque. There he fiddles with his interests—books, agriculture, art, and inventing and improving upon new devices for his home. He is known throughout the area as the man who never leaves home, and when he is seen in the street, children and adults alike rush up to kiss his hand and greet him. With them, he shows a gentleness, interest, and consideration for their welfare. With intellectual equals, he demonstrates a fast intellect, a biting cynicism, a great knowledge of the local area as well as all of Morocco, and a ready grasp of international affairs—all gleaned from radio and print media coverage. He is as skeptical about the role of the zawiya in the 1990s as he is about most politics. While he is intensely interested in the history of the River Draa and the Zawiya Nasiriyya, he somehow communicates the feeling that life passed him by. The turning point was the night he was designed successor to his father. Left on his own, he would have followed the family penchant for scholarship and today would be a professor hibernating in a book-lined office. Yet, the family responsibilities still continue. In his brother's, Sidi Sheikh's, absence, he reassumes the role of the head of the family and the zawiya.

A visiting fqih from Tazzarine, an oasis 120 kilometers to the northeast, arrived in Tamgrout to pray at the tomb. Finding the present sheikh traveling, he came immediately to Sidi Dehbi's house. There he was greeted warmly, given lunch, and invited to stay as long as he wished. The fqih, tall, big-boned, dressed in spotless white for his personal pilgrimage, declined the invitation with thanks and prepared to set off. At the door he again thanked Sidi Dehbi effusively and was answered in equally extravagant wishes for his safe travel and rapid return to Tamgrout. Then he grasped both of Sidi Dehbi's hands and kissed them, both back and palm of the hand and the forearm as well, while murmuring blessings upon the family and thanks.

REFERENCE

Marcel Bodin. 1918. "La Zaouia de Tamegrout." *Les Archives Berberes,* volume 3.

Lying, Honor, and Contradiction

Michael Gilsenan

Middle Eastern society pays close attention to status and reputa-
tion, in large part determined by one's family. One can also en-
hance one's status by honorable deeds, and, as with any society,
one can become a hero by performing extraordinary feats. Reputa-
tion is fragile and subject to manipulation. Some aspects of tradi-
tional honor systems, such as the exaggeration, even lying, of the
young Lebanese men described by Michael Gilsenan remain an
integral part of modern social behavior. However, the changes in
landowning patterns, employment, and, above all, social expecta-
tions in the twentieth century have complicated the process of
gaining a reputation by shifting the criteria for status. Whereas in
earlier times a youth was honored for avenging a wrong done to
his family, today courts or other legal authorities are expected to
rectify injustice, and one who takes the law into one's own hands
is jailed. Lying and exaggeration are tools for youths who attempt
to bridge the gap between their traditional honor systems and the
reality of their limited opportunities to gain honor or status. Con-
fusion and alienation, rather than the recognition sought, are the
result. —Eds.

This essay focuses on the ways in which meaning emerges in the practical
reality of the everyday world. With a particular concentration on the mani-
fold practices of what will be called "lying," I shall try to show the way in
which individuals in a Lebanese village negotiate and transact about the most
important area of value in any culture, social personality and the significance
with which behavior is invested. I shall go on to argue that *kizb*, the Arabic
word translated here as "lying," is a fundamental element, not only of spe-

An earlier version of this article was published in *Transaction and Meaning*, ed. Bruce Kapferer.
Philadelphia: Institute for the Study of Human Issues, 1976.

cific situations and individual actions, but also of the cultural universe as a whole; and that, further, it is the product of, and produces in turn, basic elements and contradictions in the social structure.

Precisely because kizb is a thematic and constantly used concept in the everyday world, the word itself has a wide span of meaning and reference, and as manifested in behavior kizb may take a complex form. Children rush up to other children in the street and falsely announce the death of a famous singer; a friend says he is going to a particular place and asks if he can do something for you, when in fact he will be somewhere else altogether; another has found 1,000 lire in a field, you can ask X and Y (carefully rehearsed) who were with him; and so on, to infinity. Here the lie is simply a matter of tricking another, often by coordinated group effort, and demonstrating in a simple way an ability to fool him. The essence of it consists precisely in the liar's ultimately revealing the lie and claiming his victory: I'm lying to you, you ate it! In the laughter there is the sense of superiority, the fleeting dominance of A over B. There is the risk too that it will fall flat, or even backfire on the perpetrator with direct denunciation of the kizb. These little scenes are played out constantly by children and young men among themselves, though rarely in this form by socially fully mature males.

In this aspect kizb is associated with a rich inventiveness and imagination, a verbal quick-footedness and extemporaneous wit that have strong elements of public entertainment and play about them. Players are not necessarily called to account for the factual basis of their talk, providing that an appropriate setting of banter, camaraderie, and play has been established in interaction. Even so, though the young men may indulge in the (often competitive) verbal fantastic for its own sake, it does not accord with the weight and seriousness of anyone who claims a full social "place," a "station." In such a case it would indicate a certain lightness and lack of self-respect, and a married man of, say, his middle thirties would risk becoming a joke himself if he told too many (a role, incidentally, which some, lacking prestige and social standing, settle for, thus capitalizing on verbal skills where more solid resources are lacking).

This "artificial" quality of wordplay based on kizb brings us to two more general, complementary senses of the term that relate it specifically to judgments on the nature of the world. The first may be illustrated in the words of a taxi-driver friend, twenty-seven years old, married, and known for his bravado, cockiness, and putting on the style, who had come back from a job driving people to Beirut for New Year's Eve. He returned from the capital to the quiet impoverishment of the village, and ecstatically rehearsed the extraordinary nature of the urban scene with vast enthusiasm:

> The streets were all hung in lights, decorations everywhere, people all over
> the road and pavements and filling the open-air cafes. The girls' dresses,

heaven, the girls' dresses were up to here [graphic gestures]!! There were
Buicks, Alfas, Mercedes, Porsches, and Jaguars bumper to bumper. People
were kissing in the street, it was unbelievable, it would drive you mad, you
can't imagine, it was . . . like kizb . . . absolutely . . . like kizb!

Here is a scene of glitter and artifice, style and fantasy; an ornate, baroque
extravagance of wealth, display, and ornament, of gleaming chrome and glit-
tering clothes that goes beyond reality and is totally divorced from the everyday world of common experience—in short, like kizb. My notes are full of
accounts of unusually vivid occurrences where people were all over the
place, cars, bullets whizzing everywhere (seen in person, or on film or television), that in the end were characterized and summed up by the phrase "absolutely like kizb" (*shi mithl al kizb abadan*). Lying, therefore, is not to be
understood only in terms of strategies and judgments in social relations, or as
a technique for gaining or showing superiority. It possesses its own aesthetic
of baroque invention and is part of a style, of a wide range of variations on
the cultural theme of appearance and reality, and it is recognized at once for
what it is.

Now the social world in its aspect as part of God's creation and the Muslim community bound by His revealed imperatives are part of Truth. Truth
indeed is something "preeminently real, a living force which is operating in
the very process of life and death in the world of existence." But insofar as
the world is the place of individuals' activity and a product of their own
constructing without attention to its real underlying principles, it becomes the
realm of the apparent, of what is vain and fraudulent. Though Truth is present in the revelation of the Quran and the religious law, few know the true,
either of themselves, of others, or of the world. Or perhaps more accurately it
should be said that the fact that Truth is accessible in Quran and Islamic
teaching, could be known, and yet people spend their daily lives ignoring it
shows that they are not passively ignorant but actively liars. Moreover, lying
is linked in the Revelation, as they well know, with ingratitude and hypoc-
risy, two other major and salient aspects of unbelief. Lying is thus a blasphemous act, the direct contradiction of Truth, and the active opposite of the
sacred. The sacred creates; its opposite destroys. These are not theological
statements only, for they are used to characterize a worldview by the villagers themselves, whose sense of the disjunction between apparent and real,
born of a system of dominance in which status honor is critical, is very acute.
Kizb is linked to endless reiteration of a world skepticism, and a pessimistic
and detached sense of deception: "The world is a lie, my friend, all of it's
a lie."

The village in which I worked in North Lebanon was until the late 1960s
one of the main centers of an old Bekawat family of Kurdish origin. It is still
one of the most important rural foci of the family's interests in terms of olive

groves and agriculture, even though most of the lords now live in the cities of Beirut and Tripoli, from where they have easy access to the village. Estimates of the number in the family reach as high as five thousand, and it is a family in name only. Different segments of it are the most significant local-based, landowning groups in the area, the only real material resource of which is land. Though they now live for the most part outside the villages, the family members dominate the political economy of the region almost as effectively as in the days when their horsemen exercised in the fields below their imposing, thick-walled palaces. Up to contemporary times, the "houses" of Muhammad Pasha and Mustafa Pasha ruled this land and much of the mountain and plain across what is now the border with Syria, and their influence and power are by no means dissipated, though the modalities are in the process of transformation. Their position has been dependent on the support of a staff of small landowners who have put themselves at the disposal of the ruling order as instruments for ensuring the obedience of, and the production of a surplus by, the peasants and laborers.

In the village is a group whose members claim to be of one family, let us call it Beit Ahmad, claim to be Circassian in origin (that is, from outside, non-Arab peoples), and claim to have established themselves independently as small landowners and horsemen (in the full honorific sense of the term). Their services could not be demanded through contractual or customary right; they could be obtained only by incorporating Beit Ahmad into the system of domainal rule in a position of privilege and status.

Beit Ahmad was important to the lords perhaps for two major reasons: first, the scale of the landholdings, at least in the case of the real men of power among the beys; and second, the size and nature of the ruled orders. To administer the one and to control the other, the lords themselves, scattered among their villages of the plains and hills, were insufficient in number. The staff administered villages (indeed, they still act as estate managers and bailiffs) and guarded the lands and honor of their lords against infringement by other lords or by truculent laborers.

Yet despite, or perhaps because of, their common stake in the system of domination, the relationship of lords and staff is marked by constant ambivalence. The former, often divided by the very fact that their monopoly of political and economic power concentrated the struggle and competition for that power among themselves, needed their henchmen against members of other lordly groupings. Therefore, the lords might encourage the corporate, family nature of Beit Ahmad as a mobilizable force. But to do so was hazardous, since this corporate force founded on kinship and a shared sense of status and interest might on occasion be turned against a bey's house (and even drive it from the village when a direct infringement of Beit Ahmad's privilege occurred).

In the family as a whole, some own a little land or rent it on favorable terms from a bey; some rely entirely on the lords for employment as bodyguards or chauffeurs; some are mechanics, construction workers, and truck drivers; others serve coffee and make water pipes for the lord's guests; some are not much more than casual agricultural laborers. Beit Ahmad's position is riddled with contradictions, and I would argue that it is in this gray zone of contradiction that the lie comes into its own. For the family's internal politics are highly fragmented, a series of day-to-day alliances in the context of minute fluctuations of influence and standing. Where low income, limited resources, and irregular work restrict wealth and the opportunities for real autonomy, yet where men are firmly attached to status honor and hierarchy, personality becomes critical, and the social significance and prestige of the individual are the greatest resource.

Though being of Beit Ahmad and of a certain descent has external reference, what counts within the family is the purely personal standing which a brother's or father's reputation will not make for one. The older men, in whose days the horse and gun were the dominant symbols of chevalier culture and prestige, scorned the idea of work as alien to their ethic and their being. A *qabadi* (a real man) did not work—the concept was meaningless. He simply was. To be a lord's companion, to be a hunter, to praise the bey in elaborate courtesies, to be a horseman, to be the administrator of seven villages were not work. That was left for peasants and had no place in the aristocratic code. You are So-and-so and what you can make that statement stand for by your own actions. You observe respect, hierarchy, and etiquette; you sit upright, or lean slightly forward, one hand on knee, legs uncrossed; you walk deliberately and slowly; you speak in a voice that demands attention and that silences others, assertively, emphatically.

Such men, and some of their sons as well, were *murafiqin* (companions, bodyguards, followers) to the lords, a position in which their courage and their capacity to dominate others and deter opponents would in the nature of circumstances be tested. Their position as the *aghawat* (lords; singular, *agha*) could never be legitimated merely by sitting in a certain way and observing the niceties of style, though a lord might happily relax in Tripoli or Beirut with more concern for his inheritance than for his honor. Members of Beit Ahmad depended far more on day-to-day situations, encounters and performances of honor in which claims and challenges are always possible. The lords were at least in origin Ottoman appointees, men of government, of noble rank, beys and pashas, part of the provincial politics of notables. Beit Ahmad has only what it can make of itself and is not able to command the range of alliances of the Bekawat or their economic base. The aghas are locally bound to a particular village and often individually bound to a particular bey. Their greatest deeds are usually on behalf of someone else and in response to someone else's wishes in the idiom of the heroic aesthetic.

The disruptive nature of the demands of honor is only too real in men's experience.[1] To define a situation publicly in terms of honor and to have that definition endorsed as socially authentic by the relevant performers rule out alternative choices to a large extent and entail serious risk and disruption. Within Beit Ahmad, therefore, much effort goes into preventing an event's being categorized in these ultimate terms. Any one of the family who insists on such definitions and who presses every fine point of personal honor produces a kind of social *reductio ad absurdum,* pushing the code into chaos. Individualism and fearlessness then threaten the social value of others in the family by making public and visible what should be socially masked and invisible. How can a counterdefinition be achieved? Such persons, ever likely to see an insult or a slight and ready to go for a gun, are "anonymized," despite their emphatic egoism. They are defined in such a way that their conduct, however provocative, does not demand a response, causes no infringement on another's place, but in fact socially validates that other's non-response. Such men are *makhluʿ*—reckless, mad, asocial, dislocated.[2] Their talk and conduct can therefore be received without reaction, and no social devaluation is suffered. The shame, indeed, lies in making a response or setting them off. Their individuality is neutralized by tacit social collaboration and classification.

One of the two men classified by this term in Beit Ahmad had in fact killed a member of a *fellah* (peasant; plural, *fellahin*) family because the latter had wounded a cousin in a fight. The seventeen-year-old went up the hill a few days after to the fellah quarter of the village and fired six bullets into the offender. He ran out of the shop in which the shooting had occurred and was halfway down the hill when he realized he had left his sandals in the shop in his haste. He returned through the crowd of fellahin, gun in hand, and then walked slowly down the long hill with his back to them. Members of Beit Ahmad fired off their rifles in acclamation and a senior man (brother of the wounded cousin) shouted to him: "You went up the hill a boy and came down a man!" He was jailed for seven years and since his return has been regarded as makhluʿ. (By the complex dialectic of self and others, his behavior is in fact of this type. It is said that he was always fearless but that since his sentence he has become unstable and makhluʿ.) While I was there he was shot and robbed by an ex-colleague in a gang from outside the village. The family's only concern in the internal meetings which followed was whether one of the other families of the village had done it. Had it been so, there would have been little choice but to continue the cycle of revenge, since his being makhluʿ defined him as socially anonymous with the defining group but not vis-à-vis outsiders, to whom he remained "visible" and a member of Beit Ahmad.

The second case hinges on the process of individualizing rather than on anonymizing. A member of Beit Ahmad, also now said to have been known before his death as makhluʿ and famous for a whole series of robberies and extortions (from the lords and outside the village), was killed by another member of the family. The murdered man's father, an elder of high prestige, defined his son as makhluʿ. The boy had been violent-tempered, an outlaw, reckless and unfearing. He had persistently sought to get ten thousand lire from the great lord of the village, and it was because of this that his cousin, who was the lord's bodyguard, had finally shot him in ambush. The father insisted that it was not "a killing that called for revenge," that his son was fundamentally asocial and that therefore revenge would be "out of order."[3] Peace should and must be made.

The victim had two brothers. In terms of the code, as long as a brother is unavenged one is, in a basic sense, in a state of social pollution. No one expects immediate revenge, but the situation of ultimate reference has occurred. Now, here the killing is within the family, the victim is defined as makhlu', peace has been made, and there is a collective interest in maintaining it.[4] And yet . . . .How the two brothers cope with this situation is important. The elder always carries a gun very openly and is treated with great courtesy and etiquette of social "place"; much complimentary phrasing is directed to him by the young men, his peers, and the elders. He sits at the shop where members of Beit Ahmad often gather, goes on deputations to ask favors from local leaders, is full of the verbal performances of honor, and behaves very much like the man of position he is treated as. The younger brother, an army corporal who is seldom in the village, is quiet and much respected as a man of character. It is of him that men say the killer is frightened: "Why? Because he says nothing and silence frightens.[5] The other's a liar [that is, the other brother]. That's our family for you, we're all *kazzabin* [liars] and there isn't one who is worth a franc." These remarks, which could be made publicly within the family only at the cost of confrontation, were kept for an outsider.[6]

In these cases the category of makhlu' has been used to devalue a social personality within the family. On the one hand, the actor's capacity for forcing the issue is neutralized. His behavior is defined as not requiring action in terms of the scheme of ultimate reference, which is the criterion he constantly and threateningly invokes. On the other hand, where the victim is classified as makhlu' (and is now said to have been so regarded before the killing occurred, as may or may not be accurate), his death is defined as one for which revenge is "out of order." He does not count. Yet ambiguity remains, and members cooperate to maintain and vigorously enact appropriate definitions of the relevant persons placed in this situation of ambiguity; men interact with them in the everyday world as full social, moral personalities. In both cases, the definition as makhlu' was operative within the family only. In the second case, had the victim been killed by a villager from outside the family, a very different course would probably have been followed. For then the social position of Beit Ahmad as a whole, and its claim to corporate status honor, would have been radically challenged.

How does one who has in fact lost out in the competition for prestige and regard cope with his devalued situation when the code retains its social power and importance for him? The speaker who commented sourly on the family's being worth no more than a franc is a man who had sold his inherited land and who had been prodigal in spending money on his friends until the money, and his friends, ran out. He had gone abroad following a local altercation and on his return drifted around, finishing up as an impoverished marafiq/servant at a lord's house and as an outlaw. Apart from the memory of his father, who had been a celebrated hero of Beit Ahmad, he has no weight or prestige and is regarded as something of a joker (which indeed he is, or has become). He is on the fringe of the family in terms of social significance. He constantly attacked what to me he called the kizb of Beit Ahmad,[7] and his definition and use of lying form our third case. What follows is direct from notes, and I have interpolated relevant additional information in brackets.

I had a row with Muhammad [a distant relative] in the shop. He insulted me, and I didn't return the insult because he's always drunk. A fight started and he called out Mustafa [another relative], "my brother," and Mustafa came and clouted me with his staff on the head. I grabbed the staff and then he got me with a spanner as well. People finally separated us; you should have heard the screaming and shouting. I went off to my quarter of the village to those who are most closely related, and they wouldn't do anything or go near it. My cousin even greeted Muhammad the next day!.

So I let my beard grow and said I wouldn't go into the village but would sell all I had. Everyone thought, "By heaven, he's going to kill someone." Up came several of the men saying that they'd bring Muhammad to kiss my hand in atonement. So I said I wouldn't have anything to do with them. But I knew what was going on and my heart was really happy. All the senior men came [and he proudly listed them] and Muhammad swore he meant nothing by it and there was much performance of respect behavior and he kissed my hand, et cetera, et cetera. They begged me to shave my beard, we ceremonially smoked a water pipe and drank coffee together, and off they went. But I knew I was all alone.

No, I wanted to make a road for Muhammad on which he would die while he was still alive [that is, force him to endure his own social death]. So I set out to become big friends with him. We drank arak together and became the best of friends. One day he came to me and said there's a bit of thieving we could do, so we did a few jobs in that line.

Then one of the young lords I now work for came to me and suggested a theft at the expense of another section of the behavat. So I said to myself, "Here's the chance." The boy gave me 150 lire and I went off to Muhammad and told him that they wanted us to burn the house and had given 150 each, and put the money straight into his hand. At night off he went, and I stood fifty yards off with a rifle while Muhammad stole the stuff. Muhammad fled, because he was already wanted for causing a car accident some months before and for robbery. I stayed in the village and they arrested me, though the family told me to run.

So I told them that Muhammad had set up the whole thing, because I knew the lords would get me off with a year or so and pay me no money in jail. I got out on bail before sentence after seven months and the senior men brought Muhammad and me together. I said that I had been beaten up, so what could I do but talk? And within a few days we were close friends again. The village went crazy when they saw us together again.

At the trial Muhammad was sentenced *in absentia* to fifteen years, and I to ten, but I wasn't bothered because I knew the lord could fix it.[8] That's Muhammad settled. I've finished off his children's future as well. But I keep up a show of friendship and sincerity. Yet in my heart, that's another thing. Now he's an outlaw and has no way out. That's what I call real vengeance. If he surrenders and goes to jail the kids will die of hunger. *Rujula* [manliness] does not lie in clouting someone who has clouted you [referring to his nonresponse to the blow in the first quarrel]; that is merely self-defense.

Look at the family. They're all my relatives, though I have no paternal uncle or brothers [closest in cases of honor]. I did the whole thing myself, and it all started from a blow with a staff. The rest of the family just fight and have no respect for themselves—all noise and kizb. That's the way of the village. Real manliness is destroying your enemy without all the talk and lies, doing it in secret.

Here is a man who is faced with the fact that his social biography, formed by others' judgments and his changing life situation, has become devalued over time. His father is cited as the acme of courage and honor while he, now married and of an age when men claim full social status, is virtually a servant and unable to mobilize support when threatened with a crisis. As a teenager he sold the olive groves of his inheritance and threw away the money in reckless generosity. Such generosity at that age gains him no social place, since teenagers are still dependent and not full members of the group; he also has no brothers or paternal uncles. Left with nothing, and publicly without position, he has constructed a valued self "that no one knows" which he defines as his real self. This self is constituted out of a manipulation of what is secret, not by a public performance of place claiming, for this is denied him by his social biography and the monitoring of his consociates. Everything that passes for etiquette, respect, manliness, and so forth, is for him interpreted as "all kizb." It is not that he pretends to the superiority of a different code of honor; quite the contrary: in his perspective it is he who has the greater sense of what the code of honor really is, since he understands just how far the talk and bravado of appearance is from the reality. Reality is concealed; therefore, his conduct is in the same mode of concealment. The lie which destroys—pretense of friendship based on a full intention, not mere empty form—is for him true manliness.

If we relate ideology and social structure concretely, kizb appears as an image and a source of alienation. For in the overall social setting the terms of exchange in which status is negotiated are changing. The lords have, over the years, bought up most of the independent landowners of Beit Ahmad. They have, at the same time, increased the local dependence of many of the staff by tying them to personal service and encouraging them to insist on the hierarchy of status honor. (They have also exacerbated peasant-staff relations by using Beit Ahmad where necessary against the fellahin.) Honor has become more and more a primary value and resource over which men transact, while it less and less reflects the realities of power and structural position. Its economic and political base has been undercut, since the family has been progressively separated by the lords from the independent means of administration and autonomy.

This has entailed significant transformations in the social position of the family and its different segments, transformations that are masked by kizb as well as by the public performances of claim making and honor. The younger men are acutely aware that there is one major difference between their own and their fathers' generation. The cars, tractors, and harvesters that they drive and the guns that they carry belong to others, not to them. The young men are separated, in terms of the ethic of Beit Ahmad, from what gives them significance. The boasting, talk, bravado, and kizb are now, so to say, at one remove and on a secondhand basis. Men argue about the various qualities of "their" cars, but the knowledge that they drive them for other people, that they are to be hired and fired, and that outside the village the boast of being from the family would be an insignificant claim, is a source of bitterness. The sense of everyday reality, the practice of the everyday social world, has become problematic in its relations to those values that give the social world and the self their meaning.

It is noticeable that the young men work mainly in family groups and in specific kinds of occupations. Twenty-three of them worked on the new airport runway in Beirut; five go to Syria in the summer to man a combine harvester and thresher; others travel to different areas of Lebanon in threes or fours. Wherever they go they go as members of Beit Ahmad, and only in very few cases does one take employment on his own. Furthermore, they work in a very particular kind of occupation: tractor driver, bulldozer driver, harvester driver, taxi driver, and so on. They do not go to Tripoli or Beirut to jobs in light industry or services or trades.[9] Now, the notion of "work," as I have mentioned, is alien to the chevalier ethic of status honor. Work is a reality of the life situation of many of the family, and they have become specialists in the semiskilled field of driving heavy vehicles. But in the village a man is not a driver, he is a "chauffeur." Indeed, it does not seem to me fanciful to designate them "horsemen on tractors." The young men swing a tractor up the hill, roar past those sitting outside the shop, spin it three times on its axis (to the ruin of tires they can scarcely afford), and display their driving in much the same way as their fathers did their horsemanship. Horse and tractor alike are vehicles for display. It is driving style about which one boasts; it is the make and power of the tractor or lord's car that you drive (and the make of

revolver that goes with it too) that you discuss with immense technical expertise. A "peasant" once told me that Beit Ahmad were "all mechanics," which
is true. But among themselves they are "chauffeurs," as their fathers are
qabidiyat (men of valor). Yet at the same time the complex contradictions
between ethos and reality are ever present. One friend said sardonically to
me: "Look, you saw what I was saying over there and all the showing off
about the Buick and being a chauffeur? Kizb, my friend. What am I? I'm a taxi
driver, that's what I am." Kizb bridges the gap between form and substance,
ethos and the actualities of the political economy, but at the same time men
directly experience and know that it is a false "solution" to the problem.

It is this complex situation which explains the elective affinity between
this stratum and a view of the world (the world as constituted by individuals'
actions, divorced from what is religiously right) as itself kizb. If we move
beyond the narrower definition of the term "ideology" into the realm of religion and belief, "lying" emerges as a principle opposed to, and actively in the
world opposing, the true and the sacred. "Knowing" the interior, "real"
world of the *batin* (inner, inside) becomes the supreme mark of authority for
the man of religion (the *mabruk*, or blessed); but it also, in the profane dimension, is the mark of the dangerous, manipulative skills of the liar (the *mal'un*,
or cursed). The latter is dangerous precisely because the everyday life men
live is a domain of lying, both theologically and in practice. Both mal'un and
mabruk can see behind the veil of men's acts, and they present mirror images
of each other.

Kizb thus is a vital theme in ideology and the code of honor, in social
practice and social structure, and in the worldview and belief system.[10] The
last sphere in which it is also thematic is that of dramaturgy, situational interaction, and the creating/performing of a self. It can be argued that exactly
because honor is increasingly separated from a base in political relations
much behavior described as kizb takes on the appearance of a kind of game.
Men play at and with lying, and it has its own generalized aesthetic and
styles. It might seem, therefore, that nothing is "really" at stake, that it is
"only" a game, and that statuses are not actually changed. For any given
encounter or performance, this may be quite true. But encounters and making
claims are part of processes over time participated in by your consociates, not
one-time events before different audiences. They become part of you, of your
style, of what you are. The aesthetics of honor are crucial; ritualism and individualism go together.

The honor code forms what C. Wright Mills has called a "vocabulary of
motives" with its own societal controls. Lying is important because it is part
of the language by which men set up what they hope are socially authentic
and legitimate grounds for conduct. The adequacy of their claims may at any
time be tested. One has always to think in terms of the long perspective, of
anticipated consequences for one's "name" and "place," for one's performance is expected to be relevant to future phases of social action. Games are

deadly serious after all, and none more so than those concerning honor and the significance of the person in his social world. For the ultimate stake, when all the bravado, joking, talk, swagger, word play, and kizb are over, is your self.

NOTES

1. In a killing, for example, time is open-ended, and even when blood money is paid the exchange remains ambiguous. Though there is Quranic and traditional warrant for blood price, the convertibility of blood to money is problematic: "A brother is not sold," and who knows what member of the victim's family may take it on himself, or be egged on, to seize an opportunity for revenge years later? The open-ended time span gives the situation flexibility from the revengers' point of view and allows for the maintenance of self without compromise. But it generates its own uncertainties.

2. From a verb root meaning to renounce, cast off, disown, repudiate, depose, have done with (see Wehr's Arabic dictionary).

3. However critical a circumstance killing may be, it is still of course subject to processes of social definition and transaction.

4. In one small family of the village that has no significant collective interest or collective social identity, there have been four murders of close relatives since 1935. The latest killer is in jail, and the one on whom the new duty of revenge falls is now of such an age that he is said to be waiting for the other's release. The grim cycle is expected to continue. There is no conflicting definition by which to restructure the situation so that peace may be made. Everything is visible, and each event has generated a new momentum. One man I knew well had one brother killed, and his other brother is the one currently in jail for seeking revenge.

5. Silence is of all signs the one regarded as most indicative of full intention. It was often said to me of different individuals that they would not do anything about an event, just produce a lot of talk and threats while friends rushed forward to plead and restrain. It is the one who makes no fuss of protest who is really *nawi shi* (intending something) and who may take revenge. That is when the offender keeps to his house or even leaves the village. The public declaration of sacred intention used on occasions of death or wounding is growing the beard, which is also a claim on other support in a sacred duty of revenge. As an act of self-degradation it places the person in the category of polluted until "right" in blood has been taken. It is an insistence on a very specific and narrow definition of the situation.

6. It is noteworthy that the brother of the man killed in the shop (the case discussed earlier) also makes much of carrying a gun and a staff, talks very emphatically, and is a very "public" personality in his own quarter of the village. Beit Ahmad describe him in the main as "a good man, poor fellow." The killer "respects" (avoids) the quarter altogether.

7. For example, when the young man defined as makhluᶜ in the first case insulted someone of the family, who did not reply, this man used to turn to me on the quiet and tell me that when it came to a crunch all the family's bravado and status honor were lies and show: "When this fellow goes for them, then it's mouths closed and eyes down and not a sound. Liars!" He is also, ironically, something of an expert on points of honor, the subtleties of the code, and proper behavior. He invokes the bed-

ouin heroes as "real men," can quote much classical Arabic poetry concerning them, and is a stringent and sarcastic judge of others' actions.

8. In fact, our friend jumped bail on the lord's advice and was sentenced to ten years in jail. He is now an outlaw and even more dependent on the lord, whose level of trickery exceeds his own. He does not sleep in his own house any more than does Muhammad, though he lives perpetually in the hope that the lord will arrange clemency for him. The young lord involved came out of jail after a few months.

9. It might be noted, though I shall not discuss the matter in detail, that there are very few marriages with women from outside the family, and that endogamy here is not only ideology but also actuality for Beit Ahmad.

10. Max Weber long ago pointed out the implications inherent in the utilitarian ethic which, like the ethic discussed here, has its own logic and breeds its own lies: "Honesty is useful, because it assures credit; so are punctuality, industry, frugality, and that is the reason they are virtues. A logical deduction from this would be that where, for instance, the appearance of honesty serves the same purpose, that would suffice . . . " (1958:52).

Editing *al-Fajr:* A Palestinian Newspaper in Jerusalem

Bishara Bahbah

Running a daily newspaper can be a harrowing experience under the best of circumstances. Bishara Bahbah served as editor of al-Fajr (The Dawn), a Jerusalem daily newspaper published in both English and Arabic, for the year 1983–1984. In that post he had to balance his Palestinian nationalist beliefs with the political realities of editing a newspaper under occupation. Government-imposed media censorship is a fact of life in most of the Middle East, and often ordinary citizens learn more from what the newspapers do not print than from what they do print. It took Bahbah only a short time, however, to discover that the Israeli censor was but one of the many obstacles he faced. What follows is an account of the experiences of a Western-educated editor, the challenges confronting him, and the reasons why he resigned after one year on the job. —Eds.

At the age of twenty-five I received my doctorate degree in political science from Harvard University. I was under the illusion that if I was able to earn my Ph.D. from one of the best universities in the world within ,a relatively short period of time, I could then take on the most challenging of jobs. I had not realized how pleasant (and relatively unchallenging) it was to be a student even at one of the toughest universities in the world. Of the job opportunities I had, I picked the one that had the most exposure and that provided me with the means to influence events on an almost daily basis in nowhere else than my birthplace, Jerusalem. Rather than settle into a teaching position at one of the universities, I decided to accept a position as the editor-in-chief of the Jerusalem-based *al-Fajr*, a Palestinian Arabic daily newspaper.

Al-Fajr was founded in 1972 by Yusef Nasr, a Palestinian school teacher educated in the United States. During his tenure at the paper, Nasr was often very critical, thus creating for himself many enemies among the Israeli authorities as well as among other Arabs, including some Palestinians. In 1974,

Nasr was kidnapped and presumed dead after an extensive search, during which his family offered huge rewards for information leading to his whereabouts. His brother-in-law, Paul Ajlouny, a self-made millionaire residing in the United States, took it upon himself to finance the newspaper and to run it from the United States. He delegated daily management of the newspaper to the Jerusalem-based staff, who often manipulated the power associated with running a newspaper to suit their political ideologies. In a ten-year period the newspaper had more editors-in-chief than any other paper in the occupied territories.

By the time I was appointed editor-in-chief, the political line of the newspaper was associated very strongly with the Palestine Liberation Organization, particularly with Fatah, the main faction within the PLO, which is headed by Yasser Arafat. Although I had not set *al-Fajr*'s political position, it was in agreement with my own political beliefs. I wanted *al-Fajr* to become a model newspaper to be emulated in the Middle East. I wanted it to be professional, nonfactional, thought-provoking, responsible, and credible in all eyes.

It took a short time for me to realize that my goals were idealistic and, unfortunately, somewhat impossible. On one hand, the restrictions on the freedom of the press in the occupied territories were stifling. We were forced to submit all the materials to be printed in the newspaper on a daily basis prior to publication to the Israeli military censor. The censor would determine what was to be published and what was not. Quite often our hottest news items were censored and our best news analysis and feature stories never went beyond the censor's desk. Under Israeli law, if we violated instructions given to us by the censor, we were liable to various punishments, including closure of the newspaper (which did occur on various occasions) and the suspension of our license to distribute the newspaper, particularly in the occupied territories, where our largest readership lives, in addition to a host of other punitive measures. Therefore, no matter how hard we tried to provide our readers with analysis and up-to-date news, we had to accommodate ourselves to the whims of the censor, who in my opinion, because of the powers given to him by the Israeli government, was the actual editor-in-chief not only of *al-Fajr* but of the entire Palestinian press in the occupied territories. Censorship was not the only restriction imposed upon us by the Israeli authorities. Many of our best journalists were imprisoned, others were put under town arrest, and sometimes some were even physically abused while trying to cover a story.

Being forced to deal with the Israelis and to survive under their harsh and undemocratic regulations were only part of the challenge of trying to produce a good newspaper. The other part originated in no other source than the Palestinians themselves. The fact that I was educated in the West and trained to value efficiency was part of the problem. I went to Jerusalem with expectations and visions that were difficult, if not impossible, given the circumstances, to attain.

First, many of the paper's employees had been hired for reasons other than excellence, efficiency, and qualifications. On numerous occasions some employees were hired because of their political affiliation and commitment, others because they needed a job—any job—others because they just happened to be there at the right time and in the right company. There were even those who were hired because they were persistent or willing to accept a modest salary for their services. In other words, most of the staff was hired irrespective of qualifications and productivity.

Thus my first challenge was to cope with a staff that I found inadequate. To quietly replace staff members was close to impossible. If fired, many of them would not have been able to find other jobs. Such an action would have cost such a nationalist newspaper supporters and readers. Then there were the political appointees whose patrons were so powerful that any action taken against the employees would have been viewed as an unfriendly political gesture. My only recourse was to help the staff develop and leave them no option but to work and produce. In the meantime, I was determined to replace any employee who resigned with people I believed were well qualified. I also began to hire people that I felt were assets to the paper. I hired a photographer, a translator, a political cartoonist, and a host of field reporters.

In addition to having staff problems, the newspaper needed a new printing press to replace the one of 1940s vintage that not only broke down almost daily but also was time-consuming to operate and difficult to supply with spare parts. Worse yet, our competitor had one of the most advanced printing presses in the Middle East. We tried to convince the publisher to buy a new press. The publisher insisted he would import one only if the Israelis allowed him to construct a building to house the entire newspaper operation. The Israelis naturally refused to permit the newspaper to build new offices and thus obtain a new press. From their perspective, why should they? We were a constant pain in their necks, criticizing their actions against our people and calling for the establishment of an independent, sovereign Palestinian state.

These restrictions made me realize quickly that it would be a hundred times tougher to carry out my original goals than I had earlier anticipated. In self defense, I sorted out matters over which I had no control whatsoever and those over which I had. Censorship and Israeli-imposed limitations were beyond my control, as was the acquisition of a new printing press. Other matters, however, seemed more within reach.

Although my relationship with the employees was very rocky at first, after a few months they began to recognize the purpose behind my course of action. Investments made in the newly hired employees paid off spectacularly. They motivated the others to improve their performance. Improving the quality of the newspaper moved slowly. Part of the problem was the fact that I was a trained political scientist, not a journalist. I therefore had to learn how to run a newspaper and how to administer over one hundred employees. I also had to become acquainted with the political realities and sensitivities among both the Palestinians and the Israelis. After all, I had not been in my homeland for more than six years while I was studying in the United States.

To sort out internal problems within the newspaper and to introduce changes were tough enough for any editor. However, there were other job hazards. A little over a month after I started work, I decided to fire one of the secretaries, after several warnings, for what I felt was unprofessional behavior. The same day I fired the secretary, her brother forced his way very close to my office with the intention of "beating the hell out of me." Given my small stature and the fact that he was big and furious, if he had reached me, I would have ended up with a few broken bones. In the traditional Arab manner, many people, including my own eldest brother, who had nothing to do with the newspaper, tried to intervene on the secretary's behalf and dissuade me from firing her. I told everybody that the issue was strictly an internal administrative matter and that it was not their business to interfere. I stood firmly by my decision partly because I wanted the employees to realize that things would be different from then on. An interesting twist in the case was my brother's demand, as the eldest in our family, that the family of the would-be attacker apologize to our family for having threatened me. Some of the notables in the community intervened and arranged for a *sulha,* or conciliation. During the sulha, the uncle of the young man who threatened me apologized for his nephew's behavior by kissing my brother's forehead. I was flabbergasted by the whole incident. In any case, I did not rehire the secretary.

On December 12, 1983, only a few months after I took the job, I left work about 8:30 p.m. to go home to celebrate my wife's birthday only to discover that my brand new Volkswagen had been vandalized. Somebody had slashed the tires. A few days afterward, somebody smashed the trunk with a big rock and broke a few lights. After fixing that damage, the car was hit again in various spots. All in all, within a two-month period, the car was vandalized at least six times. On one of those occasions, the rear windshield was entirely smashed while the car was parked in front of my house. I was suspicious and decided to call the police and have them check for possible bombs. Within minutes they arrived and discovered no bombs or clues as to who could have done it. I filed a complaint with the police department and, in a typical manner, I was informed that they were too busy to do anything and that if I discovered who did it then I should let them know. On that note, I realized that I would never find the vandalizer.

My personal safety was also at stake. My family and I received numerous telephone calls threatening to kill me. At that time, the publisher of the newspaper decided to hire a bodyguard for me. My entire family suffered because of the constant threats hovering over my life. Nevertheless, such intimidations never hindered me from going on with my work as I saw fit. In fact, I refused to have any information about the vandalism and threats published in the newspaper so as not to give my enemies cause to rejoice or to give them the impression that I was intimidated in any way.

Despite all that, there were many positive aspects to the job. I remember my first day on the job, when French television came for an interview on Jerusalem municipal elections. An earlier *al-Fajr* editorial had called on Palestinians in Jerusalem not to vote for the Israeli municipality of Teddy Kolek since as Palestinians we do not recognize Israel's 1967 annexation of East Jerusalem. Later in the day I granted Israeli television an interview on the same subject. I quickly discovered that I had become the spokesperson for the Palestinians on many issues of the day. In the one-year period that I was editor-in-chief, I had interviews with hundreds of visiting reporters from all over the world, including live interviews for radio stations in the United States, Canada, and the United Kingdom. It seemed that my most important success at the newspaper was in dealing with foreign reporters and, quite often, foreign diplomatic dignitaries. Our role at the newspaper was more than reporters and opinion formulators. We were also newsmakers.

Our public noted improvements in both the structure and the content of the newspaper fairly quickly. Our local news reporting quadrupled and, ironically, we became a free source of news for the foreign press as well as for the Israeli press. About six or seven o'clock in the evening we customarily received calls from Israeli journalists in charge of covering the occupied territories inquiring about the day's news events. We were always happy to assist since, more often than not, the Israeli military censor refused us permission to publish many of the news items while the Israeli press, which had an agreement to censor itself and to submit only military-related news items to the censor, could actually publish the news. We then routinely copied "our" news items from the Israeli newspaper the following day, quoting them as the source.

My decision to leave the newspaper, at the end of my first year on the job, came simply because I felt let down by the publisher, who refused to adopt my recommendations about the staff and the needs of the newspaper. I was willing to withstand all the hazards and difficulties associated with the job so long as I felt that I was moving the newspaper closer to my objective. Unquestionably, that needed support from the publisher. When I realized that it was not forthcoming, I decided to resign.

Hajj Nejm's Cures and Tales

Abdel-Salam Al Ujaili
Translated by Evelyn A. Early

Middle Eastern physicians may also be poets, historians, or musicians. Abdel-Salam Al Ujaili, a Syrian physician, is no exception. When the translator met him in his clinic in 1982, Dr. Al Ujaili was torn between discussing medical issues and discussing the history of his hometown, Raqqa, Syria, about which he has written several articles. The crowd of patients waiting in his clinic sought everything from reassurance about exhaustion to orthopedic surgery.

Contemporary Muslims usually visit modern clinics when they are ill. But they may also resort to popular remedies, much as we self-prescribe for colds with orange juice and vitamin C. Middle Eastern popular medical remedies include herbal household cures as well as those cited in Prophetic Medicine, *a collection of the Prophet Muhammad's sayings on illness and curing. Prophetic medicine is being revived by devout Muslims intent on scientifically proving its worth. The Islamic Institute of Medicine in Kuwait, equipped with the latest computerized research apparatus and using control groups of subjects, was until 1990 laboratory testing such Prophetic cures as honey.*

A Clinic in the Countryside *is a collection of short stories in which Dr. Al Ujaili gives a sympathetic, tongue-in-cheek presentation of the conflict and complementarity of folk beliefs and modern medicine. The story recounted here in first person by the physician-author presents Hajj Nejm's tale of the search for a cure by Moses. Not a part of formal tradition, this tale is from the genre of "hearsay." —Eds.*

Adapted from *A Clinic in the Countryside* [ʿiyādah fī al-rīf]. Damascus: Ministry of Culture and National Guidance, 1978.

Hajj Nejm is a lighthearted and witty man with no formal medical training. But the widespread fame he attained after making the pilgrimage to Mecca gained him an extensive following among people attracted by his wisdom, which proved to be sound advice for their lives and for healing their illnesses. I don't think that Hajj Nejm ever claimed to be a physician or a shaykh with special healing powers, although his joking and stories convinced hearers of his special powers.

Abu Sadiq, an older man suffering from chronic rheumatism of the knees, asked me once: "What is your opinion of the cure which Hajj Nejm suggested for my rheumatoid knees?" I responded: "What did Hajj Nejm prescribe?" Abu Sadiq replied: "The Hajj advised me to soak two broad strips of felt in gasoline until the cloth had absorbed a good quantity of gasoline, then wrap my two legs until both legs were enveloped in felt."

There were not many occasions for me to meet Hajj Nejm aside from his yearly or biyearly visit to my clinic, when he requested that I give him an injection which he claimed "heated up" his body. Although I don't know how Hajj Nejm benefited from this injection, according to him the injection quieted his nerves, relaxed his blood vessels, and got rid of the dampness, the rheumatism, in his body. I always complied with his request and gave him an injection as a show of my good will, even though Hajj Nejm does not always pay for my services. He does not remunerate me, that is, in the normal way; but he does pay with a captivating story or cute joke which he recounts to me or to the crowd of patients in my clinic.

One day he was waiting in the outpatient reception area when I heard him tell the patients around him a tale which I had never encountered in all the books on the Israelites I had read as a boy. Hajj Nejm related the following:

When the Prophet Moses was rescued by God on Mount Sinai, God gave him a commandment. Moses interrupted the revelation and said to God: "My Lord and master, my shoulder has hurt me for two days; can you cure this pain?" The Lord answered: "Go to a reputable doctor and he will give you medicine to cure you." Moses (whose story in the Quranic chapter "al-Kaff"—"The Hand"—is a well-known one) was incredulous and objected, saying: "Oh Lord, you created malady and medicine; you created me, and you created the doctor competent to cure. Why then do you send me to the doctor?" So the Lord said: "Come then, my dear Moses, go to the lowest valley with fig trees. Take a leaf from the tree and place it on your shoulder overnight and this will be your cure."

So Moses did as the Lord told him to do, and went down and took a leaf from a fig tree and placed it on his shoulder for three consecutive nights. But with all this, the pain did not abate. During his next revelation, Moses complained to God, saying: "The fig leaf did not cure me; what shall I do?" God responded: "Rest assured and go to a good doctor." This time Moses followed the instructions and visited a doctor, consulted him, and paid him five pounds for the consultation. Imagine Moses' surprise when he found that the doctor advised Moses to use fig tree leaves—which Moses had used before to no avail. Moses was even more amazed when he discovered that the use of the fig leaves cured him this time, and that his shoulder returned to normal strength.

When Moses, once again on Mount Sinai, inquired why the fig leaf cured him after the doctor prescribed it, even though the fig leaf had not cured him before, the Lord answered: "Be calm, Moses. Your cure was not found in a fig leaf alone, but in a fig leaf and five pounds!"

This was the story Hajj Nejm told the waiting patients. He ended the story by saying: "And this made the physician the bridge between malady and medicine. One does not arrive at the other except by way of the doctor. And that is why ancient philosophers said: 'The country without a doctor is a country without knowledge.' "

Am I wrong when I say that Hajj Nejm paid for the cost of his injection, and in full?

Islam and Hajj Brahim's World

John Waterbury

John Waterbury describes a southern Moroccan merchant, Hajj Brahim. Hajj Brahim's philosophy demonstrates the vitality of his belief system, which recognizes that other people live in different ways and answer to other codes of belief and conduct. Although other people's lives may touch him, they do not necessarily affect his own behavior.

Hajj Brahim speaks of "fate" or of one's fate being "written." However, he clearly attributes his success to hard work and recognizes the change his efforts make in his life. Belief in fate does not reduce him to laziness or inactivity, but helps him make sense of his world. We encountered a similar creative approach to fate among Egyptian mothers caring for the welfare of their families (Early, "Fertility and Fate"). One Moroccan merchant alluded to this meaning of fate when he stated that rizq (God supplying man's needs), which many Muslims liken to fate (qadar), is different from what most assume. Pointing to his brain and then to his tongue, he said, "God gave us the wherewithal to think and to speak. That's our rizq. What we do with it is our own affair." As a self-made businessman who has profited from industry and foresight, Hajj Brahim is not threatened by change. He sees enough room in the world for his beliefs to coexist with those of others, whether new or old. —Eds.

It would be simplistic to suggest that Hajj Brahim's faith is no more than an ideological device to aid him in identifying himself within the Islamic cultural tradition of Morocco. Above all else, he believes profoundly in Allah and the correctness of His prescriptions as embodied in the Quran. From his under-

Adapted from John Waterbury, *North for the Trade: The Life and Times of a Berber Merchant.* Berkeley: University of California Press, 1972. Copyright © 1972 The Regents of the University of California.

standing, he draws the perspectives that enable him to interpret the vast array of human experience which he has witnessed. It provides him with a logic to order his own priorities and to determine the causes of success and failure.

Moreover, it seems to me, Hajj Brahim's faith helps him make sense of the rapid changes he and most other Moroccans have undergone in this century. Provisionality has been a salient feature of Moroccan political and economic systems in recent decades. Hajj Brahim assumes the fragility of human relations and inconsistency of human roles and seeks the predictability and consistency that would otherwise be lacking in his life in Islam.

Hajj Brahim's life, and his interpretation of it, are testimony to his ability to thrive in what we would call inconsistent, at times incongruous, situations. Such situations appear to place no particular stress upon Hajj Brahim. He regards them as normal, as do most of his countrymen. His ability to operate with "others" simultaneously at several levels of friendship and animosity is a direct affront to our craving for certainty. Westerners treating with the Hajj Brahims of numerous countries are wont to talk of the perfidiousness, or double-dealing, of the natives. These Westerners expect relations established today to be valid and predictable years from now. They are not attuned to the *situational* changes that bring about realignments and adjustments in these relationships. It is a bit like the Lone Ranger and Tonto surrounded by Apaches. "This looks like it, Tonto; we'll go down together," intones the Lone Ranger. To which Tonto replies, "What you mean 'we,' White Man?"

The West has an obsession with undying friendships and eternal alliances, unconditional surrenders, fighting to the last man, and establishing lasting peace. Hajj Brahim marvels at our naivete. In his eyes we deny the very essence of human affairs, their provisionality. "Unconditional surrender? Just look at Germany and Japan today. Everybody has his day in the sun, but just for a little while." We in the West fly in the face of the logic God has built into His world, and it is we, rather than those who believe in the one God, who are fanatics.

Without his belief in the one God, Hajj Brahim might well succumb to the anxiety generated by the ambiguous situations through which he must propel himself. But his world is not his only frame of reference, and he is not driven to make a lasting mark upon it. Not that he lacks a craving for certainty and clarity, but he has found both in Islam. For Hajj Brahim, belief in Islam not only sustains him as he copes with his existence, but, insofar as it is *reasoned* belief more than faith, it also explains all that he must bear in this world. Islam, as propounded by Hajj Brahim, is a *logical* system, all of whose parts mesh perfectly, all of whose workings can be understood. When he talks about his religion, he is serene yet somewhat combative. He wants to communicate the beauty and the security that he sees in its logic. He wants his listener to test it and challenge it with specific problems.

Brahim exists in two worlds: the ambiguous and provisional secular world and the logically infallible world of God. However, it is not that he exists in one *or* the other; he exists in both. The secular is made palatable and is explained by the religious, and each secular act has significance in the world of God. Islam allows Brahim to make the best of both worlds.

* * *

"No one knows God's will; no one can predict the future. You say that in a couple of hours you will get in your car and drive to Rabat. That, you say, you can predict. But do you know what you will see on the road? In fact we know very little, and it is our pride that makes us think we know a lot. When a man who has succeeded in business says 'It's thanks to Sidi Ahmed ou Moussa [a saint of the Tazeroualt] that I did well,' that is a sin. And if a man says 'It's thanks to my efforts alone,' that is worse yet. There are no associates in God's will. It is always thanks to God's will alone."

* * *

In Hajj Brahim's discussion of Islam there is an undeniable element of fatalism centered on the futility of human efforts in the face of the inscrutability of God's will. Throughout much of the literature dealing with the Middle East in general and Morocco in particular, the inertia that various observers discern in the traditional or peasant society is attributed to religious fatalism. Moroccans themselves are wont to shrug off situations that they cannot control with the simple phrase "It is written" (*maktub*). Quite clearly, however, Hajj Brahim has never acted as if all were beyond his control. He does not passively submit to his fate; rather, he actively submits to his fate.

"We are not helpless, and we make choices to try to better ourselves. When you hear people talking about maktub, what this really means is that everything that is done is done with the knowledge and consent of God. What is written always has a cause, and we know that cause. He who does not sow will not reap. Maktub means that we can do absolutely nothing against the will of God, but that we are capable of everything with His will.

"So you see it is not Islam that ties us down. Really the problem is discipline. It takes discipline to work hard. In the great age of Islam our religion provided that discipline. And it still does to the extent that there are Muslims who practice it. Religion is very practical and necessary in that sense. In the countryside, it is not the police who keep order but religion. In the cities, if a man is drunk or a woman indecent, it is not the police who prevent immorality. Good Muslims prevent it themselves. But this social discipline is dwindling, what with the youth and the hippies and our attachment to world civilization. And as it dwindles we are capable of less and less."

* * *

"If only we all understood our religion, then we could meet the modern world with serenity. Our problem is not too much religion but too little, and what there is, is misunderstood."

* * *

"When I look at the future, all I can see is confusion. Our people are adrift; they don't understand their own values. On the one hand, the young abandon all their principles, and on the other, the traditionalists feel that all can be put right by a blind imposition of rigid rules. No wonder that our societies have gone astray! Islam is great precisely because it is not a tradition. It does not say that what our elders have done is necessarily good for us. The most traditional Muslims are the most ignorant. They become obsessed by what is unimportant. Neither clothes nor haircuts are religion. How can we face real problems when Muslims worry about miniskirts?

"I cannot blame Europeans for not understanding Islam when so few Muslims understand it. This has been a problem for Islam from the beginning. The simpleminded want easy solutions and magic. They don't realize that there is no magic, that everything has a cause and can be explained. That is the real magic, the rationality of God's universe. Bukhari recounts that at the time the Prophet went to Medina, a bedouin went to visit him at his camp. The bedouin was prepared to believe anything and probably wanted the Prophet to perform a few miracles. He rode up on his camel outside the praying grounds and was greeted by the Prophet, who invited him to prayer. The bedouin asked him if he should tie up his camel or count on God to keep the beast from wandering off. The Prophet said, 'Count on God, and tie up your camel.' "

Suqs of the Middle East: Commercial Centers Past and Present

Robert Fernea

The suq, *or market, is the traditional heart of a Middle Eastern city's life. This article situates the suq, historically a center of production and international commerce, in the contemporary world marketing system. Robert Fernea discusses the importance of its preindustrial features and traditional goods. He suggests that, although today's suqs sell blue jeans and videos, they remain a distinct, and perhaps more resilient, economic institution than do retail outlets in modern Western cities. —Eds.*

The suqs of Middle Eastern cities and towns are the traditional markets where people come to buy the material needs of daily life.[1] Today, Western-style retailing, with large department stores and shops, has become the predominant form of commercial life in the major cities of the Middle East and North Africa, but suqs are still to be found in the older sections of these same cities, the visible expression of the Middle East's preindustrial commercial past.

My first acquaintance with a suq was in a small southern Iraqi town where I lived from 1956 to 1958, and since then I have enjoyed becoming acquainted with suqs and the "people of the suq" (*nas es-suq*, as they are called in Arabic) in Cairo, Ballana, Nubia, and Aswan, Egypt; Marrakesh, Morocco; Hail, Saudi Arabia; Herat, Afghanistan; and more briefly in a number of other Middle Eastern cities and villages. Suqs are public places; everybody, stranger and native, has to go to the suq at some time or another, even if one has servants to do the daily shopping. Wherever they are found in the Middle East, suqs share some basic characteristics. Much of what I saw in the suqs I have visited would have been present in some degree one hundred or even five hundred years ago. Many of the physical and cultural features of the Middle Eastern suqs have remained the same; the backstage, however, has changed.

The preindustrial suqs began to change with the advent of colonialism and the subsequent Western economic hegemony in the area. Today, international corporate capitalism produces much of what suq shops sell. The suq is now a part of the world marketing system, and a political authority stands behind the suq, protecting and governing much of its activity. And in all Middle Eastern countries, the so-called Western sectors are found, in the banks and engineering firms where the local elites are employed.

THE SETTING

In small towns or villages, the suq may be only a row or two of small shops. In big cities a suq includes hundreds of shops in the center of town, and there are also smaller suqs near the old city gates and in residential areas. Physically, however, the pattern is generally the same: the establishments are small, located side by side, and one can easily walk from one to another.

Some Westerners have noted that suqs are like our modern shopping malls. There is some resemblance: in larger suqs the lanes between the small shops are often roofed so that shoppers can walk along from store to store protected from the summer sun or the winter rains. This market design came into existence long before motorized traffic, and the narrow streets and lanes in many suqs are closed to cars and trucks.

The American shopping mall is the result of the shift of retail markets to the suburbs, from the high real estate costs and limited parking of overcrowded downtown areas. In contrast, the major Middle Eastern suqs are typically in the *madina*(s), or old sections, of the region's modern cities.

Suqs, like malls, also offer places to buy food and drink, and they frequently present a tumultuous social scene, with plenty of opportunity for visiting and people-watching. Going to the suq is something that young Middle Easterners look forward to doing and, as in American malls, young people may "hang out" in the suq. Regular visits to the suqs are an important and enjoyable part of adult life as well. Mosques and religious shrines are often in or next to suqs, and visitors often combine shopping with a visit to those religious centers. For a woman, a trip to the market is a respectable outing even in very conservative settings, providing also an opportunity to visit with friends and see a bit of the public world.

MERCHANDISING

To a stranger in Marrakesh, the urban center of southern Morocco, all shops seem to be part of one large market in the middle of the old city. For the native Marrakshi, however, the market is a collection of many suqs, which seem to be one because over the centuries of urban growth the spaces between the specialized markets have been filled by new shops and workshops.

One Moroccan friend of mine, who worked in the rug suq, could name forty-two major suqs in Marrakesh, including five fruit and vegetable markets, seven cloth markets, three animal markets, and twenty-seven other suqs for such things as dates, silks, automobile wheels, *babouches* (slippers), knives, copper wares, shoes, radios, furniture, gold, cosmetics, herbs, belts and purses, and many other kinds of goods.[2]

The aggregation of the same commodities in the same place is a distinctive feature of the Middle Eastern marketplace—that is, shops selling similar kinds of goods and services located side by side. In the American shopping mall stores selling the same thing are usually as far apart as possible. Why are stores in the Middle East arranged so that many establishments selling the same things are located in the same place? Would it not be better for competing shops, selling the same goods, to be spread about in different locations, as is the case in American cities? After all, in the Middle East, as in America, shopkeepers compete for some of the same customers.

The different approach of Middle Eastern merchants is related to social and historical as well as economic factors. The shape of the suq, its internal arrangements, and its structural characteristics are all intrinsically related to the preindustrial context in which the suq developed. First was the question of scale and size. These commercial establishments lacked the accumulation of financial capital found in "big business" today. Without banks to make loans or corporations to make investments, both the workshops and the stores in the suq were of a size which could be financed through familial and personal ties.

Suq shops did offer credit to the customers, however. In the Iraqi village where I lived, shopkeepers sold goods to impoverished farmers up to the expected value of the future harvest. Though payment of interest is forbidden by Islamic law, the higher prices constituted a form of hidden interest. Each shopkeeper would take only a certain number of farmers on credit, a percentage of his annual business, since he had to buy stock and support himself between the farmers' harvest-time payments. Credit was based on reputation and was extended to persons known to the shopkeeper directly or indirectly. A customer's failure to pay could oblige him to run away and try to get established elsewhere, as loss of credit could mean starvation. On the other hand, customers who paid cash regularly were highly valued and the same merchant would encourage their patronage by offering lower than average prices.

In premodern times, the possibility of higher taxes or civil uprisings, or both, always present in the area, had never encouraged the development of large stores with big inventories on display; just as madina homes do not show off the wealth of their occupants from the outside, so also did suq stores not fully reveal the actual wealth of the merchants. Taxation, whether the sultan's tariff or "protection" money paid to tribes in troubled times, was usually based on how much a merchant had in stock when the government agents came to look over the store. The lesson was clear; a small stock in evidence meant lower taxes.

Before the twentieth century the population of preindustrial Middle Eastern cities was densely settled within the city walls and numbered in the tens of thousands; even in 1971 the city of Marrakesh, whose population (220,000) was approximately the same as that of Austin, Texas, occupied one-fifth of the space. Unlike American cities today, these preindustrial cities were for walking, not driving. No one lived far from the centrally located suqs, and having shops selling the same products located next to one another offered the opportunity to shop comparatively—as well as to patronize conveniently one's favorite shopkeeper, who had to "stay honest" since his fellow merchants were literally next door. At the same time, however, Middle Eastern merchants also have interests in common that encourage them to stay together, including selling neither too cheap nor too dear, maintaining the same hours, and seeing to their common safety, some of the things many Western merchant associations also consider. Thus, the old suqs often had gates which were closed at night, rules about who could sell goods in the suq, and rules covering other common concerns. In 1971, the merchants of most Marrakesh suqs belonged to a *hunta*, an association with an *amin*, or leader, who represented their interests. Both merchants and artisans had hunta associations, which were of varying importance in arbitrating such things as rental disputes and in setting wholesale prices. The strongest huntas were those of suqs dealing in goods subject to government price controls, such as gold and meat.

As centers of production, Middle Eastern suqs traditionally combined a number of activities which in industrialized societies have become dispersed both geographically and economically. True, the preindustrial suqs did not produce all that they offered for sale; they also served as ports of entry for the caravans bringing salt, spices, gold, and slaves from distant lands to Cairo, Fez, Damascus, and other cities. From the great suqs these exotic goods were sold to merchants from smaller markets in the surrounding regions. However, in preindustrial times, the suq was where most of the production of goods took place: there, raw materials from the countryside were processed into finished products, which were then sold to the merchants, who in turn sold them to the customers. Finally, it was among the people of the suq that the financial investments for all these activities were organized.

Behind or near the shops of the Middle Eastern suq were the workshops where goods for sale were made. Thus, the metal suqs were not only the places to buy copper trays and charcoal braziers; they were also where coppersmiths and tinsmiths made and repaired such products, where blacksmiths forged plowshares, knives, and gun barrels as well as goods needed for other trades—such as hinges and door handles used in carpentry. Not far from the shops of the cloth merchants were the workshops of weavers, cordmakers, silk spinners; the shoe and purse makers were a short walk from the suqs selling leather products.

The presence of production and retail distribution in the same place is perhaps the most fundamental difference between the modern mall and the preindustrial suq. Indeed, the suqs of contemporary Middle Eastern cities have not entirely lost this function, even though local production of goods has become secondary to the sale of goods produced by the international capitalist enterprises which dominate the contemporary market economy.

LABOR RELATIONS

In Marrakesh, in the workshops where cloth is still woven, a dozen or more men and boys can be found working on the looms together. Here we would expect to find one to be the owner and the others, his employees. However, in the traditional suq this was not generally the case. Labor relations were seen as "partnerships"—one-to-one agreements between individuals. The employee, then, worked with other persons rather than for a company (Geertz et al. 1979:191). This kind of relationship is deeply rooted in the region's history, mentioned specifically in the twelfth century (Goitein 1967:170).

Both as a form of investment and as the basis for employment, the idea of partnership colors the obvious differences in status between master craftsmen and the journeymen or apprentices, who all work together. The master craftsmen, who may own the means of production, such as looms or other special tools, as well as the premises in which the work is done, obviously are in a position superior to that of the junior partners in the enterprise. Abuses and rewards remain a personal matter in the workshops of the suq; the suq of today is the antithesis of bureaucratic relationships, in which "the company" is the focus of responsibility.

In the Marrakesh suq, at the time I observed it, the terms of employment depended on what skills and resources each individual brought to the partnership. If all one had was the need to work, the terms would not be very favorable, especially in times of high unemployment. However, the ideology of employment, the idea of partnership, did make relations of production in the suq subjectively different from those of the factory worker. The factory worker works for a company; the suq artisan was working with his partners, unequal though their status may have been. The hope for future advancement is present in both cases; the difference in scale may have made advancement in status seem more likely in the suqs.

How would an artisan improve his position in a partnership? How does a blacksmith's assistant, for instance, come to own the tools of the blacksmith? The problem of acquiring preindustrial means of production has never had a simple answer. A carpenter I knew in Herat, Afghanistan, finally came to own his tools when his master-partner retired and gave him his equipment. Before this happened, however, he had gone back and forth from carpentry to other jobs several times. Others inherited from their relatives.

Formal apprenticing, in which one learned a craft and earned the right to practice it by working for a set number of years at low wages or, sometimes, merely for one's keep, may have been a common form of advancement to the status of master craftsman in the old Middle Eastern suqs. Today, the route to success seems less well structured. A man starts out pushing a cart around with a few potatoes for sale and hopes to be a merchant with a proper shop some day. Most men seem to have worked in a variety of jobs as they moved up the scale of artisanal or mercantile employment, learning the ways of the suq.

Just as every artisan in the suq did not own the tools of his trade, the objects made in the suq were often not the product of individual artisans. Several men might work on the same products—such as men's robes or inlaid trays. Furthermore, suq workshops were not like craftshops or artists' studios, where the personal identity of the individual who made the product was forever attached to the fruits of his or her labor. Artisans might do jobs on consignment for individual clients, but artisans were not themselves merchants, and what they made generally went to retail merchants.

However, a major difference existed between the suq and the modern market insofar as the relationship between the producer and consumer was concerned because production and marketing responsibility remained within the same social space for producer, merchant, and customer. Bad workmanship could be traced back to particular individuals if necessary, as could overpricing, cheating, and failure to pay debts. The products of a suq did not acquire spurious value through the exaggerations of advertising. In the suq, reputations of individuals, not companies, rose and fell according to the quality of goods produced and sold.

The major division of labor in the suq is between the artisan (*snay³i*) and the merchant (*taajir*). The merchants are always "on stage" in the suq, well dressed and well spoken, better able than the artisan to fulfill the ideal of the proper Middle Eastern gentleman in presentation of self, though the merchant is not necessarily wealthier than the artisan. In preindustrial suqs, shops were usually owned by the men who sat in them, though they might have an assistant or two and a little boy to run errands and fetch tea or coffee for the owner, his friends, and important customers. These last two categories of people were often the same, since customers were indeed customary; usually the same people came back to the same merchants. With strangers, the merchant bargained and raised his prices; for the regular customer-friend, the backbone of his business, the price was always right and was not discussed.

How was the relatively self-contained universe of the suq tied together? How did materials move around until they were purchased by customers? Today, many of the products produced in the suq are for tourists, but the production and distribution pattern is much as in times past.

In Moroccan markets, the auction (*dillal*) played and continues to play a central role in moving goods from raw materials to finished products and distributing them to the merchants for sale. The auction sets the sale prices of materials; it is literally a stockmarket with real stocks, not pieces of paper and electronic boards.

In the Marrakesh rug suq, where prices are high and expertise is essential, the service of a good *dlaal* (auctioneer) is particularly important, as rug buying and selling is a complex matter, involving much discussion of the various qualities of the merchandise. In what seems to be a way of restricting the auction to the professional merchants, the bidding is conducted in currency values which are not in common usage. This is like using "bits" in English— two bits equals twenty-five cents, four bits equals fifty cents, and so on—but much more elaborate and very confusing if one is not familiar with the system. Thus, most of the bidders are rug merchants, who, like other merchants, sit in their open shopfronts and inspect the goods as the dlaal carries them by. However, other men—merchants from out of town or private purchasers— may also bid. A good dlaal is clever and knows his customers and his merchandise well. He knows what is needed to get top price at an auction and may expect an extra financial incentive before he agrees to sell a particular batch of goods.

CONTEMPORARY ADAPTIONS

Today foreign tourists are a conspicuous element among the thousands of people who visit the Marrakesh suq. But the suq also remains a major attraction for the rural people of southern Morocco, who come to Marrakesh by bus, truck, and taxi to buy and sell and often to look for jobs. Although many dry goods and hardware items are now imported, the suq in Marrakesh still depends on its environs as the source of fresh foods, raw materials, and some finished goods. The father of the young rug dealer spent much of his time traveling in the villages of the Atlas Mountains near Marrakesh, picking up from the local weavers the kinds of rugs he felt would appeal to the European tourists who frequented his store.

Suq goods are also produced in the surrounding city. In 1972, more than half the adult women in Marrakesh were estimated to be employed doing piece work—embroidery, machine sewing, crocheting, basket work, and hand finishing of caftans and jallabas. Young boys and girls carry materials from the merchants to their mothers and older sisters, then return the finished items. Piecework was an important source of family income; indeed, I was told that in this way more women were able to work in Marrakesh than men, for whom jobs were very scarce. Many younger men stated that they were only working in the suq until a better paying job opened up—in a tourist hotel, at a bank, or even in France, where many Moroccan men work as migrant laborers. The suq today in Morocco is for many a way station between jobs in the Western sectors of the economy, but the suq is not able to take care of all the unemployed, many of whom wait at designated stations day after day in hope of finding work.

Yet many men are still deeply committed to the suq as a way of life and have become rich despite the changing circumstances of contemporary Morocco. Real estate values in the madina have greatly increased, so that anyone with suq property is likely to be well off from rent alone. But being a property owner is not the only source of wealth. For example, one elderly merchant had a partnership in a coffee shop, a partnership in a photography store, and a part interest in a postcard kiosk, and he owned a food shop which he rented out. He also had a share of a farm he inherited from his mother. Nevertheless, he was to be found every day in his shop, sewing and selling purses. Though only a small part of his income came from purse making, it was what he had always done and he continued to do it.

Today, if one wanders into the suq in Marrakesh or the Khan al-Khalili suq in Cairo, one might be romantic enough to feel transported back to the mid-nineteenth century or before, since the small shops are about the same in appearance and the streets are as narrow and twisting as in the past. However, the small shops dating from so long ago offer polyester cloth woven in Korea; silk from Taiwan; Japanese radios and TV sets; French stationery and ball point pens. The only items locally made are those which local taste continues to demand and mass producers find unprofitable to make. Such products are an expression of cultural differences still resistant to change, such as the jellabas and distinctive shoes worn in southern Morocco. The leather goods still made in Marrakesh are mostly designed for the tastes of French visitors who frequent the suq on visits from the nearby Club Méditerranée. In Khan al-Khalili bazaar in Cairo, trays and braziers are made largely for foreign consumption, as are inlaid wooden boxes and carved wooden screens. The setting and the methods of retailing are the same but the customers are different; many of the tourist goods are sold to exporters or produced on commissions from tourist shops in the Hilton, Sheraton, and other luxury hotels.

The strength and endurance of the suq must never be underestimated, for it is at once a self-sustaining embodiment of historical practices and attitudes and an expression of new conditions of economic and social life. Far from being obsolete, the suqs of large cities are still the bargain basement for most local shoppers, full of inexpensive food, clothing, and housewares. Lower overhead means that many new products can be sold at lower costs in the suqs than in department stores.

Much of the traditional behavior of the suq continues; tea is still served if the transaction is of importance or the friendship is valued. The customer in a hurry is an anomaly among merchants who may still value good conversation as much as higher profits and who criticize hustlers who are out to skin the unsuspecting visitor. Less obvious to the foreign visitor is that the suq is also a tightly packed center of human communication. Fact and rumor sometimes mix together in an extremely volatile fashion; young men can seem to materialize from nowhere and storm through the narrow lanes pursued by police, while merchants hastily slam down the metal shutters in front of their shops. Indeed, when the merchants start to close up their shops in the middle of the day (other than at times for prayer), it is a good indication that something violent is about to happen. Some observers have argued that the Teheran bazaar was the flash point of the public uprising in the Khomeini revolution in Iran. Opinions—about people and about politics—take shape in the network of communications in the suq; even the most severe government censorship cannot stand up against the whispered asides which pass from person to person in the suq.

Compared with the suq, one of the oldest commercial institutions in human history, the mall and the department store are mere arrivistes. The suq's importance as a center of production has declined during the last hundred years. Yet, given a worldwide depression, or a major war, the suq could easily regain local importance while "Western sectors," the outposts of foreign interests, wither away. In Cairo, Khan al-Khalili still has thousands of people shopping in its streets every day, as does the suq of Marrakesh. Although the suqs of the Middle East and North Africa may seem to be overshadowed by modern commercial centers, they are not quaint survivals from the past but rather are still the lively, vital hubs of many forms of economic and social activity. Middle Eastern suqs may still be busy making goods and selling them some day when the dust is settling in the empty corridors of our nonproductive Western shopping malls.

NOTES

1. *Suq* (singular) and *aswaq* (plural) are the correct transliterations of this term from Arabic. See Elizabeth Warnock Fernea (1975) for detailed descriptions of the madina.

2. Food stores are located in different sections of the city near local residential districts, while individual "convenience" stores—small shops selling cooking fuel, sugar, salt, matches, and other items of daily use—are to be found among the houses along residential streets. The old "mom and pop" stores of America were like these small, handy establishments.

REFERENCES

Fernea, Elizabeth Warnock. 1975, 1990. *A Street in Marrakech.* New York: Doubleday/ Anchor (1975), Waveland Press (1990).

Geertz, Clifford, Hildred Geertz, and Lawrence Rosen. 1979. *Meaning and Order in Moroccan Society.* Cambridge: Cambridge University Press.

Goitein, S. D. 1967. *A Mediterranean Society.* Vol. I. *Economic Foundations.* Berkeley: University of California Press.

Movie signboards in downtown Cairo, Egypt. *Photo Evelyn A. Early*

Merchants display wares in the *suq* (market) in Taroudannt, Morocco.
Photo Dorothy Andrake

A woman merchant in Wad Medani, Sudan. *Photo Evelyn A. Early*

Beef and lamb for sale in a Moroccan market. *Photo Dorothy Andrake*

A sweet shop in Egypt. *Photo Evelyn A. Early*

A small shop in a village near Shiraz, Iran. *Photo Mary Hegland*

The Hannou department store in the business district of Cairo, Egypt. *Photo Evelyn A. Early*

A northern Egyptian peasant leads the family's water buffaloes past cut sugar cane. *Photo Evelyn A. Early*

A Moroccan architect drawing blueprints. *Photo Evelyn A. Early*

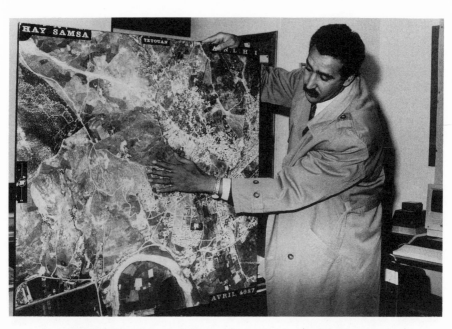

An engineer explains an urban renewal project in Tetouan, Morocco.
Photo Muhammad Hamushi

An electrical engineer in Morocco. *Photo Muhammad Hamushi*

Ablutions in the Qarawiyiin mosque, Fez, Morocco. *Photo Evelyn A. Early*

A villager in Iran greets a pilgrim returning from Mecca. *Photo Mary Hegland*

Bus travelers arrive in Meknes, Morocco. *Photo Dorothy Andrake*

Teams compete in a soccer match in Rabat, Morocco. *Photo Dorothy Andrake*

The commander of the Camel Corps for the south central region of Morocco and the mayor of a small outpost town. *Photo Dorothy Andrake*

A seamstress in Cairo, Egypt. *Photo Evelyn A. Early*

A reporter interviews a guitarist in Morocco. *Photo Muhammad Hamushi*

A television crew interviews the governor (to right of cameraman) of Kordofan, Sudan. *Photo Evelyn A. Early*

Government officials present the deed of a house to a woman in Tetouan, Morocco. *Photo Evelyn A. Early*

PART FOUR

Popular Expression of Religion

INTRODUCTION

The Middle East is the birthplace of monotheistic religion—Islam, Christianity, Judaism, Zoroastrianism—and practitioners of each of these religions can be found throughout the area. The majority of the population, roughly ninety percent, are Muslims, believers in Islam.

Islam means to surrender oneself, to submit to another's will, in this case to the will of God. Islam teaches believers the meaning of this submission to God and how to conform to the Creator's will. Anyone who recognizes God and follows God's admonitions is a Muslim.

Islam's first principle is belief in one God. Arabs at the rise of Islam professed different faiths: some were Christian and some were Jewish, but the majority were pagans who worshipped numerous gods. The revelations to Muhammad, the first prophet of Islam, stressed that there is but one God (in Arabic, *Allah*; literally, "the God"). God created human beings, the world, and all that it contains; he guided the earlier prophets (whose records are found also in the Jewish Torah and the Christian Scriptures); and revealed the Quran to furnish believers with precepts to guide them on the proper path. The Quran, the Muslim scripture, is revered as God's word; it is a compilation of the 114 revelations given to Muhammad. Two essential Quranic *sura*s (chapters) are presented here to give a sense of the Quran's language and content. Kristina Nelson, in her article, points out the vital significance of the sounds of the recited Quran.

The worst sin a Muslim can commit is polytheism: to deny the unity of God or to attribute God's powers to any other being. The muezzin's five-times-daily call to prayer emphasizes the acknowledgment of God's supremacy as he calls, "God is the greatest. God is the greatest. Come to prayer."

The Muslim *shahada*, or statement of belief, professes the belief in one God and in Muhammad as the prophet of God. Each Muslim repeats this creed to testify that God is one, that He was not born, neither can He give birth, nor can He be compared to any other creature. In Islam God is defined by ninety-nine attributes: omnipotent, omniscient, merciful, beneficent, and so on. Muslims recite these qualities as they work their way three times around their string of thirty-three prayer beads. Religious posters list the ninety-nine traits in elaborate calligraphy. Every document and meal and many other actions begin by invoking God's name—"In the name of God, the beneficent, the merciful."

The second line of the shahada affirms Muhammad as the final prophet of Islam. God spoke to humans through all the prophets, from Adam to Muhammad, and demonstrated his concern for people and his desire that they be led properly through the vicissitudes of life. If individuals follow God's commandments, they will be rewarded on Judgment Day. The Quran vividly describes the paradise of the believers and the hellfire of the wrongdoers.

God chose prophets to preach his laws to the people. Muhammad emerged as the leader of the Arab community and organized a community of believers which replaced the community of blood relations and wealth, common in the Arabian Peninsula until that time. The Quran speaks of the *umma*, the community of believers which replaces all other types of community organization. Membership in the umma is based upon belief; all Muslims are equal in the umma whatever their birth, rank, nationality, or wealth.

The second major principle of Islam recognizes the need to follow a just social and economic order in the community. Muslims are expected to follow the moral order outlined in the Quran. This moral order defines membership in and responsibilities to the Muslim community, such as caring for the poor, the orphaned, and the needy. Islam established a social and economic order inextricable from religious duties, largely by instituting a system of Islamic law, the *shariʿa* (literally, "path," or "way"). Islamic law is derived first from the Quran and second from the idealized example set by Muhammad and his early community. By following these sources of the law (combined with other jurisprudential techniques of community affirmation and recourse to precedent and collected into massive jurisprudence texts), which encompass such areas of life as worship, family relations, social codes, political regulations, commercial contracts, law of warfare, and community government, Muslims express their submission to God's will.

The Quran specifies as obligatory for Muslims five religious practices which are thought to characterize the essence of faithful practice. These five pillars of Islam are the creed, prayer, *zakat* (tithes), fasting during the month of Ramadan, and the *hajj* (pilgrimage to Mecca). Each religious duty speaks to two aspects of worship: the spiritual or transcendent side of Islam and the community-oriented practice which involves a communal experience.

The creed "There is no God but God and Muhammad is the messenger of God" states the core beliefs of Islam: the unity of God and the prophethood of Muhammad. Muslims hear and recite it in Arabic repeatedly throughout their lives. Rather than repeating the formula unthinkingly, once in every believer's life he or she must declare the phrase with full knowledge of what is being stated and thereby commit to the tenets of Islam. Conversion to Islam is accomplished simply by pronouncing the creed before witnesses with full knowledge of what is being said.

In Islam there are two types of prayer: *salat*, the ritualized prayer, and *du'a*, a personal plea to God. Each salat incorporates a short du'a, or prayer touching on personal concerns, in its ritual. The salat is performed communally five times each day. In the mosque the worshippers line up in rows, shoulder to shoulder, rich and poor, young and old, merchant and peasant. They bow and kneel together to recognize the greatness of God.

Originally, *zakat*, a tithe on wealth, provided the economic base for the umma. Rich and poor were to provide an equal share of their resources to support the community, specifically to care for orphans and widows—those with no family to rely upon. Even though zakat is rarely paid as a tax these days, the obligation to care for the poor is graphically illustrated in the story of Abu Illya, included below.

During Ramadan Muslims fast from sunrise to sunset to cleanse the body, recognize God's bounty, and feel kinship with the deprived. At the same time, community solidarity is never stronger than when Muslims worldwide await the signal that the sun has set and that they may begin to eat. In Morocco, all break the fast with *harira*, a soup, so that all, rich and poor, in cities and villages, break their fast at the same time with the same food.

All Muslims everywhere, circumstances permitting, are commanded to make at some point in their lifetime the hajj to the sites of the revelation of Islam. Close to one million Muslims arrive in Saudi Arabia each year by plane, ship, and truck, don *ihram*—plain white garments worn for the duration of the pilgrimage—and follow the path of pilgrims from centuries ago. At this point, whether peasants or kings, all Muslims are dressed alike and follow the same ritual—all united in Islam. An American convert to Islam, Michael E. Jansen, explains both the ritual of the pilgrimage and the emotions evoked by her presence in Mecca.

Muslims view Islam as both *din* (religion) and *dawla* (state). Ablution for prayer or formulation of business contracts—all actions are defined by Islam. Thus Islam becomes a standard for society as well as a standard for worship.

In the centuries following Muhammad's death, Muslims elaborated on the Quranic injunctions and incorporated other practices as part of Muslim religious expression. Scholars systematized Islamic jurisprudence, developed approaches to theology, and generated Islamic philosophy based on Greek sources.

A widely quoted *hadith* (saying) of Muhammad states that the community will divide into seventy-seven sects of which only one will be correct. While a variety of sectarian groupings have emerged over the centuries, the two major movements within Islam are the Sunni (*Ahl al-Sunna wal-Jama'a*, The People of the Prophet's Sunna, or practice, and Community) and Shi'i (*Shi'at Ali*, Party of Ali). At Muhammad's death, the community divided over the basis of selecting the new head of the fledgling Muslim community. The Sunni position ultimately evolved into one of consultation among the community elders; the Shi'is claimed that Ali, the Prophet's cousin and son-in-law (husband of Muhammad's daughter Fatima and father of the Prophet's grand-sons, Hassan and Hussein) should succeed Muhammad by virtue of blood ties. Over the years, political conflicts exacerbated differences between the groups. While the basic theology and jurisprudence of both groups are very close, there are instructive differences in their beliefs about community governance, derivation of juridical positions, ritual practice, and other subjects. Sunni Muslims, the majority (about 70 percent) of the world's Muslims, consider themselves the mainstream of Islam. Shi'i Muslims compose a majority of the population in Iran and Iraq and about 40 percent of that of Lebanon. There are also large numbers of Shi'i Muslims in parts of the Arabian Peninsula, Pakistan, and East Africa.

A highly significant development of Islamic belief was the formulation of sufism (*altasawwuf*), or mysticism, as Islamic precepts were influenced by Christian, Jewish, Hindu, and Buddhist mysticism. Elaborate schools of mystical thought grew up around famous mystics, and branches of their *tariqa*s (mystical orders) spread throughout the Muslim world. The works of such mystics as the poets Hafez, Rumi, Attar, and others constitute a world-famous body of poetry addressed to God and celebrating his glory.

Local peoples added their traditional holy spots to their new religion, and pious men or mystics were identified with sacred streams and trees and commemorated by shrines. While the formal Islam of scholars and jurisprudents seemed remote and far removed, the shrines, as focal points for pilgrims requesting help, thus served to make their religion accessible to individual needs. A shrine may be a humble, unwhitewashed, mud house, a pile of stones, or an elaborate, gilded edifice. Local saints are believed to respond to pleas, and all shrines exhibit scraps of cloth knotted to window grilles, folded papers shoved into cracks, or locks of hair which pilgrims have left as signs of their vows. Although many local saints were originally pious men or women from the village or neighborhood, the family of Muhammad—his daughter Fatima, son-in-law Ali, and grandchildren—are revered worldwide. Popular stories are told and written about their lives. Excerpts from Muhammad Fahmi Abdul's pamphlet on Zainab, Muhammad's granddaughter; emphasize her piety and courage.

Both Sunni and Shi'i Muslims make minor pilgrimages to smaller shrines. A popular time for these visits is the *mawlid*, the birth or death day of a saint. The ritual practices of local pilgrimages mirror some aspects of the Meccan pilgrimage. For instance, worshippers commonly circumambulate the tomb seven times counterclockwise as is done at the Kaaba. Although pilgrims to Mecca always sacrifice sheep, pilgrims to other shrines may bring poultry, goats, or other foodstuffs as well as sheep to present to the guardian of the shrine or, as vowed, to the poor when their vows are fulfilled. Robert L. Canfield and Anne H. Betteridge give accounts of shrine visits. Canfield describes the holiday nature of the celebration, and Betteridge notes that women's religious observances may differ from those of men.

Other types of religious observance, practice, and expression include drama, the *ta'ziyeh,* or passion play, of the Shi'ites, the Sufi mysticism of the various orders, formal traditions of Islamic education, the elaboration of jurisprudence, architecture and art, house paintings which tell the story of the resident's pilgrimage to Mecca, pamphlets which apply the lives and teachings of Muslim historical figures or prominent preachers to present-day concerns, treatises on the interpretation of the Quran. All of these pull the individual Muslim into the larger context of Islam while at the same time answer an individual call for guidance, help, comfort, celebration, or spiritual sustenance.

Selections from the Quran

Translated by Juan E. Campo

Muslims believe the Quran to be God's miraculous gift to mankind as revealed to Muhammad through the Angel Gabriel. Thus, it is the axis of Islam, the source for all its laws and doctrines. Below are selections from the 114 suras, or chapters, of the Quran. Muslims listen to selections from the Quran on the radio, at all religious ceremonies, at funerals, at holiday celebrations, and on many other occasions. The proper form of reciting the Quran is of great importance to the Muslim, and recitation schools teach proper methods. Correct recitation is a highly valued art form.

Because of its sacred status, the Quran is never referred to by Muslims as simply a "book." It is called "the Glorious Quran" or "the Copy," meaning a copy of the archetypal Quran, which coexists eternally with God. Muslims treat their scripture with great respect, placing it in an honored position in their homes and handling it carefully. When Muslims move into a new house, a copy of the Quran is the first item carried across the threshold. For them its physical presence conveys the power of blessing and prevents misfortune. —Eds.

I. SURA 1 *AL-FATIHA* ("OPENING")   MECCA

In the name of God (Allah), most compassionate and
   merciful.
Praise be to God, the lord of the worlds.
Most compassionate and merciful,
Lord of judgment day.
It is you whom we worship,
You to whom we turn for aid.
Guide us on the straight path,
The path of those whom you favor; not those who have
   incurred your wrath, nor those who have gone astray.

II. *AYAT AL-KURSI* ("THRONE VERSE")

From Sura 2 al-Baqara ("Cow") 255 *Medina*

God, there is no other god, the living, the eternal. He neither slumbers nor sleeps. To him belongs all that is in heaven and earth. Who intercedes with him unless it is with his permission? He knows what they do in open and in secret, and they cannot grasp anything of his knowledge, unless he wills it. His throne encompasses heaven and earth; preserving them is no burden for him. He is the high and mighty one.

III. SURA 109 *AL-KAFIRUN* ("DENIERS") MECCA

In the name of God, most compassionate and merciful.
Say: O deniers!
I do not worship what you worship.
You will not worship what I worship.
I will not worship what you worshipped.
You are not worshipping what I worship.
You have your religion and I have mine.

IV. SURA 112 *AL-IKHLAS* ("SINCERITY") MECCA

In the name of God, most compassionate and merciful.
Say: He is God, the one.
God is the eternal.
He does not procreate, nor is he procreated.
He has no equal.

V. SURA 113 *AL-FALAQ* ("DAYBREAK") MECCA

In the name of God, most compassionate and merciful.
Say: I seek protection through the lord of daybreak
From the evil of what he has created,
From the evil of twilight,
From the evil of women who blow on knots,
From the evil of the envious when he envies.

VI. SURA 114 *AL-NAS* (''HUMANS'') MECCA

In the name of God, most compassionate and merciful.
Say: I seek protection through the lord of humans,
King of humans,
God of humans,
From the evil of the whisperer—who withdraws when
    God's name is mentioned,
Who whispers into the hearts of humans,
Of jinns and humans.

The Sound of the Divine in Daily Life

Kristina Nelson

Muslims declare that the Quran is proof of Muhammad's prophethood: only a divine source could explain the miraculous power and beauty of its language, for Muhammad was an illiterate merchant. Kristina Nelson writes here of the significance of the sound of the language of the recited Quran and of the many levels of meaning it has for listening Muslims, and explains the pervasiveness of that sound in daily life. —Eds.

Muslims believe that the Quran is the word of God revealed in Arabic to the Prophet Muhammad, and that it is the last of a series of revelations, including the Torah and the Gospels. The Quran has been compared to those holy books, but Muslims consider the Quran to be more than a book of scripture in which is set down God's law and promise for humanity, and the history of creation. For the Quran must be heard, not merely read. As the word of God transmitted to the Prophet Muhammad, it is considered to be the actual sound of the Divine, the model of perfect beauty, and a testimony to the miracle of human and divine interaction. The revelation was not even written down, except in bits and pieces, until after the Prophet's death, and then, the authoritative reference for the written text was the recited Quran as it had been memorized by the followers of the Prophet.

An indication of the primary importance of the sound is the fact that the official text distributed to each community was accompanied by a reciter. Since then, the primary source for learning the Quran has been its recitation. Learning the Quran is equated with reciting it from memory. Preschool children learn the verses of the Quran and the correct phrases with which to begin and end a recitation. But they memorize more than words: they are encouraged to master the sound of the Quran, even before they can comprehend its meaning. Throughout the Islamic world children are rewarded for their memorizing the Quran with cash prizes, media exposure, and the respect of their communities. The child with a pleasing voice is encouraged to become a public reciter.

The actual learning process is rote memorization: the teacher recites and the student imitates. The teacher corrects until the student has it right. This tradition has great authority, for it is believed that the Prophet Muhammad was himself thus instructed by the Angel Gabriel over the twenty-year period during which the Quran was revealed, and that when the revelation was complete, the accuracy of the revelation was confirmed in a final review in which the Prophet was made to recite the Quran in full. Traditionally, the student may or may not refer to the written text, depending on the student's age and experience. But the basic premise of Quranic learning is that the written text is an aid to the oral tradition, and that to achieve full mastery, one must ultimately depend on what one hears.

To guard against the distortions and variants of oral tradition, Muslim scholars devised a code of rules which preserve the Quran in its oral manifestation. This code, called *tajwid*, regulates Quranic recitation in detail. Muslims believe that the sound thus preserved is that of the actual revelation; it is the language of God. Whereas the written text preserves the words, syntax, and order of materials, tajwid preserves the sound, from the pronunciation of each phoneme to the length and timbre or voice quality of each syllable. It is tajwid which differentiates Quranic Arabic from literary Arabic and gives the recitation its unique and characteristic sound. Even children have learned that, whether in the context of formal speech or informal conversation, the words of the Quran demand special rhythmic and pitch patterns which mark its divine origin.

The Quran is considered the miracle of Muhammad's prophethood. The proof of its divine source is in its inimitable euphony, eloquence, and wisdom, for Muhammad was neither poet nor sage, but an unlettered merchant. Most Westerners find the claim to the Quran's inimitable beauty baffling, for they have had access only to the written text, whether in translation or in the original Arabic. The ears hear more than the eyes see in the written text, and it is only in the sound that the full miracle is realized. Thus, while the meaning of each word may be translated from the Arabic, the Quran itself is untranslatable. In recognition of this, A. J. Arberry, an English scholar who tried to render something of the poetry, the imagery and rhythms, of the Quran into English, titled his work *The Koran Interpreted*. The point is made clear in comparing translations and the written Arabic text of a passage consisting of a simple list with the recitation of the same passage. What reads as a prosaic and boringly repetitive passage on who can marry whom (Quran 24/26) is, when recited, a lilting verse that draws one's attention to the subject with alternating rhymes, parallel syntax, and a catchy rhythm.

What does the Quran sound like? There are basically two sounds (and the following description should be considered a supplement to your listening), depending on whether the context is pedagogic and devotional or performative. *Murattal* is the style of recitation learned by all Muslims who want to recite correctly, that is, according to the rules of tajwid. Emphasis is on rendering the text correctly and clearly. The text is recited straight through, without repetition. Although differing from that of conversation, intonation is within the same range or even more restricted. The voice is pitched at conversation level or a bit higher. It is the characteristic rhythm of the text which dominates and most obviously marks this style. The sound of murattal has been variously described as "sing-song," soothing, restful, refreshing, and hypnotic. Except for radio broadcasting, murattal is usually heard only in the contexts of prayer, private devotions, and learning. Murattal is what most Muslims use when they recite.

What Muslims listen to, and what you, as a visitor to most Islamic communities, are likely to hear, is the *mujawwad* style, which is used for public performance. In this style, clear and correct rendering of the text is taken for granted. The intent of the mujawwad reciter is to exploit the inherent beauty of the text with melody and artistry in order to "reach the hearts" of the listeners. This style is marked by repetition, elaborate melody, ornamentation, full voice, and, sometimes, an almost unbearable intensity. The audible release of tension on the part of listeners when the reciter comes to the end of a phrase is also characteristic of this style. Audience response may range from sighs and murmurs to weeping to ecstatic shouts.

Like all great art, recitation can be transforming, the participants touched and changed. But Quranic recitation is more than art. Indeed, Muslim scholars and reciters are careful to distinguish between recitation and "mere" music. The late Shaikh Mustafa Ismail, one of the more elaborately melodic reciters, told of a meeting with a prominent Egyptian musician who handed him a lute and asked him to sing. "I don't sing," said Shaikh Mustafa. Later the musician asked him, in effect, how he could make such sublime music when reciting and then say he does not sing. "I believe in God," said Shaikh Mustafa.

The public reciter is sensitive to what distinguishes him from the singer. He is not taught how to put text and melody together. He does not memorize melodies or set pieces. In performance, he has no backup chorus or instrumental accompaniment. Although he may command as great a fee as the most popular singers, it is paid by a patron or group of sponsors, and his performance is free to the public. Whereas the singer may bend the text to his melodic inspiration, the reciter has no such license. He must not be carried away by melodic improvisation at the expense of the correctly rendered text. For it is not just any text, nor even just any religious text; it is the Quran.

The meaning of the Quran is not restricted to the words: the meaning transcends the words. In listening to the recited story of Joseph and his brothers, for example, one hears not only a particular narrative but also the sound of the Divine, the moment of revelation. No wonder listeners have been known to weep, swoon, and even expire on hearing the recited Quran.

Indeed, the approved response to Quranic recitation is weeping; it is a sign that one is profoundly moved by the experience. An extensive tradition of stories attests to the affecting power of recitation, and anecdotes are continually being added to this tradition. I was told, for example, that every Christmas season the BBC used to broadcast the late Shaykh Muhammad Rif'at's recitation of the story of the birth of Jesus. An American heard five minutes of such a broadcast and "dropped everything to come to Egypt and devote himself to the study of Islam." It is said of the same reciter that, when it was time for his regular broadcast, "all of Cairo fell silent, listening, even the foreigners in restaurants." A well-respected patron of Quranic recitation told me that he used to drink heavily, and while drinking, would often listen to recitation. "My friends told me this was blasphemous [it is forbidden to drink alcohol in Islam], but gradually, I began to listen more and to drink less. Now I don't drink at all." You do not have to be Muslim to appreciate the recited Quran. Jews, Christians, and nonbelievers have all testified to the power of the sound. Comments of non-Muslims often acknowledge that the recitation is somehow more than music, and they include references to the character of the reciter, his piety, sincerity, or lack thereof.

Obviously not every recitation fulfills the ideal. There are reciters who misuse their skills to attract a following, whose inspiration is not the Quran, but financial reward and personal popularity, just as there are listeners who seek out performances for the thrill of a particular reciter's music genius. ("He is like a tightrope walker: when he goes high, you are breathless.") In some Islamic countries Quranic recitation is severely restricted melodically to preclude such transgressions, and even in Egypt there is continuing discussion over the appropriateness of the use of artistry in recitation. But none of this affects the essential orality of the Quran, nor its impact on the listener. Whatever the style of the recitation, the basic reality is that the Quran is recited.

Quranic recitation is a common, daily event, not restricted to special occasions, nor even to strictly religious contexts. You may hear a beggar, sitting with palm outstretched on a corner in a residential neighborhood, reciting in full voice. You may take a taxi to the accompaniment of recitation played on cassette tape. You may deliver your laundry, buy meat, and find that most shopkeepers along your route have their radios turned to Quranic recitation. Halfway up the block, a group of men, sitting formally on small stools which spill out of the store onto the sidewalk, are listening to a recording of recitation. They are there to honor the memory of a deceased colleague. A business is opened, and the event is marked with lights, flowers, and the sound of a reciter broadcast into the surrounding streets. At a summit conference in Tunisia, reciters representing the participating countries perform in turn. Radio stations open and close their daily programming with recitation. Radio and television stations program recitation regularly during the course of the day. On the religious radio station in Egypt, you can listen to live performances of recitation in the context of commemorative and official events, or of religious liturgy. Or you may listen to a program that presents selections from a heritage of forty years of recordings of Quranic recitation.

Think of the characteristic sounds that define your day . . . the sound of the alarm clock, of dishes clattering, of disc jockeys and newscasters, the noise of traffic, of telephones and xerox machines and typewriters. Whereas you might be lucky enough to hear a piece of sublime beauty in a concert of religious music, or in the context of religious liturgy, or to hear even a Bach cantata in your local delicatessen, it would be a rare occasion, and it would not be the Quran. Imagine what it would be like to have, as an integral part of your day, a sound with all the implications and power and beauty and prestige of the recited Quran. There is no equivalent to that experience.

Abu Illya and Zakat

Donna Lee Bowen

The teachings of the Quran emphasize the responsibility of the individual to society and of society to the individual. The indigent, widows, orphans—those without a family to supply their needs are to be watched out for by the community as a whole. Sayyid Qutb, a twentieth-century Muslim ideologue and activist, stated in his book Social Justice in Islam: *"Again every individual is charged with the care of society, as if he were the watchman over it, responsible for its safety. Life is like a ship at sea, whose crew are all concerned for her safety. . . . No individual, then, can be exempt from this care for the general interest. Similarly the welfare of the community must be promoted by mutual help between individuals—always within the limits of honesty and uprightness. 'Help one another in innocence and piety, but do not help one another in crime and hostility' (Quran 5:3)."*

Each adult Muslim is expected to pay annually one-fortieth of his property for the care and welfare of the less fortunate in the Muslim community. In most parts of the Muslim world zakat (tithes) is no longer collected by the state as it was during the early years of Islam. Its donation has become voluntary and is given directly to the needy as well as being dispensed through a mosque.
—Eds.

Abu Illya, the father of my friend Illya Muhammad, is the baker for the Moroccan town of Bou Jad. Each morning he rises at 3:30 a.m. and begins work at the bakery at 4:00 a.m. He and his second oldest son, Abdul Latif, mix, knead, and bake hundreds of loaves of bread in large hot ovens set in the walls of the bakery. When the doors of the oven are opened to retrieve the bread, the bakery resembles an inferno. Despite the strength needed to operate the bakery, Abu Illya is a slight, quiet, unassuming man. In family gatherings he sits quietly and contributes little to the conversation, preferring to puff on his pipe. The more time I spent with Abu Illya, the more I grew to respect him and the values that guided his life. My first meeting with him, however, was unusual.

At the family party preceding the wedding of Illya's second cousin Fatima's daughter, puffs of illicit *kif* (hashish) smoke drifted past Illya, me, and a few others. We sniffed, paused, and looked at each other. I began to scan the room for a tell-tale huddle of young kif smokers, but I was stopped by a blushing Illya. "It's my father," he said. "I wish he would stop smoking." Abdul Latif joined in. "Don't you think it is bad for his health? No father should smoke in front of company. Talk with him, help him see he'd be better off without kif." Both sons were clearly embarrassed and worried about their father's pastime, but could do nothing more than gently tease him about it.

Later Fatima and I cornered Abu Illya and asked about the kif. "Don't you know that it's illegal in America?" I asked. Fatima countered with "What kind of example are you setting for your sons? Do you want them to turn into kif smokers too?"

He smiled. "I get up before dawn every day of the week and work hard to prepare bread for the town. The work is strenuous, routine, and with the heat of those giant ovens, I feel like I face the fires of hell each day. I return home at lunchtime exhausted and wanting only some quiet for a few hours. Furthermore, Bou Jad is the most boring town in Morocco. What else is there to do? Can I be blamed for smoking to relax? Haven't I earned the right to be left alone in peace with my pipe and my thoughts?"

From then on, Abu Illya and I sat together in the salon after lunch. He smoked and I read books and generally tried to make sense of all I saw in Bou Jad.

One afternoon a knock at the door shattered our quiet and the rest of the family's siesta. Illya's sister, Khadija, ran to the door and admitted a woman dressed in a shabby gray caftan. They held a whispered conference and then Khadija came into the salon to consult her father. He reached for his wallet, pulled out several bills, and handed them to Khadija, who ran back to the entryway and pressed them into the woman's hand. The woman called out thanks to Abu Illya and faded back into the alleyway.

That evening I asked Illya and Abdul Latif about the woman. They answered in an off-hand fashion that it must have been Lalla Fatiha needing something for her son's schooling since autumn classes had just begun. Who was Lalla Fatiha? No, she isn't a relative; she is our neighbor. Down the *derb* (alley), the doorway on the right. The one painted orange for her daughter's wedding. You've seen her younger children playing soldiers and soccer in the street. She is a widow. My father pays his *zakat* to her.

Zakat? No it isn't zakat as in the Prophet's time when it was paid as a tax to the community coffers. We don't have any collection of zakat in Morocco now. Instead we pay income tax to the government. And then we give alms to the poor. Most people don't pay zakat regularly, just give alms during

Ramadan or perhaps support a particular beggar, although Bou Jad has far fewer beggars than Marrakesh or Casablanca Medina.

Abu Illya, it seemed, believed in the responsibility of Muslims to pay zakat whether or not it duplicated income tax. He also believed that one should pay zakat as it says in the Quran, that Muslims should know their neighbor's situation and look after their welfare without being asked for help.

Abu Illya had known Lalla Fatiha and her husband, Si Mukhtar, since he was a boy. Si Mukhtar had been a clerk in the super caid's office making a low but sufficient wage. After he had fathered seven children, two of whom died before they reached one year of age, he developed unexplained pains in his stomach, was treated by a variety of doctors from Bou Jad to Khenifra, but died within the year. A horde of relatives descended upon Lalla Fatiha to mourn her husband's death, but within a week they had all left for their homes having eaten enough food to feed her children for three months.

Lalla Fatiha quietly went about her life. Gradually her children's clothes grew shabbier; the older boys stayed in school, but each year Lalla Fatiha looked more worn as she struggled to buy them shoes and books from the small savings her husband left. Finally, Um Illya, Illya's mother, in conversation with Lalla Fatiha about an upcoming feast, discovered that she was not planning to sacrifice a sheep but to purchase a little meat for brochettes instead. In Morocco, failing to buy a sheep for sacrifice on 'Id al-Adha is a sure sign of financial insolvency. Um Illya rushed home to consult with Abu Illya, and the next day Illya and Abdul Latif delivered a small sheep to Lalla Fatiha's door. That began the systematic zakat.

From then on, Lalla Fatiha and her children could hardly make a move without Abu Illya, his wife, or his children knowing. When money was short for the coming school term, an envelope was delivered to the orange door. When the oldest married daughter fell ill during the final months of her pregnancy and needed special food and medicine her husband couldn't afford, Abu Illya set up a credit line at the pharmacist. When the second youngest daughter discussed leaving school to apprentice herself as a maid, Um Illya was sent to speak to Lalla Fatiha about the need for her daughter's education in the fast-changing world that was modern Morocco. Each week, Abu Illya deposits sacks of flour at the orange door on his way home from the bakery. Illya's sister Khadija tutors the little girls in mathematics; Khalid, the youngest brother, tutors the children in English, his best subject.

After a few years of help, Lalla Fatiha reconciled herself to the omnipresence of Abu Illya's zakat after she tired of the lectures she received when he realized that she had not sent word to him when she lacked for anything. Again and again he told her: "This is only temporary. When your Abdul Rahman finishes the Bac then he can be responsible for you. If he or his brothers don't get an education, how can they support you or the little girls on an errand boy's or a dustman's wages? Little ventured, little gained. We must be willing to invest if we want a return. What would Si Mukhtar say if he knew you thought of sacrificing the children's education?" Weary Lalla Fatiha would nod her head, try to kiss Abu Illya's hand, and be brusquely told to get back to her work.

"But what about Lalla Fatiha?" I asked. "Doesn't she resent all the charity? Always taking from others?" Illya was astonished at the question. "This isn't charity," he retorted. "This is zakat. Our honor is to proffer zakat, her honor is to use the zakat. All is provided by God, not by us. This time we have sufficient for our needs; later it may be Lalla Fatiha's turn to provide for us when her children are educated and work as doctors and engineers, and Abdul Latif and I are worn out from working in the bakery. God provides for us; he gives us our wherewithal, our brains, our health with which we work. If we have enough, then we share with our neighbor. If we lack, our neighbor is to share with us. Lalla Fatiha helps us be better Muslims, and in turn is a good Muslim herself. Isn't this the way Islam is to be lived?"

An American Woman on the Hajj

Michael E. Jansen

Each year, between the eighth and thirteenth days of the twelfth month (Dhu al-Hijjah), more than 800,000 Muslims from all parts of the world arrive in the Hijaz, the area where the holy cities of Mecca and Medina are located, for the pilgrimage (hajj). A lesser pilgrimage (umra) can be made at any time of the year and marks the respect the Prophet Muhammad paid to the city of Mecca. —Eds.

I was in Mecca at last.

Before me was the *Ka'ba*, a great black cube partly submerged in a torrent of white-robed pilgrims circling round and round. Around us, like a dam containing the torrent, stood the massive walls and the seven slim minarets of the Sacred Mosque. High above, the muezzin began the evening call to prayer: *"Allahu, Akbar!*—God is Most Great!" Up on the hills the thin reedy voices of the muezzins in the smaller mosques joined in, each voice picking up the call in a fugue of prayer soaring into the golden crest of the afternoon.

In response, the crowds circling the Ka'ba slowed and stopped while new thousands flooded into the courtyard. In unison we bowed, fell to our knees and touched our foreheads to the earth, the familiar words of prayer filling the courtyard and cloisters with the hoarse whisper that spilled out into the streets of the hushed city.

Like most pilgrims, I could barely resist the desire to pay my formal respects at the Ka'ba immediately, but the crowds were so dense that I thought it wiser to wait. In the interim I stood in the arched cloisters and looked out at the marvelous spectacle taking place in the great courtyard before me.

The center of the spectacle, of course, was the Ka'ba, shrouded in black silk, with a wide band of golden calligraphy two-thirds of the way to the top. Just that morning, the Ka'ba had received its ceremonial washing and, as is

Adapted from "An American Girl on the Hajj," *Aramco World Magazine* 25, no. 6 (November-December 1974).

customary, the corners of the covering had been raised for the duration of the Pilgrimage, exposing the dark-gray blocks of Mecca stone, of which it is constructed, roughly cemented together.

Around the Ka'ba, following their *mutawwifs* (guides for pilgrims) and repeating the customary prayers, swirled men and women of every race and nation, from every corner of the earth. There were brown men, black men, yellow men, and white men; some young, some old; some with the bearing of ancient patriarchs, others with the faces of medieval peasants and warriors, many with the clean-shaven look of modern businessmen. It was as if the sea had risen in a great tide around the world and swept us all to Mecca and into the whirlpool spinning about the massive black cube.

After a short time I realized that the crowds were not going to diminish, and decided to delay no longer. Leaving the cloisters, I walked along one of the nine broad stone walks that lead to the wide marble oval pavement which surrounds the Ka'ba. I tucked my sandals (which I had removed before entering the mosque) into the gravel near a bench. Then I engaged a mutawwif and, left shoulder to the Ka'ba, edged into the current.

Although this first ceremony is a moving experience for a pilgrim, the *Tawaf*, or "the Circling"—that is, making seven circuits around the Ka'ba—is not, at that point, considered part of the Hajj. Along with the *Sa'y*, or "the Running," it comprises the *Umra*, or "Lesser Pilgrimage," which is a gesture of respect to the Holy City made by the pilgrim on his first visit. It begins, traditionally, with the pilgrim's kissing or touching the Black Stone, but on that night there was no question of my getting near enough to touch it. The throng, gently but firmly, had carried me off.

Despite its size, the Hajj multitude is surprisingly gentle. Occasionally, as one group or another would attempt to cross the mighty stream, there would be an angry wave of pushing and jostling, but even that was understandable. To many pilgrims, who may never have gone further than the next village before making the Hajj, getting lost or separated was an experience too terrifying to contemplate.

On the seventh circuit the mutawwif steered me from the center of the stream to the outer bank and found a place for us to perform *Salat*—the recitation of a prayer while bowing, kneeling, and touching the forehead to the earth. This Salat, which completes the Circling, is performed near the Place of Abraham, a spot where Abraham prayed.

For the next rite I mounted the small rocky hillock called al-Safa, turned toward the Ka'ba, raised my hands in salutation, and declared my intention to perform the rite of Sa'y. Then, descending from al-Safa, I entered the Mas'a, a spacious promenade bisected lengthwise by two narrow, railed pathways for the wheelchairs of the infirm, and joined another throng of believers, walking briskly to al-Marwa, another hillock, in the first of seven Runnings between the hills.

This throng, I found, was more relaxed than the crowds outside. Although there were occasional groups of determined peasants from the Anatolian steppes or the plains of the Punjab who, arms firmly interlocked, swept other pilgrims aside as they rushed at a headlong pace down the Mas'a, most were exceptionally considerate. Children unconcernedly followed their parents; proud fathers bore infants in their arms and on their shoulders; the old, the blind and the crippled, who either could not afford or would not countenance wheelchairs, slowly but safely made their way.

After the Sa'y, I visited the Well of Zamzam, where Hagar, the mother of Ishmael, found water. I descended the white marble steps to a large, divided chamber with a long pipe equipped with brass spiggots running along its back and side walls. Crowding round the taps were ample Egyptian women, who wept as they splashed themselves and everyone else with the warm water, which I found had a slightly brackish smell but little or no taste. At the top of the steps I saw two men wringing out a long piece of white material: "A burial shroud," someone said, explaining that some simple folk bring their shrouds to Zamzam because they believe that a shroud bathed in its waters will help them gain entrance to Paradise.

In the dark corners of the mosque, pilgrims slept wrapped in blankets, shawls, and even prayer rugs. During the Pilgrimage, the Sacred Mosque becomes a part of the daily life of the pilgrims as well as a center of Pilgrimage. This may seem surprising to Westerners, but to a Muslim religion is a part of living; it is not folded up like a churchgoer's Sunday best until the next service. A prayer rug may serve as a bed, blanket, shawl, or turban, as well as for devotions. Only the Quran is kept apart, wrapped carefully in a cloth and placed respectfully on top of one's goods.

As I walked on, the peace and serenity of the mosque crept into my heart. At the rail of the dim gallery above the cloisters, a man sat facing the Ka'ba, transfixed, a Quran in his lap; and an Iranian woman stood alone quietly weeping. In the courtyard, where great throngs still circled the Ka'ba, the sedan chairs of pilgrims unable to perform the Tawaf on foot bobbed above the heads of the multitude like boats plying through waters.

The next morning, with the thunderous refrain *"Labbayk, Allahumma, Labbayk!"* the Pilgrimage began. Thundering through the streets of Mecca, the crowds swept out of the city in a great river that flowed along the broad road to Mina and past Jabal al-Nur, "the Mountain of Light."

For many, the Pilgrimage begins with this first glimpse of Jabal al-Nur, where Muhammad received his first revelation. To them, the mountain where the Prophet was summoned to God's service finally becomes a reality. Here Muhammad was commanded, "Read: In the name of thy Lord Who createth; createth man from a clot. Read: And thy Lord is the Most Bounteous, Who teacheth by the pen, teacheth man that which he knew not." Here, with these words spoken in this place, Islam began, and here we joyfully responded—*"Labbayk, Allahumma, Labbayk!"*—knowing that God was indeed with us in this lonely, inhospitable valley. The sky was a hard ice blue and the air like crystal, sparkling with the rising dust. Yes, this was indeed a place fit for revelation, an intense solitary place, brown and blue and filled with white-robed believers as far as the eye could see.

With new understanding in our hearts, we streamed into the little desert town of Mina, where Muhammad and his Companions spent the night on their way to Arafat. Following in his footsteps we halted at Mina, set in a steep-sided wadi, barren and brown, only three-quarters of a mile across on the Mecca side but widening into the plain of Muzdalifah. At the narrow end of the wadi stand the three stone pillars, the Jamarat, which represent the three attempts made by Satan to prevent Abraham from sacrificing his son. As the wadi broadens there are streets of pastel-painted buildings, three to four stories high, in which pilgrims are housed. At the edge of the built-up area are the Mina field hospital, the public bathhouse, blocks housing the Hajj Administration, and the vast tent city, sprawling as far as you can see, filling the wadi, creeping up its rugged sides and spilling forth upon Muzdalifah.

I immediately set out to explore Mina and found it fascinating. Stalls selling iced drinks, cloth, ready-made clothing, toys, and strings of beads lined the streets. There were goods from the world over: watches from Japan, bananas from Guatemala, apples from Lebanon, citrus fruits from Jordan, bolts of cloth from Hong Kong and India, dresses and shirts from Africa, chocolates from Switzerland, sandals from China—an accumulation of goods as heterogenous in origin as the pilgrims themselves.

In the afternoon I also explored the tent city where most of the pilgrims live—and found that it was a city in every sense of the word, with broad avenues and narrow streets, sanitation facilities, and running water. Along the highway I saw free dispensaries, first-aid tents, a small Swiss plane spraying the area against fleas and flies, and some helicopters hovering overhead to help ambulance teams find pilgrims in need of medical attention. The tents were of all shapes and sizes, and for many purposes. There were striped tents and flowered tents and multicolored tents; soaring pavilions with beautiful patterns inside and long low halls with partitioned rooms; tents for sleeping and tents for eating; privy tents and bathing tents.

Before dawn the next day—the ninth of *Dhu al-Hijjah* and the second day of the Hajj—I rose to the call of prayer, made my ablutions and performed the Salat, and opened my Quran to the introduction to refresh my memory on the life of the Prophet, particularly on his Farewell Pilgrimage, which Muslims have ever since tried to emulate. Thus, it became my practice during the Pilgrimage to turn to the Quran, or to a book on the meaning of the Prophet's message, whenever I felt puzzled or when I had a problem.

At about eight o'clock I tossed my gear onto the roof of one of our mutawwif's little coaster buses, climbed up, and made myself comfortable among the bedrolls and bundles of the pilgrims inside the bus. The street was jammed with cars, buses and trucks brimming with hajjis and their goods waiting for the signal to begin the journey to Arafat. The din of the engines drowned out this signal—but there must have been one, for in one instant we all were moving, sailing smartly and smoothly above the traffic, waving gaily to other happy passengers, all part of the mighty river flowing from Mina to Arafat. *"Labbayk, Allahumma, Labbayk!"* cried a group of Africans from the back of a small truck, and the multitude joined in, each nationality responding in its own accent, to the divine call issued more than thirteen centuries before: "And proclaim unto mankind the Pilgrimage. They will come to thee on foot and on every lean camel; they will come from every deep ravine" (Quran 22:27).

At Arafat I set out at once for Jabal al-Rahmah, the Mount of Mercy, where, at the foot of a dark granite hill on the edge of the plain, the Prophet had stood to deliver the sermon during his Farewell Pilgrimage. At the base stood many pilgrims, eyes uplifted to the dazzling white pillar erected near the top of the two-hundred-foot slope. Some prayed, others sat on mats talking, family groups had their photographs taken, and a knot of Africans, crowded beneath a striped beach umbrella, chanted *"Labbayk."* One mutawwif, leading a long line of Turks, exhorted them through a loudspeaker. Television cameras scanned the goings-on from a scaffold, perched high above our heads. Keeping pace with me was an obviously sophisticated pilgrim, chatting animatedly to his wife, apparently oblivious of where he was and what was happening around him. But then he looked up and, seeing the Mount just before him, stopped in his tracks and burst into a flood of tears.

As I began to ascend the Mount, a tall African generously shared the shade of his green silk umbrella with me and I recalled the Prophet's words: "Above all else, never forget that each Muslim is the brother of all others: for all Muslims in this world form one race of brothers."

Back in the tent, I found that the Pakistani ladies—now part of my group—had not visited the Mount of Mercy. Instead, they sat on their bedrolls, reading their Qurans. For me, the meaning of those words was enhanced outside in the streets of Arafat, at the foot of the Mount, and on the barren plain enclosed by stark, azure mountains on three sides. I went out and walked alone until I found a place I could peacefully stand and gaze at the Mount, in my own private commemoration of the *Wuquf*, or "the Standing," of the congregation for the Prophet's sermon. There were many of us who stood in the streets of Arafat that day, under the noon sun, recalling that God had given His last revelation to Muhammad at Arafat: "This day I have perfected your religion for you, completed My favor upon you, and have chosen for you Islam as your religion" (Quran 5:4). When they heard those words, the Prophet's Companions wept, for they knew that he would not remain with them long, and every pilgrim who has "stood" at Arafat since has felt the same sense of loss.

After the noon prayer, the multitude at Arafat seemed to heave a great sigh of relief, and the atmosphere changed from grave devotion to lighthearted serenity. There is a lovely story about the Prophet which explains the transformation at Arafat, a story few pilgrims know, but the essence of which they all feel in their hearts.

While he was at Mina during his Farewell Pilgrimage, Muhammad seemed glum, but his Companions, who felt his mood, hesitated to ask him why. At Arafat the next day, however, the Prophet's face glowed with happiness. One of the Companions asked him what had happened, why his spirits had changed from gloom to gaiety. The Prophet replied that the day before he had been depressed because he had asked God to forgive the pilgrims all their sins and God had replied that He could forgive only the sins against Himself. He could not forgive the sins they had committed against one another. But now He had said that He would forgive all the sins of the pilgrims at Arafat. And from that day onward pilgrims have left Arafat free men and women, reborn and without sin, for there is no concept of original sin in Islam.

Back in our compound, I found the magic of Arafat had made everyone serenely happy. A picnic atmosphere had swept across the plain. In our tent we were served enormous dishes of lamb and chicken cooked in spices with rice, and a sweet saffron-rice pudding. After lunch the streets filled with people, long trains of pilgrims marching behind banners proclaiming their nationalities, families gathering in the shade of the little striped awnings attached to their cars, men and women sipping tea in refreshment tents.

At dawn a cannon announced the morning prayer. In the chill mist that blanketed the plain, I began to walk from Muzdalifah to the pillars at Mina. In order to keep their little groups together, some hajjis had raised distinctive standards on long poles: teapots and paper bags, rags and plastic bottles, posters and flags were solemnly held aloft. The problem of losing hajjis was solved by the mutawwifs in various ways. Some gave their charges little cards with their addresses at Mina which lost hajjis could present to the nearest Boy Scout or policeman so that they could be sent to the correct tent. Desert tribesmen traveled in tight little rings, women and children on the inside, men forming an elastic outer circle. But it was the Iranians who had devised the most ingenious way of keeping track of their ladies: they simply stitched their addresses onto the back of the billowing white cloaks in which the women enveloped themselves from top to toe.

Because I was well ahead of the mass of pilgrims coming from Muzdalifah, I was able to approach the Jamrah quite easily. I took careful aim and cast the first seven pebbles home: one . . . two . . . three. They flew in shallow arcs . . . tic . . . tic . . . tic as they hit the pillar. I felt complete solidarity with the people all around, both great and humble; people who were at that moment striking out at their weaknesses, their misdeeds against God and one another . . . tac . . . tac . . . tac against the pillar. The earnestness with which the majority of the pilgrims—peasants and villagers of Africa and Asia—approached the Jamrah shamed the more worldly of us who, feeling foolish, initially hesitated on the edges of the crowd. But with each stone I felt more strongly the link between past and present, between the Patriarch Abraham and this vast assemblage: the millennia dissolved and the good intentions and resolutions of all the pilgrims who had cast their stones over the ages were fused into the collective Muslim will to follow "the Right Path."

As it was now time for the Sacrifice, I explained to my companion that I would perform it only if I could arrange to have the animal cooked, eat a part of the meat, and give the remainder to someone who was less fortunate than I. (Some hajjis follow this procedure, but most leave the carcass with the attendants at the Place of Sacrifice for distribution among the poor.) We proceeded, therefore, to the Place of Sacrifice, purchased a sheep from one of the bedouin shepherds who were selling their flocks, sacrificed it, and took it, cleaned and ready for cooking, to the proprietor of a shop where a charming rascal called Hajj Muhammad Atiq had agreed to cook it for me.

As we watched the meat cook, an old man, obviously without means, drifted by, clutching a loaf of bread from the bakery next door, and asked Hajj Muhammad timidly the price of the meat. But it was too costly and he turned to go. My companion leapt up and offered him some of our meat as it lay simmering in the dish. Shakily the old man held out a nylon bag while Hajj Muhammad spooned in pieces from the pan. "Go in peace," the old man said as he ambled away.

After eating our fill, we left the shop of Hajj Muhammad in search of a recipient for the rest of the Sacrifice. As we thrust through the crowd in the street, a thin dark hand reached up from the pavement and plucked at my sleeve: "Some bread please, some bread." And we gave the lot to this crippled man, sitting on a mat with his crutches beside him.

After packing some clean clothing into a bag, I caught a bus to Mecca to perform the Tawaf and Sa'y of the Pilgrimage. The ride gave me a moment to reflect on what had happened to me since I had left Mecca two days earlier. Before I had embarked on the Pilgrimage, its rituals seemed to me just so many curious exercises. But as I participated in the events of the Pilgrimage, the meaning of these rites unfolded, my understanding of Islam was deepened, and I learned more fully what it meant to be a Muslim. Indeed, this is why God had commanded Muhammad to issue the call for the Pilgrimage: "That they [the pilgrims] may witness things that are of benefit to them" (Quran 22:28).

Back at the Mecca Hotel, the time had come to doff the Ihram, shower, and put on fresh clothing for the Tawaf: "Let them make an end of their unkemptness and pay their vows and go around the Ancient House" (Quran 22:29).

The courtyard was not so crowded as it had been when we performed the Umra. After engaging a mutawwif I began the circuits, graceful gray and white pigeons fluttering overhead. From the minarets above us the call to prayer pierced the silence of the Sacred Mosque and my guide led us to the edge of the oval floor, where we prepared for the congregational devotions of the evening Salat. In the radiant evening the throng stood and knelt in unison round the house built by Abraham to proclaim the oneness of God and the unity of mankind. At that moment I understood why Muslims turn toward this great black cube in prayer.

Back in Mina I called on a man recommended to me by a friend, a man learned in the ways of religion, whose face simply radiates his inner peace and goodness. "When you come here," he said, "you are calling on God, you are entering His House. The *Talbiya* is your application for admittance to His House, a request for an appointment with Him. And that you were able to make the Pilgrimage at all is a sign of God's willingness to accept you. It is a very great blessing for you, for all of us."

Sayyida Zainab: The Chosen of Bani Hashim

Muhammad Fahmi Abd al-Wahab
Translated by Evelyn A. Early

Sidewalk vendors sell popular religious tracts outside all major mosques. These include pamphlets on the lives of Muslim saints; collections of Prophetic sayings; and discussions of Islamic morals, Islamic medicine, Islamic astrology, and so on. Some of the more popularized may be a random collection of Islamic and folk traditions on such diverse subjects as appropriate foods for a pregnant woman, auspicious astrological times to travel or cut business deals, and proper duties of wives and husbands.

While some collections may reflect heterodox views and are probably not condoned by religious authorities, the lives of Muslim saints and the collections of Prophetic sayings recount standard interpretations of history which diverge from standard versions only to add human interest. Such a pamphlet is "Sayyida Zainab: The Chosen of Bani Hashim," by Muhammad Fahmi Abd al-Wahab. The particular copy used for the translation was purchased near the Hussein mosque in Cairo in 1977 from a pushcart bookseller who was doing a lively trade with middle- and lower-class Egyptians.

The pamphlet recounts the story of Zainab, an early Islamic heroine, the daughter of Fatima (the daughter of the Prophet Muhammad) and Ali (the nephew of the Prophet and the fourth ruler of the Muslim community). All were in the Bani Hashim clan. Zainab is lauded for her keen insight derived from her deep faith, a common feature of Muslim and other saints. She is also renowned for her bravery at the battle of Karbala. There, Zainab's brother Hussein was martyred and followed in the line of Shi'a Imams— the first of whom was Zainab's father, Ali.

The following two selections, on Zainab's prophetic insight and on her bravery at Karbala, chronicle some of the traits which have made Zainab a revered saint in Islam. —Eds.

Excerpted and translated from the pamphlet *Sayyida Zainab: The Chosen of Bani Hashim* [al-Sayyidah Zainab ʿaqīla Banī Hāshim]. Cairo: Dar al-Salām, n.d.

THE PROPHETIC INSIGHT OF YOUNG ZAINAB

Zainab was the best and the purest—springing from the Holy Family and placed in the care of her famous grandfather, the Prophet Muhammad. The beneficent God showered Zainab with His grace. With exquisite care from her renowned father and her mother, Fatima Zahara, no other young woman could succeed as much as the child Zainab did in her refined environment.

Her pure upbringing and her unshakable faith revealed for her the light of truth, which was then her companion from the dawn of her birth.

The child's capabilities increased until she grasped, through her deep insight, the inspired, prophetic wisdom of her pure descent.

History mentions that, as a child, Zainab was able to recite passages from the Quran—after listening to her father. At such a moment God inspired Zainab with the meaning of the verses, and the understanding shone in her face. Even as her father explained the Quranic meaning to her, her face reflected understanding. Her father was amazed when the Chosen One, the child Zainab, said to him seriously and with dignity: "I already know that, father. Mother explained it to me, as she prepared me for the future." And the father did not know what to say. He remained silent, and his heart trembled with compassion and affection.

THE STORM OF EVENTS

And the Chosen One, the child, matured and witnessed the most critical events in the history of Islam. Before she became an adult, earthshaking events had washed over her from every direction. And the child stayed in her family's house, caring for her siblings.

And the days passed until the day when the Prophet died, a day heavy with misery. And Zainab, the Chosen One, sat on her mother's high bed, a blanket of fear and emotions swirling around her, until the house recovered from the loss of the presence of the Prophet. History mentions that Zainab's mother, Fatima Zahara, initially rejected and denied the news of her father's, the Prophet's, death. We know that Zainab did not leave her bed except to go to the Prophet's tomb to cry. And every time, she took a handful of earth from the tomb and put it on her eyes and face as she implored and recited:

> Whoever smells the earth of Ahmad, smells calamities poured out on disasters the extent of time, the days the nights.

And Zainab cried, and her weeping caused her brothers and sisters to cry, as well as the entire household, and all Muslims, until they all cried—the exemplar of grief, "the five in history."

> Adam cried of grief and regret.
> And Noah cried.
> And Jacob cried, as did his son Joseph.
> And Yahya cried, fearing the fire.
> And Fatima.

And historians add to these Ali Zayn al-Abidin and the father of Hussein.

Only a few months had passed when Zainab's mother joined her father, the Prophet. The disaster of losing her mother distressed Zainab's soul. As pain engulfed her from every side, she remembered her mother's last wish on the deathbed, for Zainab to stay with her brothers and be a mother to them. And when was that?

That happened when Zainab was only ten, but her Islamic upbringing had matured her earlier than usual so that she did not lack for nurturing emotions. So this child Zainab took the place of her departed mother. She was to Hassan and Hussein, as they grew up, the equivalent of their mother, as she was also to her young sister, Um Kulthum.

KARBALA AND THE VALLEY OF DEATH

Hussein and his family came to the valley of death—Karbala, with the Chosen One, Zainab, and her sons close by, surrounding him, and with his sons and brothers and friends; and behind them the women and children. And Hussein stood before 4,000 from the army of Ibn Zayad and the People of Kufa. . . .

Hussein called in a loud voice: "Listen to my words and do not make haste. Then, judge and do not hesitate. God, from whom the Quran descended, is my protector. He is the protector of the faithful."

And when the voices of his wife and brothers and children, all crying, reached the Imam Hussein, he sent them Ali Akhbar and Abbas, instructing the two of them: "Quiet them. Do not let them carry on with their crying." When the family had quieted, the Imam turned to the Kufa army and said: "Look at who I am. Then ask yourselves whether my death is warranted. Protect the women of your Prophet, and the family of the believers in the Prophet."

. . .

And the Imam remained patient in the desire to do God's will. And he said as he lifted his hand to the sky, blood flowing from it: "God will avenge this killing of kinfolk and this sacrilege."

And thus happened the assassination of Hussein and his companions one by one, and the bodies of the martyrs were carried to the tent of the long-suffering Zainab. And she saw every martyr—from the least significant to her brother, the Imam.

It was not long before they carried in and placed the bodies of her four dead sons before her.

She had lost her family. There was nothing for her to do but to recite the words: "I am the Lord God and all that is in this world returns to me."

For the entire concern of Zainab was to be faithful to her brother, the Imam.

New Year's Day at Ali's Shrine

Robert L. Canfield

Celebrations marking the birth or death anniversaries of saints are held throughout the Muslim world. These festivals (mawlids) resemble large fairs. If they are held in a rural locale, tents are erected to shelter different groups of saintly descendants or pilgrims from afar. Merchants flock to the festivals, displaying all kinds of wares to tempt young and old—trinkets, toys, foods, drinks, lotions, cloth, amulets, souvenirs, and services to the passersby. Sometimes carousels and carnival rides are carted in. Every day different folklore groups perform, and traditional music blends with the contemporary sounds emanating from portable radios. Children are treated with firecrackers, dolls, drums, or new clothes and always—whatever the occasion—sweets.

The air of suppressed excitement also causes tensions to run high. Parents, nerves weakened by days of their children's anticipation of the pleasures to come, react with irritation at the slightest snag in their plans. Children plot their escape to the street with their saved pennies. Extended families arrange complicated logistics of departures, arrivals, and meeting places for tea, refreshment, and other needs. —Eds.

The most elaborate celebration of a saint in Afghanistan takes place annually at the shrine of Ali in Mazar-i Sharif on *Naw Roz*, or New Year's Day.[1] I was privileged to witness the activities there in 1968.[2] Naw Roz takes place at the time of the spring equinox each year and technically is not a religious holiday—at least for Sunni Muslims, the sect which dominates Afghanistan. But in Mazar-i-Sharif the day is celebrated by Sunni and Shi'i Muslims alike. The Shi'a have always observed it as a holiday, believing it to have been the day on which Ali, their hero (and the son-in-law and cousin of Muhammad), finally took office as the Caliph of the Muslim community after years of being deprived of it. Naw Roz is lavishly celebrated by Shi'a elsewhere in Afghanistan and, of course, in Iran, where most people are Shi'a. But in predominately Sunni Afghanistan the Naw Roz ceremonies held at this shrine, the nation's greatest, have fallen into Sunni hands; as long as anyone can remember it has been a Sunni-controlled event.

What I saw and heard there combined importunate solitication for grace with all the elements of a carnival. My memory of Mazar-i-Sharif is not of a place but of an experience—sights, sounds, smells, claustrophobic fears amidst the shoving crowds. Legions of people of all classes had come from everywhere: Herat, Hazarajat, Kandahar, even Pakistan and India. There were Sunnis and Shi'a (but no Isma'ilis); men in starched suits but without a head covering (symbolizing their Westernized orientation), their wives in brightly colored Western dresses, their children in new clothes; women in saris; men in suits not pressed for a year, wearing Karakul hats (the badge of the bureaucratic class and petite bourgeoisie); and, of course, thousands of ordinary Afghan peasants and nomads—Pushtuns, Tajiks, Hazaras, all in pantaloons and wearing their distinctive turbans, their wives in chadaris, the ankle-length veils that secluded them from the gaze of strangers. The streets were filled with the mingled odor of human flesh, kabab, smoke, urine, feces, and hashish and with the sounds of crackling charcoal fires being fanned in long trays on the sidewalks, the clanging bells of horsedrawn carts warning the throngs ahead, and the shouts of boys selling fruits, bread, nuts, sweets from carts that blocked the sidewalks or from overladen trays carried on their heads.

Tea houses resounded with the shouting of waiters and guests calling out orders; with the raucous jokes of reunited friends; with the friendly warmth of total strangers (when I came into the place where I stayed people crowded up a bit to make room for my sleeping bag). The buzz of conversation continued long into the night: about the auspicious timing of this Naw Roz, as it fell on a Thursday, that is, the eve of Friday, the Muslim sabbath; about an old *malang* (someone who has withdrawn himself from the world and might have supernatural power) who had always come every year, they said, and never asked for anything, always insisting that he had no needs, but who this year, ominously, had not appeared. People commented on the inflated prices—a young religious student gathered up his things and left when he learned that there was an extra charge for spending the night in our tea shop.

The religious focus of all this busy humanity was the shrine itself, a building of intricately crafted blue tile, which workmen painted and trimmed and cleaned long into the night of Naw Roz Eve. Here Ali is buried—one of seven places where he is buried (to spread the blessing around to more people, I was told). Here many other, lesser-known saints are also buried—one of them in a tomb forty steps under the shrine, a martyr who lies as he fell, still bleeding, they say. Around such dazzling architecture and holiness a thousand pigeons swarm, in the trees, on the roof, in the courtyard and on the walls, but leaving scarcely any droppings, so sacred a shrine it is, the Sunnis say (Shi'a say that the pigeons fly to the grave of Abu Hanifa, who formulated the brand of Sunnism to which the Afghan Sunnis subscribe, to defecate there).

The rituals evinced the religious purposes of the holiday. The muezzin's call to prayer five times a day was familiar but loud and distorted as it blared from speakers mounted on the shrine roof. Less familiar to me were the amulet hawkers in the park that surrounded the shrine. For ten afghanis you could have an amulet with your name on it and, always, your mother's name—they won't work right without your mother's name. For the same price, or less, you could buy a more ornate one, longer, with all the names of God printed on it, and the seal of the Prophet, to boot (all of the ones I saw had been printed in Lahore). These you could hang on a string around your neck, pin to your blouse, nail to a doorway, or attach to your cow.

And there were preachers. A man who had no jaw shouted vigorously to a crowd that listened respectfully but, I believe, without understanding. A man who apparently had almost no voice chanted through a microphone attached to his throat, which added a crackling-radio quality to his already raspy voice. A well-fed Shi'ite, wearing a khaki U.S. Army coat and big scarf, preached in the courtyard of the shrine. Singing the achievements of Ali, he held a battle axe in his right hand; with his left he diffidently accepted gifts of cash from his listeners. Two of his students chanted, taking turns, one wearing a black turban, the other a white one. Poor and rich alike listened attentively. Only those of the upper and bureaucratic class really noticed that a foreigner stood in their midst.

But the common laity were not mere spectators. They had not come mainly to hear sermons or to buy amulets; that much they could have done at home, even if the sermons and amulets at home were not as good. They had come to perform rituals. And they did. On the wide court surrounding the shrine, hundreds of people walked around and around the shrine, moving in both directions all night long on Naw Roz Eve. Each person circumambulated the shrine forty times, to bring blessings for the coming year, I was told, or to be cured of some affliction. As the parents walked, their children played tag and romped in the courtyard away from the crowds. In quieter corners of the courtyard men prayed, sometimes singly or in twos and threes, each in the stylized form of Islamic prayer, whispering greetings to the angels on his shoulders, silently reciting verses of the Quran and prayers of supplication and praise, kneeling and bowing, pressing his forehead to the ground. Four men, one of them bareheaded (a mark of the progressive middle class), sat crosslegged on the pavement and recited rhythmically the name of God for several hours: "Allah! Ho! Allah! Ho! . . . " Larger groups of men locked their arms over their shoulders and swayed as they chanted the names of God. Others, mostly women, stood at the doors of the tombs and wept. They shook the locks and chains barring the doors, rattling them to arouse the dead saints so that they would pray for them, hoping that perchance a lock might fall open as evidence that their prayer would be answered.

A less obvious, but no less intense, ritual was the waiting. An old man sat in the dark throughout Naw Roz Eve, coughing and spitting; I didn't see him the next day. Scores of blind people drifted around, as they did all through the holidays, hoping against hope that their turn for healing would come; some of them had kept a vow for a whole year for this occasion, they said. There was talk about the healings; seven on Naw Roz Eve, I heard; more the next day. I witnessed one of them on Naw Roz morning. There was a shout that someone had been healed, and a mass of humanity pounced upon one pitiful soul, scuffling to tear scraps from his clothing while it still held the supernatural essence that had healed him. Somewhere beneath that mass he sought desperately to breathe; when the mass finally dispersed fifteen minutes later, he emerged, his clothing badly rumpled but intact, his face white and taut. He bolted out of sight.

All that was the disorganized activity of individual religious quests. But the ceremony of the Naw Roz morning pulled the mass into one coordinated ritual. Thousands crowded the courtyard; hundreds more watched from second-story windows in buildings across the street. The ceremonies began with the thump and blare of a military band, headed by an honor guard whose right guide was Afghanistan's tricolor flag and whose left was the hand of Ali on a staff, which is said to have supernatural power. An eminent ʿalim (a learned religious authority) sanctimoniously intoned an invocation from the Quran. The military commandant of the province conveyed messages from the king and his prime minister. A mullah exhorted the crowds to morality and uprightness in the coming year, closing with the shout, "Long live His Majesty the King! Long life Afghanistan! Long live the holy law of democracy!" (That cry might again be made today; but in those days Prime Minister Maywandwal was trying to teach the nation "Islamic democracy.")

The climactic moment of the holiday, for which everyone had come, was the raising of a great pole in the courtyard of the shrine. The pole, topped with a large bulb to which colorful scarves had been tied (by people who had donated heavily for the privilege), was wrapped all the way down in bright green silk (donated by a wealthy cloth merchant). Four venerable religious authorities tried to raise the massive pole as a symbol of public worship. As they pulled on guy wires the crowd watched breathlessly, straining vicariously in hope that no mishap or difficulty in the raising would bode ill for the coming year. It took two tries: after the pole had been raised part way, for some reason it fell into the crowd, striking someone who, I heard, was carried away dead; the next time it went up without difficulty. Everyone clapped and threw coins into the air. Some rushed to pull portions of cloth from it. Young men, bareheaded and in expensive clothing, shinnied up the pole to tear more and more of the cloth from it for it was believed now to have holy power. People rubbed handkerchiefs on the pole for the rest of the day, to get blessing, they said. For that they had come from afar.

NOTES

1. An excellent recent study of the history of the shrine is Robert D. McChesney, *Waqf in Central Asia: Four Hundred Years in the History of a Muslim Shrine, 1480–1889* (Princeton: Princeton University Press, 1991).

2. I am indebted to Drs. Mark and Gretta Slobin for enabling me to attend this celebration.

Women and Shrines in Shiraz

Anne H. Betteridge

Islam is often described as a male-dominated religion and most forms of public worship—prayers, Ramadan sacrifices—are predominantly attended by men. The woman's daily tasks and schedule preclude her attendance at the mosque to pray; she typically snatches a few moments when the large noon meal is finished and children are quiet to pray in a corner of her house. Group religious activity is regarded as a favorite outing, and relatives or neighbors like to take a short pilgrimage to a local shrine to gain general religious devotion, or in times of stress, a solitary visit to pray for aid. —Eds.

Muslim women in Shiraz, Iran, are more likely to enter into local pilgrimage (*ziarat*) than are men. In writing about pilgrimage in Shiraz, I at first regarded this fact as rather unimportant, meriting only brief mention and cursory explanation. However, in the course of piecing together the relationship between women and ziarat, I began to realize that the relationship is significant and fundamental to understanding local pilgrimage as I observed it in Iran.

The nature of the association of women with pilgrimage is twofold. First, on a social or behavioral level, women make pilgrimage to local shrines more often than men. Doing so enriches their lives both spiritually and socially. Second, women's local pilgrimages have a cultural aspect which touches the realm of belief and assumptions about the way the world is constituted. Because local pilgrimage is regarded as basically female in character, it is a ritual practice simultaneously suspect and beloved, not totally orthodox but to which many Iranians have a deep-rooted emotional attachment.

Shiraz is located in southwestern Iran; at the time of my residence there the population numbered just over 400,000. The character of religious obser-

Adapted from *Mormons and Muslims,* ed. Spencer Palmer. Provo, Utah: Brigham Young University Religious Studies Center, 1983.

vances in Shiraz, including local pilgrimage, is colored by the fact that most Iranians adhere to the Shi'i sect of Islam and revere the Shi'i imams, a series of men regarded as the rightful leaders of the Islamic community after the death of the Prophet Muhammad. The majority of Shi'a recognize a succession of twelve imams, and the people of Shiraz are no exception to this rule. Most of the shrines located in the city are the tombs of men and women supposed to be the descendants of the Shi'i imams. These descendants of the imams, or *imamzadeh*s, are respected for their nearness to God by virtue of their descent and their great piety. On account of their privileged position, these saints are often appealed to by Shirazis who are in need of assistance, both material and spiritual. Men and women visit the shrines seeking cures, help with personal and family problems, and forgiveness of sins.

Men tend to frequent larger, more important shrines which are considered legitimate from a formal religious point of view. Women predominate at small, backstreet shrines, often ramshackle sanctuaries of doubtful antecedents, mocked by men.

The extent of a woman's participation in and devotion to pilgrimage activity depends on a number of factors. The degree of her religious orthodoxy is important; those with strict backgrounds and orthodox education may regard the practice as a distortion of religion based on ignorance or misunderstanding. Others with a more strictly businesslike or scientific outlook may see it either as a diversion for women who don't know better or simply as a waste of time. A woman's age and stage of life also influence her ability to spend time visiting shrines. It is difficult for those with extensive responsibilities for young children or meal preparation to get away as often as they might like. Class membership alone appears to be less relevant; women tend to show fewer status-group differences in religious behavior than do men. At the shrines one sees well-to-do women as well as those with tattered veils. The expense of their vows and the status of the shrines they visit may vary, but the women are differentiated more by dress and wealth than by the degree of their attachment to pilgrimage.

One of the attractions of visiting local shrines is that it is not a formal, highly structured religious activity. Muslim women's participation in formal religious activities is to some extent circumscribed by rules pertaining to their sex. A woman may not pray, enter a mosque, or touch a line of the Quran while menstruating. For young mothers the care of children and household duties make attendance at the mosque difficult. Should women, usually older or childless, go to the mosque, it is often very hard for them to become deeply involved in the services. There women are physically separated from the men, who sit in the central part of the mosque in front of the speaker. The women may, for example, be on a high balcony at the rear of the hall or seated in a side section of the mosque, often marked off by a curtain. In either case, it is none too easy to see the speaker or hear clearly, especially if the sound is piped to the women's section by a faulty loudspeaker. The occasional presence of children in the women's area and the social atmosphere which may prevail can also affect the seriousness of women's attendance.

Interested in hearing a sermon, I went to the mosque one evening and was directed to a balcony over the courtyard where the men were gathered at the feet of the speaker, who was already seated on the minbar (stepped pulpit). The women around me were chatting, cracking the shells of seeds, and arranging themselves comfortably with a good view. I felt as though I were at the movie house rather than at a serious religious gathering. Needless to say, I was not able to attend to the sermon in detail. This is not to suggest that I agree with the view men sometimes state that women are constitutionally unable to involve themselves in the serious business of Islam. It is simply that the formal, public setting of the mosque, even when a woman is able to attend, works against her involvement.

Rather than attempt to integrate themselves into the male pattern of religious behavior, where they are often assigned the role of spectators and kept on the ceremonial sidelines, women have become very much involved in their own forms of religious activity, which give them greater scope for religious expression and allow them full ritual participation. Among these activities are the preparation and serving of ritual meals, sermons recited by and for women, classes conducted especially for women and girls, and pilgrimage to local shrines. On these occasions women are not relegated to peripheral positions and passive roles.

In contrast to the mosque setting, the structure of shrines and the way in which they are used encourage informal religious activity and allow women more freedom of movement. Particularly during those times of day when men are at work, local shrines become women's territory, popular places to gather and to perform their religious activities, ranging from prayer to Quran-reading classes.

Saturday evening is set aside as the time for visits to Qadamgah, a very popular shrine in Shiraz. At that time a great deal goes on within the shrine building and in its courtyard. Inside, women circumambulate the glass case which marks the footprint of Abbas, half-brother of the third Shi'i imam, Hussein. Off to the side a group of women may be praying while others are seated on the floor playing with children and exchanging news. A few women may prefer to sit alone and weep. Some listen to a sermon which they have paid a blind man to recite for them. Outside in the courtyard people are seated on the ground eating, drinking tea, and sharing a sweet, halva, which they have made in fulfillment of vows.

On one Saturday night when I was seated inside the shrine, two young men entered the building to pay their respects. As they went straight to the glass case, and encircled it, they were the object of intense and decidedly unfriendly scrutiny by the assembled women. The young men soon became uncomfortable, no doubt aware that they, apart from a blind man and the shrine employee, were the only men present. They left abruptly. I was later told by an old man who works at the shrine that men visit it on Fridays when they are not at work.

Even at those times when men are also present at a shrine, women are not cut off from participation in that which is taking place at the sanctuary. In larger shrines, separate rooms, alcoves, or large areas to one side of the entrance or tomb become women's areas as a result of popular usage. There they can enjoy nearness to the tomb and the company of other women without compromising themselves by coming too close to the men who are also paying their respects to the saint.

There is usually no formal central activity, such as a sermon, from which women can be excluded. Activities at a shrine are more a matter of personal choice than group involvement. Women freely circumambulate the tomb and register their requests with the saints;[1] they may also pray, sit a while with friends, or nap if they choose.

There are many reasons for women to be fond of visiting shrines. The opportunity to get out of the house is not least among them. An older woman, not able to get about as easily as she used to, envied me the time I spent visiting shrines in the city. As she put it, "You see something. You say something." In making local pilgrimages, women are able to escape their household tasks and domestic responsibilities for a time and come into contact with new people and situations. While men have varied experience of people in the course of their workday lives, women come into contact with such variety only on outings, such as shopping, visiting, and pilgrimage. Shopping is an end-oriented activity and one in which men often assume an important role. Too much visiting would compromise a woman's reputation, suggesting that she was not seeing to her duties at home, but visiting shrines is a praiseworthy religious act and one which the men of the house or other women would find hard to oppose.

Still, shrine visiting is not viewed uncritically by all men and women. The relative freedom with which women may visit shrines has led to their being viewed as places of assignation. Shrines may be the sites of innocent flirtations or more questionable encounters. I was told, although I was unable to verify the report, that at major shrines such as the tomb of the eighth imam, Reza, in Mashhad or that of his sister Ma'sumeh in Qum a woman may indicate that she is available by wearing her veil (*chador*) inside out. Author Ibrahim Golestan has described illicit goings-on at a shrine in his short story *Sefar-e 'Esmat* (Esmat's Trip). In this story a destitute woman visits a shrine and is approached by a low-level clergyman, who as it turns out is actually a thinly veiled pimp recruiting women. It is sometimes said that the possibility of temporary marriage (*sigheh*) in Shi'i Islam has been exploited to facilitate this kind of relationship. However, these doubts about pilgrimage tend to surface in jokes and offhand remarks. I never encountered a woman who had been prevented from frequenting a shrine because of suspicions regarding her motives.

Apart from the obvious opportunity to get out of the house, women go to shrines for a number of different types of activities—religious, social, and personal. Regularly scheduled events such as Quran-reading classes, prayer sessions, and particular visits are frequently arranged exclusively for women. Women and girls are welcome to take part in others. At these times, women know that programs of religious interest will occur and that a particular shrine will be crowded. The women gathered there are likely to include friends, all contributing to a convivial and supportive atmosphere. The women who visit the shrine share their faith and their sympathy. For example, on one visit to a small underground shrine I met an elderly woman who recounted to every other woman at the shrine in turn the story of her son's automobile accident. Her son was at that moment in the hospital. In each instance, the women comforted her and assured her that her son would be fine, giving her the solace and encouragement she so much needed at the time.

Other pilgrimages occur as a woman chooses and not according to a specific schedule. A woman may prefer to avoid busy days and instead go to a shrine at a time when she knows it will be quiet, facilitating private prayer and communion with the saint. The immaterial benefits of pilgrimage were described to me in various ways. One woman told me that she enjoys ziarat because it is soothing, another described the experience as "heart-opening," and a third assured me that my heart would be enlightened by taking part in pilgrimage.

Anyone having a problem—emotional, spiritual, or material—may take it to a saint in the hope of achieving some solution. The saints are felt to sympathize with men and women whose situations in some way parallel their own in life. Accordingly, women in Shiraz are able to find a sympathetic ear when appealing to female saints. Two shrines in Shiraz specialize in bringing about marriages, and at both the saint in residence was in life an unmarried woman. At another shrine it is said that the pregnant wife of its saint is also entombed there. Not surprisingly, the saint himself is inclined to assist women hoping for an easy childbirth and the birth of a son.

If a woman finds a particular imamzadeh to be helpful, she may continue to seek help at his or her tomb. The relationship established between the woman and the saint may last a lifetime and prove very comforting to her in times of need. She knows that there will always be someone to whom she can appeal.

The relationship individuals have with the imamzadehs is intensely personal, and one of its strengths lies in this quality. On one occasion I was surprised to find a woman shaking the grating around the tomb of Imamzadeh-ye Ibrahim demanding his help. She threatened that if he failed, she would inform his father, the seventh imam. I subsequently learned that the pattern of alternately imploring and haranguing is very common and that people often have personal conversations with the saints and address letters to them.

Clearly one attractive element in the local pilgrimage is the fact that pilgrims can make requests of the imamzadehs. The way in which the asking for and potentially receiving favors proceeds is also important and, as Fatima Mernissi has pointed out, is particularly appealing to women. In making vows at the shrines, women are able to take charge over some aspect of their lives and attempt to bring control into their own hands. A doctor must be paid for his services regardless of success, but a saint is recompensed only in the event that he or she proves to be of help. This is especially important to women who, for one reason or another, be it social, economic, or political, are unable to exert much control in their everyday lives. Even for those strong women who conduct their daily affairs as they wish, there are always discrete events which do not yield to conventional means of redress and on account of which women may seek divine aid. Difficult in-laws, barrenness, the desire for a son, and problems with a husband all may prompt visits to shrines.

The performance of local pilgrimage, then, has much to offer women. On a religious level, it allows them to play a central role in ritual; on a social level, it provides women with an opportunity to visit with one another in an approved setting; and on a personal level, it offers women a place in which to experience contact with divinity and attempt to control their lives in ways meaningful to them as individuals in their own right.

Discussions with men in Shiraz suggested a basic connection between beliefs about women and the character of local pilgrimage. In general, men tended to make disparaging remarks about women's participation in pilgrimage activity. They attributed the amount of time women were able to spend visiting shrines as due to women's leisure, unburdened by men's important tasks. This opinion is related to the general understanding of the nature of women I encountered in Shiraz. On numerous occasions I was told that women are emotional creatures, easily swayed by sentiment and inclined to be irrational. Men were described as serious, likely to reason clearly, immune to emotional concerns. In support of this stereotypical view, I was referred to passages in the Quran concerning women (4:34) and reminded that a woman cannot act as a legal witness (2:282). Two women can serve as one witness, I was told, because two would correct the emotionally colored report provided by only one. I found that women generally accepted this view of their nature, some feeling that the weaknesses were inevitable, others regarding them as tendencies which could be surmounted.

These beliefs are related to views of women's religious behavior. Most men I consulted felt that women place too much emphasis on the social aspects of religious gatherings and are less well educated about Islam in general. Considering the pleasure women derive from the social atmosphere sometimes present at shrines and the fact that they find attendance at the mosque so problematic, these criticisms are not entirely without foundation. However, women's religious activities may be viewed in other, more flattering lights. Women who live opposite the shrine of Seyyed Fakhr al-Din in the south of Shiraz agreed that women make local pilgrimages more often than men (although men could do it too) but felt that, since women have more time for these activities, they developed more faith by doing them.

A more penetrating explanation of women's involvement in pilgrimage was implied by a young man who worked at a local handicrafts shop. He had made a vow to a popular local saint but had not gone to the saint's tomb at a local shrine to do so. When I questioned further, he first voiced the same scorn as other men had: "Women everywhere devote more time to practices such as ziarat than men; women are more idle than men." Then he added a revealing example: If he has a request for a saint, he may send his wife to the shrine to make it for him. She has the time to go, but also "women are without pride." Men have pride and do not like to display weakness or need in public.

It is in keeping with the view of women as more emotional and less rational than men that women perform ziarat to local shrines on behalf of their family members. In doing so they discharge part of their responsibility for the health and well-being of their relatives. This is not to suggest that men are not interested in local pilgrimage or in making vows, just that they express their religiousness in different ways.

The young man's remarks also suggest that much of the behavior at a shrine, such as expressing deep emotion and stating one's needs and perhaps shortcomings publicly, is not in keeping with notions of manliness. In effect, much of what takes place at a shrine involves a female mode of behavior, regardless of whether the pilgrim is a man or a woman. It is these "female" aspects of the pilgrimage which are often called into question. In the course of discussion I had with men at a religious bookstore in Shiraz, the man behind the counter recommended a book to me: *Ziarat: Truth or Superstition?* The title indicates the crux of the problem. Men and some women formally educated in religion are ill at ease with the practice, while many other women are devoted to it. There is no definite proscription of the practice, and some traditions (*hadiths*) support and encourage it. Paying one's respects at a gravesite is laudable, but the way in which it is done during the performance of local pilgrimage is regarded by many as questionable.

In making pilgrimage to local shrines, men and women have the opportunity to argue with their "betters" and, within limits, to challenge the given order of things. They are also able to express their feelings in ways that are otherwise inappropriate. In so doing they are able to shape their ritual practice to their own requirements. The pattern of challenge, harangue, expression of deep emotion, and voluntarism in ritual is foreign to the mosque. The opposition between shrine and mosque is described by Brian Spooner in connection with his descriptions of the religion of the shrine and the official religion, which "contains rules of ritual prayers, fasting, celebration, mourning and general conduct, which concern the will rather than the heart." He identifies the first of these two strains of religion in Iran as unconscious, while the official religion is the conscious religion. I suggest that this opposition is at base a description of the difference between female and male modes elaborated in a religious context.

It is not surprising that funeral observances in which women are involved are more likely to take place within the home or in a shrine than in a mosque. It is not a time for dry observance of the passing of a fellow human being and loved one but a time to rage and lament, in so doing accentuating the sense of one's own life, and this is inappropriate in the formal setting of a mosque.

The way in which shrine space is used at a funeral reflects differences in the styles of interaction between men and women, patterns reflected in overall religious behavior. Men's style tends to be restrained and formal. They sit on folding chairs in the shrine courtyard, facing the officiating priest. They look down, their hands held over their eyes. At times they sob quietly or perhaps engage in muted conversation with the men seated in adjacent chairs. Tea is placed on small tables between the folding chairs. The atmosphere is highly formal and subdued; spaces are clearly defined in keeping with the nature of official religion as Spooner describes it.

In contrast, women at a shrine funeral sit on the floor inside the wall and perhaps around the central tomb. At one end of the room, backs against the wall, sit the grieving women of the deceased's family. Women attending the funeral first approach them, pay their respects and extend condolences, and perhaps sit with the bereaved women for a time and weep with them. Then the women move back as others come to take their place in the "receiving line." As the guests move outward through the rows of seated women, the tone of the gathering becomes less somber until, in the outer circles, women are busily gossiping, catching up on the news of those more distant relatives and friends whom they see only on such formal occasions. All the while the seated women enjoy the tea and ice cream or sherbet that is served to the guests. The intimacy which prevails at women's gatherings is both physical, enforced by the pressure of bodies against one another as women plop down on the crowded floor, and social, as women exchange information and embraces and discuss their personal problems, aches, and pains. Just as the men's behavior suits the character of the "official religion," so do women behave in a way more consonant with the "religion of the shrine."

The fact that women are associated with local pilgrimage in Iran is neither accidental nor incidental. Men are associated with the mosque, religious texts, reasoned theological discussions, formal ritual assemblies—in short, with intellectual aspects of religion. Women's association with local pilgrimage points out that it is bound up with things of the heart, the troubling aspect of life which questions, unsettles, and answers obliquely. Women in Muslim Iran are regarded as frivolous, emotional, irrational, and at times dangerous; the things with which they are associated are consequently dismissed as either inconsequential or at times downright suspect. Even women's dreams are described in Persian as *chap* (unreliable, off the mark; literally, "left").

Women are ritually polluted with the messy business of menstruation and childbirth, but these polluting elements are paradoxically life-giving. Similarly, local pilgrimage is disorderly and informal, but what goes on at the local shrines energizes religion. Ziarat gives scope to the personal and difficult aspects of life and allows both men and especially women to express their emotional sides—to grieve and wail in an approved setting and to celebrate joyously with others.

NOTE

1. I was advised that, to avoid pressing against men performing the same action, women should hold back and not circumambulate the tomb when a shrine is crowded. In this instance, as in so many others, ideal prescriptions and actual behavior often differ markedly.

PART FIVE

Performance and Entertainment

INTRODUCTION

In the Middle East, as elsewhere, art and popular culture express the community's spiritual and intellectual concerns in many varied forms, both public and personal. Cultural expressions may occur in small gatherings, quite private and hidden. Lila Abu-Lughod tells of the women of Awlad Ali in the Egyptian desert, who express their feelings in the private venue of personal poetry—oral lyrics recited in conversations with intimate friends or sung while working alone. Poetry and other expressions may be popularized in public recitations or in the media. Art for the masses can be subject to ideological manipulations. In the public venue of tribal politics in Yemen, described by Stephen C. Caton, war is waged with words as well as with weapons. Here, the poets are shaykhs, the tribal political leaders, and their poetry is a vibrant element of political discourse. Less lively, but of equal political importance, is the bedouin poetry programmed on Syrian, Iraqi, or Gulf television by governments aiming to publicize pure Arab, bedouin heritage.

Some performances depend heavily on shared understandings of key personalities and symbols among participants. The Syrian satirist Darid Laham, profiled by Evelyn A. Early, delights pan-Arab audiences by poking fun at bungling Arab governments. Afaf Lufti al-Sayyid Marsot explains how political jokes serve as agents of social change by creating a repertoire of gallows humor directed at the enemy or occupier.

Radio and television are freely used as channels of political propaganda by most Middle East governments. Television news producers who neglect to lead off the evening news with the head of state's daily routine risk rebuke or even dismissal. Leaders of coups simultaneously storm radio and military headquarters; military dirges on the radio signal an overthrown government more often than a funeral.

The proliferation of home videos and of smuggled satellite dishes still banned by repressive regimes has not only allowed citizens to mitigate government media control but has also forced governments to alter propaganda techniques. For example, Sudanese television featured lengthy speeches by the new military council in the first few weeks following the June 30, 1989, coup. However, when leaders realized that bored Sudanese had turned off the station and taken to renting videos, the ever-popular Egyptian serials reappeared in prime time.

The video has made mass culture accessible, not only in video-junky paradises such as the electronic-age Gulf, but also in remote Syrian and Algerian villages without electricity where generators provide power for crowds huddled around sets. Peasants know of James Bond and Dallas as well as all-time favorite Egyptian movie stars such as Suad Hussni and Mahmud Yassin. The prominence of Egyptian films and television serials means that from Casablanca to Karbala speakers of mutually unintelligible Arab dialects can break into a facsimile of Egyptian colloquial. Egyptian television production has become a multimillion-dollar enterprise, with filming in Greece, Europe, and other locales and featuring favorite Egyptian stars in film after film.

Mass consumption of media brings not only linguistic borrowing, but also shared political and cultural socialization. Egyptian movie classics, known throughout the Arab world, have portrayed preindependence exploitation of the peasant (*Al-Ard*), the new woman with rights to divorce and to personal independence (*Aridu Halan*), and the betrayal of the Palestinians and of the Egyptian post-Nasser bourgeois governments (films of Youssef Chaheen). Egyptian films in the 1950s portrayed the Algerian revolution against colonialism, graphically focusing on the trysts and fortunes of such nationalist heroines as "Djamila." The Nobel Prize–winning Egyptian novelist Naguib Mahfouz is known to many Middle Easterners through his sociological novels of traditional Egypt; his books have been rendered into such popular films as *Wikalat al-Balah*, about a scrap-iron warehouse proprietress, and *Sukkariyya*, about a traditional family embroiled in the life of the back streets of Cairo.

As videos revolutionized electronic media, so some Middle Eastern musicians have electrified instruments and modified presentation to meet the demands of new audiences and venues. For example, in the 1970s in Egypt the *muwashahat* of Sayyid Darwish made their way to the casino stages of Cairo to be crooned to electric guitar by a popular singer who kept the restaurant packed until three in the morning. Until then, the famous Egyptian composer's pieces, classical poetry set to an oriental tonal version of madrigal music, had been performed at a concert hall by a choral group.

The mix of traditional and modern, of old and new expressive forms is inevitable. Philip D. Schuyler demonstrates the creativity of that mix in his discussion of the revival of folk music in Morocco, where traditional melodies have been recast in a new form to appeal to a modern audience. The folk revival has encouraged amateur musicianship; in towns all over Morocco, young men and even young women play instruments and sing—merging their personal music with classic and folk forms. Likewise, as Schuyler notes in his article on marketplace entertainment in Marrakesh, traditional popular locales for art can be adapted as well as the forms of art themselves.

Some selections in this section peer at the inner soul of private songs and poetry, and others look at the mass soul of film and music. But all present examples of expressive experiences in a realm set apart from everyday life. All allow us to see the affective side of Middle Easterners as they laugh, cry, triumph, and despair.

Humor: The Two-Edged Sword

Afaf Lutfi al-Sayyid Marsot

Very little in the Middle East can be separated from politics or religion. Jokes are no exception. Humor revolves around daily events and springs from contradictions and error. Laughter buffers many difficulties and makes the seemingly unbearable— overpacked buses, long lines at the municipal government offices, lost wars—bearable. Luckily for Middle Eastern humorists, politics furnish a store of material suitable for stories, quips, political cartoons, and satire. Here, then, we read about another level of discourse: person to person, "in the street." If in the past satire was the domain of the poet, today it is the domain of the ordinary person. As the author demonstrates, jokes are a window to Egyptian culture. —Eds.

The subject of this essay is one that impinges on our lives every day, a subject that has given politicians and governments many sleeplessness nights, the second question that every Egyptian asks of another Egyptian: namely, the joke, or *nuqta*.

Studying jokes of various nations suggests that we can learn much about the internal situation of a country from its brand of humor. Obviously this is not a brilliant discovery on my part, but I believe that, although there are studies of humor in general, none has been applied to political humor in Egypt or any other Arab country. Thus, the brand of humor or jokes that I consider here pertain to that variety of humor directed either at the person of a political figure; or at an institution having a political function, such as the government, the army, the police; or at a political situation or event of one sort or another. The common ingredient among all these is the element of politics.

A longer version of this article was presented as the presidential address for the Middle East Studies Association in 1980 and published in the *Middle East Studies Association Bulletin* 14, no. 1 (July 1980).

Why, then, examine the joke? Why not be content with examining the political event or the individual concerned? The answer is supplied by Freud and derives from much the same reasons for which a psychiatrist will examine a patient's dreams as an indication of his or her subconscious condition. So, in the same way, by analyzing jokes, one can get evidence of national reactions, that is, social evidence that may otherwise go undiscovered because it is hidden through fear and emerges only in the disguise of a joke. That evidence ranks alongside folk tales, mawwal and zajal, forming the bulk of a folk history and oral evidence.

The crux of my research led me to inquire why Egypt abounds in jokes and has in consequence a reputation, even a notoriety, among its fellow Arab states for levity. What is the fountainhead of all these jokes and, above all, what political function do they perform? And in positing the question and trying to find an answer for it, I learned a number of disturbing things about humor, wit, and the use of both in terms of power relationships within a society, and in terms of the political equilibrium of that society.

"Laughter is after speech the chief thing that holds a society together," we are told. It is part of man's gregarious instinct and its chief manifestation in the form of jokes is one that is social, for a joke must be shared; otherwise, it has no value. The reasons for which we laugh are again different among different authors. Where Voltaire thought laughter "to arise from a gaiety of disposition that is absolutely incompatible with contempt or indignation," Bergson, on the other hand, claimed that in laughter we always find an unavowed intention to humiliate. The ancient Greeks would have agreed with Bergson. Aristophanes, who used satire at the expense of his rival Euripides—as unmercifully as did Voltaire, incidentally—would have agreed that derisive humor is a fine weapon to use against an opponent, for with it one laughs "with the pale ghost of a sneer."

Most of the Greek philosophers and some of the less ancient philosophers such as Hobbes and the Victorians showed a disapproval of laughter and levity as a manner inconsistent with higher thoughts and grave ponderation. They thus ranked it low on the scale of intellectual exercise, scarcely even considering it to be one. One author gave us a reason for this: they were men who hated to be laughed at. Indeed, many of us hate to be laughed at. Those of us who pride ourselves in our ability "to see a joke" and to laugh at ourselves, nevertheless, do so only if the joke is not excessive or too unfavorable. The reason is that when we became the butt of a joke, we experience a feeling of inferiority. Even when the laughter is not derisive, but is "friendly laughter," it is built on the premise of a moment of inferiority on our part and on an impulse for hostility on the part of the person telling the joke at our expense. Freud was the first of many to tell us that humor is generated by hostile impulses. Humorists have even been described as sadists. Certainly an evening of listening to a stand-up comic often confirms that.

Aggression, which in primitive times was overtly expressed by acts of violence, was curbed through the ages, the effects of civilization, and the creation of laws. Today a child may manage to express aggression openly in action or in abusive language; for which the child is presumably punished by censorious adults and is taught to repress natural feelings of aggression toward others, in much the same fashion as one is taught to repress sexual urges. Thus, the instinct for brutal hostility, forbidden by law and society, is replaced either by verbal invective (if one thinks one can get away with it) or by humor.

In brief, wit and humor begin with an intention to injure, which culture requires us to repress and which is censored or inhibited by the superego. There in the unconscious it is disguised, thus escaping the watchful censor, the superego, and emerges in the form of a joke. The release of psychic energy that is no longer needed to suppress the feelings of aggression is laughed off as humor. The better the disguise of the aggressive impulse, the better the joke, for the chief pleasure derived from a joke is the release of the inhibition or the repression. But the anxiety that aroused the original feeling of aggression must be mastered and controlled before reference to it may be enjoyed as humor. A traumatic incident can only, if ever, become the subject of humor when some time has elapsed to allow the wound time to start healing. Some wounds never heal, and humor about them is always offensive.

By surfacing through the sublimation of unwanted impulses, humor becomes a defense against anxiety, a shock absorber, a healthy debunking process, an agent of social change, a means of controlling group behavior (as in times of war or national crises), a means of fostering conflict, a means of building up morale in a group (as in a people under occupation), or a means of demoralizing another group (for instance, the occupiers, in situations giving rise to a repertoire of gallows humor that becomes the symbol of resistance used by a national group against the enemy or the occupier).

That every joke, therefore, has a public of its own and is based on the new interests of the day explains why good jokes frequently fall into oblivion, although years later they may resurface in a new guise to fit the new interest of the day. In the 1960s in Egypt, when supplies of staples, fuel, and cooking oils were scarce, a joke that is familiar in all East European countries that faced the same shortages made the rounds of Cairo. The joke was about a fisherman who caught a fish and brought it to his wife to cook, but she had no oil with which to cook it and no fuel on which to cook it, so the man, in a rage of frustration, threw the fish back into the sea. Whereupon, the fish surfaced and shouted, "Three cheers for Gamal Abdul Nasser!"

Another joke, which I had thought to be a profoundly Egyptian one, was apparently used in some other countries also. The joke appeared in 1955, after the revolution, when the members of the Revolutionary Command Council had become too well known to the Egyptian public, who then stereotyped them all. The story goes that

Abdul Hakim Amir, the Commander-in-Chief of the army, who was said to enjoy hashish, was returning home one night somewhat stoned, when he passed by the statue of the nationalist hero, Mustafa Kamil, who stands pointing in the direction of another square where there is an equestrian statue of Ibrahim Pasha, the son of Muhammad Ali. The statue then called out to Abdul Hakim, "Psst-psst, Abdul Hakim." "Wha-what?" asked a be-fuddled Abdul Hakim. Reproachfully the statue said, "Abdul Hakim, are you not ashamed that I, the hero of the nationalist movement, should have to stand on my feet for eternity when that exploiter of the masses, the feu-dalist, Ibrahim Pasha, is riding a horse? Go tell the Rais that I demand a white horse." A bewildered Abdul Hakim went home and the following morning went to the Rais, Abdul Nasser, and told him what had happened, so Nasser decided to go with him to the statue that night to see if it had really talked. As the two men approached the statue, they heard it say in a resigned voice, "I said a white horse, not a black donkey!"

Jokes in Egypt from time immemorial have been directed against the gov-ernment, against authority in whatever guise it appeared, because it was al-ways oppressive. With authoritarian governments being the rule, aggression or criticism against authority was always dangerous; the joke therefore made an aggression against authority possible. The joke thus represents rebellion against authority and liberation from its pressures. The greater the number of jokes directed at an individual or at an institution, the greater the degree of aggression toward it that motivates such outbursts of humor. In the past, rulers who had recognized that humor was a safety valve, had allowed them to go unpunished. Others, who had understood the incipient rebellion that lay behind them (for instance, Caliph al-Hakim), sent the soldiers out to pun-ish the population. It was said that Nasser made a collection of the all-too-numerous jokes that were cracked at his expense. Few rulers realized that these jokes were not innocent outbursts of hilarity coming from lighthearted subjects, or from people under the influence of hashish, but were really ex-pressions of deep-rooted antagonisms or feelings of resistance, if not rebel-lion, against them. How is that so?

Belittling enemies or the objects of the feelings of aggression, thus making them seem small, inferior, despicable, or comic, is, in a roundabout way, a means of dominating them through laughter when they cannot openly and consciously be attacked. Humor is therefore the unconscious means of reveal-ing opposition toward the object of the joke. When that degree of aggression is heightened, as after some traumatic experience, then the reaction differs among different peoples and, consequently, among different countries.

In Egypt, and in the rest of the Arab world, humor is then aimed not solely at the person or persons held responsible for the catastrophe, but also at his wife or mother, so that not only is the person diminished, but also his manhood is called into question, and his *asl* (lineage) is equally slighted. That is a theme that might well go back in the past to pre-Islamic practices and the use of satirical poetry, *hija'*, the poetry par excellence of the Arabs.

Hija' was an element of tribal warfare as important as the fighting itself. The satirical verses of a poet in Jahiliyya days were believed, through his oral magic, to be as fatal as an arrow that had hit its mark or as fatal as a curse pronounced by a priest. When, later on, the magical utterance of the poet gave way to the lampoon or joke, it retained some of these atavistic associations. Where tribes were said to have withdrawn in shame after listening to satirical verses made up about them, individuals would feel as bad at the lampoons of themselves. Just as one of the bitterest lines of satire in the repertoire of hija' refers to the mother of a *qawm* (group), today that trait appears in jokes against Arab political leaders and their maternal ancestry. But the change in family relationships from the extended family to the single unit has caused that satirical trait to be transferred also to the wife, who becomes more frequently the butt of the joke, thereby casting doubts on her husband's masculinity so that, in a way, the joke castrates him, or renders him impotent by questioning his maleness, and belittles him.

For example, after the war of 1967, Nasser, in an attempt to rally a demoralized nation, used as a slogan the expression, *kulluna Nasir* ("We are all Nasser"), meaning that all Egyptians should unite in a joint endeavor to face the common enemy. The reaction to that slogan was a joke that said a man crept into Mme. Nasser's bedroom and tried to make love to her. She objected and said, "I will call for Nasser." "But, Madame," was the rejoinder, "we are all Nasser."

Where in the past satire or hija' was the domain of the poet with his magical gift of verse, today satire as a lampoon is the domain of the man-in-the-street with his natural gift of wit. It is firmly in the hands of the people, where it cuts across class lines and is a great social leveler; hence, the importance of studying it. We then have the ambivalent situation of a presumably greatly beloved leader such as Nasser, who was the butt of the bitterest satirical jokes invented by the people, expressing simultaneous feelings of admiration and aversion. And because Nasser came from the people, these jokes about him were all the more significant, as it was a recognition in him of elements within themselves that the people disliked. It was the unmasking of one of them rather than the verbal tomato thrown at a king waving from a terrace high above the heads of the crowd. Had these jokes been invented solely by a discontented and dispossessed *ancien régime bourgeoisie* and resented by the mass of the people, they would not have been as widespread as they were; for some degree of benevolence—or the absence of an inhibiting factor that could provoke feelings opposed to the purpose of the joke—must exist as an indispensable condition to the success of the joke. A totally beloved leader would not have been the butt of jokes, or the jokes would not have circulated with such rapidity, unless there were a deep current of hostility toward him among the people.

Moreover, the jokes would not have had the cutting flavor that some of them had. One joke of a particularly offensive nature was told about a new postage stamp that was supposed to have a picture of Nasser. The people complained that the stamp did not stick to the envelopes. Nasser then called in the Postmaster General to investigate the case, and the man spat on the back of the stamp to show that it did stick. "Then why are the people complaining that it does not stick?" asked Nasser. "They are spitting at the wrong side," was the answer.

One can compare the feelings of animosity behind this joke, as well as behind the joke of the "black donkey," for the public well knew that Nasser was a very clever and intelligent man and was certainly not a "black donkey," whatever else he may have been. Both jokes were meant to communicate feelings of hostility towards him, unlike the many jokes that are told about Tito of Yugoslavia, for instance. There, in contrast, the jokes today have lost whatever elements of animosity they may have had in the past and make fun of Tito, but in an admiring fashion, laughing at his sexual prowess and his longevity.

Jokes after 1967 were so numerous in Egypt that Nasser publicly rebuked the population for an excess of wit at a time of crisis. The wit was predominantly at his expense and at that of his generals, who were caught unprepared, although some of it was also at the expense of Israel. There was a psychological need for humor on the part of the Egyptians after the trauma of the Six Day War, for as their collective spirits sank, the need for humor rose. The opposite is sometimes true. Where the Egyptians wanted to lash out in rage against their government and the army that had let them down, but could not, they sublimated their feelings of anger into humor and a multitude of jokes. And while Israel and much of the Western world were trumpeting Israel's victory over Nasser and Egypt, the Egyptians, impotent and helpless for the time being, could only seek spiritual equilibrium by venting their aggression in waves of humor.

I happened to be in New York shortly after that war broke out and saw a button that read, "Visit Israel and see the Pyramids." Like an outraged Queen Victoria, I could only mutter, "We are not amused!" It was too soon after the event to be able to cope with it humorously. On my return to Egypt a few weeks later, enough time had elapsed for humor to circulate and the country overflowed with jokes; and the more Nasser objected to such levity, the faster the jokes flowed.

One of the best jokes was supposed to be a television interview with Moshe Dayan, where a reporter asked Dayan, "General, why did you not occupy the other bank of the Suez Canal as well?" Dayan then (putting one hand over his blind eye to simulate the patch), asked in bewilderment, "Other bank? Where? Where?" The purpose of this joke was obviously to make fun of Dayan's infirmity. However, it also reflected the Egyptian feeling that perhaps Israel could have taken over further chunks of Egyptian territory with as little resistance as they had met in the Sinai, even when they were led by a general who could see through only one eye! By laughing at the whole experience, the Egyptians were exorcising the pain of a military occupation and reducing an unbearable reality to the level of an illusion. This was not self-deception, but an attempt to cope with an unbearable trauma. Far from remonstrating against jokes, Nasser should have encouraged them; for without the safety valve of humor, the population might have risen against him. That such humor was not enough of a safety valve among the generals of the army is clear from the fact that Abdul Hakim Amir was rumored to have attempted a coup against Nasser, for which he was then "suicided."

The fact that humor may deflect overt acts of aggression, or worse still, channel energy away from action of any kind, as happens with mentally disturbed people, is precisely the reason for which fellow Arabs criticized Egyptian levity. I remember some earnest Algerians saying disapprovingly— as indeed did many Egyptians at the time—that Egyptians can do nothing but joke at a disaster. Whereupon, an irrepressible wit said something to the effect that "he who fights and runs away lives to joke another day," a paraphrase that was totally wasted on his audience, who could not understand how anyone could laugh at a time of defeat. They did not laugh when they were fighting their war of independence!

That question opens up new avenues of research as to why some people choose to laugh at a calamity, which is a form of covert action, and others will choose brutal or overt action instead. Is it an either-or situation, or does one follow the other? Is laughter the characteristic of a people that seems constantly oppressed and has thus renounced the option of action? Or does it reveal a greater degree of aggression and hostility, but allied with *hilm* (forbearance)? "Revenge," goes a French saying, "is a dish that is savored cold." Is it simply a different manner of licking national wounds? Or are all of these put together arising from the principle of pleasure deriving from unpleasure? Can humor be linked to a particular class, so that we have working-class humor, bourgeois humor, or urban and rural humor? Is there a qualitative difference in the humor of the *mujamaʿ* (administration building in Cairo) and in that of the *qahwa baladi* (popular cafe)?

When all the jokes come to an end, what then? That is the lull before the storm and is a danger signal that the aggression and anger that are brewing under the surface may boil over, and we have civil disturbance or war.

Eighteenth-century Egypt reveals a pattern of uprisings every decade or so, a pattern that diminished only with the British occupation and the presence of an army in occupation, but continued in the form of brigandage and, after 1918, as riots and demonstrations that went on until World War II. At the same time, humor had become channeled into publications such as *Abu Naddara Zarqa*, which introduced the cartoon at the time of Ismail Pasha; or the writings of Abdallah al-Nadim, the orator of the Urabi revolution, who was said to be capable of arousing a revolution through his oratory, but who also wrote some of the wittiest verses of zajal and the funniest satire. Satire continued to find an outlet in Rose al-Yusuf, in al-Kashkul and Al-Ba'kuka, in the cartoons of Saroukhan and in those of Salah Jahin in *Al-Ahram*. The public, for a joke, was thus widely expanded, just as the pattern of civil disturbance continued in one form or another and was expanded to cover a number of elements of the society that had never before demonstrated—such as the government employees in 1919. The most recent outbreaks were the bread riots of January 1977, when a distressed population took to the streets to demonstrate its anger.

The premise I would like to lay before you then is this: when tensions within a state build to a high level, jokes and wit also build to a high level, frequently bordering on the unrestrained. That level, however, cannot be sustained without damaging the national psyche, and the alternative to excessive humor, coming after a situation of stress, is a period of no jokes; for when they are no longer sufficient as a safety valve, the only release of tension is through action. Humor itself is a release of tension, but in some cases it is not a sufficient enough release because the tension is too high, and action must follow it in the shape of civil disturbance or war. The tension buildup is then turned either outward against a real or invented enemy or inward against those in authority, or against a scapegoat blamed by the people for creating the national stress.

How to measure the degree of tension that could predict action of one kind or another, I leave to a generation of quantitative historians who can compare the speed and number of joke production before and after a crisis and quantify them in such a manner as to measure the degree of national aggression behind the humor. Studies of Black humor, religious humor, the humor of children and the socially disturbed abound, so why not political humor in Egypt or in any of the Arab countries? By using humor as an index for the study of a society, we may be able to predict national reactions and come to an understanding as to the way in which public opinion is molded, as well as to the relationship between those in power and those who have none.

There will always be a normal undercurrent of humor that peoples will have as a consequence of their own internal psychic conditions. There will always be institutions to tilt at—marriage, alimony, mothers-in-law, parent-child relationships—which are constants within a society and about which jokes will vary in their degree of acerbity depending on the strength of the institution in question. But the humor I am talking about is the kind that we can call political humor and which is primarily aimed at the government or at authority figures within a state. It is one thing to joke about mothers-in-law in general and another to joke at Sadat and his wife; and the more jokes there are at his or her expense, the greater the degree of animosity toward them on the part of the population. A certain degree of animosity is standard for a people who have always resented their government, with good reason, since they have seldom, if ever, had good government.

But an excessive degree of humor is a revealing factor that is of a more deep-rooted consequence than the overt adulation that the man-in-the-street vociferously offers when he lines up to watch a motorcade pass. When *ibn al-balad* (the urban man) watches Sadat and waves and shouts "Hurrah for the hero of peace"—in much the same way as he waved for Nasser and for numerous kings before him—and then makes a bitter joke at the expense of Sadat or at the expense of his government, that is a situation that should be watched carefully. At one time when Sadat was in Upper Egypt conferring with Kissinger, a joke was invented which said that while Sadat and his entire cabinet were in Aswan, someone phoned to tell Sadat that his palace had been burgled and everything in it stolen. Sadat said, "Wait a minute." He went to count his cabinet members and returned to the phone to say, "Impossible! I have all the thieves here with me!"

When all the overt adulation is laid aside or unmasked, are we not left with a people which is basically, even unconsciously, hostile to their government, which is seeking to express its hostility through social terms, but fears repression and so disguises it and brings it out exteriorized as a joke, who then communicates these hostile feelings to the rest of that society, even while making them laugh, so as to equalize the tensions which constitute a menace to existence? If that is the case, we can expect such feelings of aggression to build up or to defuse whenever a change of circumstances takes place, when the feelings of hostility change into an acceptance of an improved lot, or explode into outrage at a lot that has worsened or that may have improved but not sufficiently to meet the people's expectations.

Humor is therefore a two-edged sword in society, because of its intimate connection with feelings of anxiety and because most comic phenomena are bound up with past conflicts of the ego. Humor is a warning sign that a people offers its government and those set in authority over it; it is a safety valve which allows the ego to overcome its past fears and it is a means of letting off steam. It is also the clearest indication that a great deal of steam is building up and needs to be treated before it erupts into violence. Perhaps in the future we might be able to quantify the degree of humor that precedes outbreaks of civil violence or the degree of humor that tells a government, "Enough! You have gone too far!" Perhaps we may never be able to do that.

What applies to Egyptian humor applies equally to that of other countries, and makes a study and analysis of humor a valid and necessary chapter in our study of the social histories of peoples. This study will tell us a great deal about the common folk, the ones who are mere statistics in the archives we all love to consult and quote; and who are seldom, if ever, viewed as living, dynamic entities who interact with that institution called the government and who exert pressure on it, even when it exerts pressure on them. For one can never claim to understand a people or its mental condition unless one has grasped the sense of humor and the hostilities it reveals. Let me leave you with a final joke that needs no analysis in order to understand it. It was first told about Charles De Gaulle and later adapted to fit the case of Nasser:

When Nasser died, the question of where to bury him arose during a cabinet meeting. One minister said, "Let us bury him in the tomb of the Unknown Soldier." Another objected, saying, "You can't bury a colonel with a common soldier." A third suggested that he be buried in one of the tombs of the Mamluk sultans. "No! No!" was the objection. "You can't bury the Rais with a slave." Finally running out of burial sites, someone suggested Jerusalem. Whereupon, the rest of the cabinet rose in horror and said, "Never! The last time they buried someone there, he came back after three days!"

Darid Laham: Political Satirist as Modern Storyteller

Evelyn A. Early

The Syrian film and television character "Gawar" has been played over the last two decades by the Syrian actor Darid Laham. During that time, Darid Laham has transformed Gawar from a social comedian to a political satirist whose mounting fury is in step with increasingly sharp criticism of Arab governments by ordinary citizens fed up with the Arab-Israeli conflict and with corruption in home governments. It is small wonder that the theaters in the Gulf and North Africa are packed when Darid Laham's plays come to town; Gawar speaks aloud the thoughts of many Middle Easterners. Some of the more recent Gawar productions are reminiscent of "Saturday Night Live" or of "Monty Python." This article is based on research conducted in Syria in 1982 on popular expressive culture and includes excerpts from interviews with the actor Darid Laham. —Eds.

The contemporary Syrian political comedian Darid Laham's television play videos are always rented out in Syrian video shops as well as in those throughout the rest of the Arab world. His stage personality "Gawar" is that of a lovable, but incompetent, village buffoon. In his trials lie truths, and in his naive comments lie critiques. The critiques are of Arab governments in general but can be seen as barbs at the Syrian Socialist Baathist government in particular. Darid Laham denies any specific criticism of Syria in his work and also discounts suggestions that the Syrians tolerate the personality of Gawar as a harmless escape valve for their frustrations.

Whatever the reason for Gawar's existence as the sole political comedian in Syria, his popularity is undeniable. Here I explore the social background of the actor Darid Laham, the development of his stage personality "Gawar," and the tradition of critique and satire in Syrian culture. Both traditional theatrical forms—such as the coffee house storyteller (*hakawati*) and shadow puppets (*karikos*)—and Gawar use an acceptable art form to satirize and critique a government in power.

THE SON OF A DAMASCENE CHARCOAL MAKER

Today's Syria is ruled by the Baathist party, a party so deeply committed to Arab nationalism that it calls Syria a "region" of the Arab "nation." Regardless of politics, Syrians are steeped in Arab culture and heritage, and the Syrian intelligentsia is a rich blend of cosmopolitanism and classical Arabism. Darid Laham is no exception with respect to his Arabism; however, his background is humbler than that of many other prominent Syrians.

The son of an impoverished charcoal maker, Darid Laham grew up in a traditional district of Damascus and attended the Teacher's College. Upon graduation, he began to teach physics and to act in television comedy. With time, he found his two roles in conflict, and he chose acting. Today, he is a movie star and comedian admired throughout the Arab world. His recent television plays such as *Cheers, My Country* represent development of his stage personality "Gawar" from a comic slapstick figure of the early 1960s to a serious political critic of the 1980s. Left free to operate in what appears to outsiders to be a tightly controlled society, Darid Laham has coined an invincible comic figure.

In a 1982 interview, Darid Laham recounted his youth:

> I was born here in Damascus in a popular quarter in 1934. We had ten children in my family. We were living in a house built in the old Arab style. If you walked through the streets of Damascus in those days, you would find houses built so close together that you could reach out and touch them with your hands.
>
> I was the youngest son. I studied in the Muhsiniyya primary school. In 1945 we moved into the Salahiyya quarter, where I completed preparatory and secondary schools and then the university. During my studies I always worked during the summer at many professions, including as a tailor and as a blacksmith. My father was a charcoal salesman; he traveled to Lebanon on a ninety-kilometer trip—there and back in one trip in one day and night. In the university I studied physics. I developed the hobby of music.
>
> When I graduated with a diploma in physics, I became an instructor because I was one of the highest-ranking students. In 1959 the television director invited me to appear on television with my musical group. It became hard to teach organic chemistry at the university and to appear on television. My students could not believe that their teacher would say funny things on television and then lecture on chemistry. In 1960 I decided to leave the university and become a full-time artist.
>
> In the beginning, my work in television was horrible. We had no idea about television: the people would accept anything because it was new. They would sit mesmerized by the television because it was a novel experience, but with time it became necessary to create substantial programs.

The 1967 war propelled realistic, local-based drama to the forefront and produced new playwrights such as Mamduh Awdah and Muhammad Magut, the poet who writes my scripts. In 1969 we began to think in grander terms and began political comedy, and that is why today you find Gawar known everywhere in the Arab world.[1]

THE DEVELOPMENT OF THE STAGE PERSONALITY GAWAR

Gawar's stage personality underwent a marked development from his first years in the early 1960s, when he was little more than a buffoon, to the late 1970s, when he had become a political satirist. Darid Laham explains that he created a Gawar whom everyone loved; if the authorities had tried to stop the performances of Gawar, the people most likely would have protested. When Darid Laham began to portray Gawar in the early 1960s, the simple comic figure evoked viewer sympathy and affection as he was battered by ill fortune, sometimes brought on by his own tricks. In an early film, *Gawar James Bond*, Gawar joins the daughter of a barber and another adventurous man to play such pranks as bank holdups with a hair-dryer-turned-pistol. The trio has a workroom with exaggeratedly mechanized instruments such as one to call the partner downstairs (drop a ball down a chute to raise a weight to hit a bell). The film's unreconstituted slapstick seldom rises above the waves of shaving cream. However, the lovable personality of Gawar as the proverbial, well-meaning fool so far gone he verges on the clever shines through in the same way it does in later political films. In both kinds of films, he mutters to himself, to the machines, and to the world in general. In earlier films the message is comedy, but Darid Laham's middle-period films have coherent scenarios. For example, in *Samak Bila Hassik*, Gawar is the confidant and protector of a widow woman fishmonger and her daughter. When the unmarried daughter becomes pregnant, Gawar offers to save her reputation and marry her. He tells her: "I will be your husband in front of people and remain your brother before God."

In the beginning, Darid Laham and his group were not sure of the reception they would find. He noted in an interview:

> In 1966 when we presented *Misrah al-Shawq*, we were ready to go to prison. We used the opportunity of a Festival. Some officials wanted to imprison us; some supported us. Hafez al-Assad, then the Minister of Defense (today the president of Syria), and Dr. Nur al-Din Attasi, the President, requested that the officials let us go. They said that we were free artists and that people must listen to us. From there we began our serious political plays, including *Dayya Tishrin* in 1974 and *Dayya Ghurba* in 1976.

Darid Laham attributes his turn from slapstick to political comedy to the situation in Syria:

When we began, we did not want to talk about politics. But the loaf of bread was moldy. [Darid Laham had earlier quoted the Chinese proverb "If you have two piasters, buy a loaf of bread and a flower," saying that when he was a child he had only one piaster and no time for art.] Political events were affecting the price of bread. Now the radio is every place—in the office, the car, the house. When I grew up, there was one radio in my lane. One is not able to escape the radio. Our generation has lived through six wars—1948, 1956, 1967, 1973, 1982, and World War Two. I was five years old when World War Two occurred. It is impossible to live far from these events. Our plays must reflect them.

By the 1970s Gawar had become a political comedian and satirist. *Dayya Tishrin* is a television play in which the village rulers and their regulations are the trials and tribulations of Arab politics (particularly Palestine) writ local. They are writ not only in village governance but also in such village social events as marriages and, of course, feasts. The action unfolds in the square in front of the village *mukhtar* (mayor's) house. In the opening scenes, a soldier plans to marry; the fathers-in-law disagree, not on the dowry, but on what to cook for the festivities. "Political plans" are made for marital happiness whereas a curfew is imposed for "scientific reasons." Since this is a comedy, we learn of these events by group songs and dances, and by Gawar's side comments to the audience. The mixing of politics, science, and the price of meat becomes more tangled in the play before it is resolved.

In *Kassak Ya Watan* (*Cheers, My Homeland;* 1979), the format is similar to a *Saturday Night Live* presentation with "Radio Monte Arab" newscasts interspersed with skits. (The name is an obvious takeoff on Radio Monte Carlo, famed Western/Arabic pop music station with excellent Middle Eastern news coverage.) Gawar portrays a common man fighting with the institutions of the day. When his wife becomes pregnant he clucks over her stomach and talks to the baby in her womb. When Gawar cannot find a job, the government officials say that it is Gawar's fault. When his child dies, the physician denies that the child is dead.

The Gawar of *Cheers, My Homeland* is definitely not the Gawar of *James Bond*. As the actor himself explain in a magazine interview: "Gawar is a pawn; his role changes. The Gawar in *Cheers, My Homeland* is different from the Gawar in the television series, and so on. He is both intelligent and stupid, but despite his clowning there is something quite daring and serious in what he says."[2]

COFFEE HOUSE STORYTELLERS AND SHADOW PUPPETS:
GAWAR AS A CONTINUATION OF SYRIAN CULTURAL
HERITAGE

Why is the personality of Gawar so appealing? Does he strike a chord of classical heritage in the hearts of his Syrian and other Arab audiences? Does he appeal as a slapstick figure in much the same way that Charlie Chaplin appeals to Western audiences? Darid Laham, who denies that there is any influence from either quarter, remarked in an interview that cultural traditions such as shadow puppets were also social critiques but could not have influenced him because he rarely saw them: "I heard about shadow puppets when I was very young. It was a form of television at that time. An old man would bring puppets and a white screen on which to cast their shadows." The presentations were so bawdy that they were restricted to coffee houses, where Darid Laham could not go as a young boy. "Without a doubt, during the days of Ottoman and then French imperialism, the shadow puppet performances opposed the occupying powers and called them foul, derogatory names." As for the hakawati, or coffee house storyteller:

> The hakawati had become much less prevalent. The original reason for the hakawati was the widespread illiteracy of the people. He would sit on an elevated chair and read stories of Antar, Abla, Abu Zayd al-Hilali, and other heroic knights. People love stories of heroes, particularly ones as dramatic as Antar.
>
> The hakawati would read the story of Antar and, as they do in television today, he would stop reading the story at a suspense-filled point. Of course, if the people were literate, they could have taken the book about Antar and read it themselves. But in that time you had maybe two literate people in a lane.
>
> Sometimes the coffee house crowd would divide into proponents and opponents of Antar; sometimes the two groups would fight and splinter chairs on each others' heads. Antar's proponents might prevail on the reader to read one more page until he came to a point where Antar's side won. They would then go home happy and relaxed.
>
> I heard a story once; I don't know if it is true, but it is certainly conceivable. A hakawati reached a stopping place in the story and said: "Come tomorrow for the next installment." At that point in the story, Antar was imprisoned and one of his supporters was so upset that he could not sleep. He had become a part of the story. He dressed, went to the hakawati's house, knocked on his door, gave him money, and said: "Take this money and read another page or so until Antar is freed from the prison." Surely this story or its equivalent happened.

Whether or not Darid Laham senses that his character Gawar represents continuity with past cultural forms, both genres mock human folly and bear an explicit relation to the ruling powers. The only remaining shadow puppeteer in Syria explained to me in an interview:

> Shadow puppets were originally shadow gods who were dummy figures to whom the priests spoke and for whom the priests asked sacrifices. Those who refused risked hell and the priests' curses. . . . Shadow puppetry thrived for thousands of years as one of the secrets of the priests and sooth-

sayers. . . . Its audiences laugh and learn at the same time and so in the past
shadow puppets were used to solve social problems."[3]

GAWAR: THE CRITIC OF HUMAN ERROR

Darid Laham sees his character Gawar as a medium by which to critique no
government in particular but rather the corruption of bureaucrats and the
treachery of Arab governments who have abandoned the Palestinians in general. He described how he felt about Syria and the Arab nation:

> Although you find in the Arab world in general that a Tunisian thinks in
> a Tunisian way, and a Kuwaiti thinks in a Kuwaiti way, our problem in
> Syria is that we think in an Arab way. We forget Syria. I don't know why.
> Perhaps because Syria is progressive. We understand that the nation
> (*watan*), is people first and foremost. Land by itself means nothing more
> than rocks, mountains, or plains. Only when people interact with that land
> is it worth something. For instance, Aristotle Onassis bought an island, but
> that island is not a nation. It is just stones and hills. A nation is composed of
> people and their relation to the land. This relation makes what would other-
> wise be mere land into a nation.
>
> This is why all our plays are based on a people and on their relation to
> the land. Without this relation—be it agricultural, organizational, or some-
> thing else—the people are lost, without a nation. They are estranged from
> their nation while they are living in it, which is why they can so easily leave
> it. They can gather their memories, cares, joys, and dreams in a suitcase,
> take the first plane, and leave. Our theater troupe clarified this best in *Dayya
> Ghurba*. We also dealt with it in *Dayya Tishrin*. There the mayor asks the
> army, "Why didn't you fight?" Gawar says: "Why should we fight and
> defend? I will fight to defend my freedom and honor. I will not fight to
> defend a prison or tyranny."

While it true that Gawar critiques tyranny, some spectators feel that he is
the one social critic allowed to speak in Syria. Riad Ismat, Syrian theater
critic, asked the following in an interview with Darid Laham: "I hear that
some people, particularly the leftists, are against you and your works. They
say that rather than stimulating people to revolt, you make them more relaxed with your laughter." Darid Laham reaffirmed his belief that his Gawar
is political:

> If we are going to talk about political theater, I think I am quite justified
> in calling our theater political. Personally I see political theatre in two
> forms; it can be the mouthpiece of the regime or it can criticize the regime. If
> there is another form, I do not know about it. I think it is quite easy to define
> which branch we represent. We not only criticize our government but

others as well. All the Arab governments would prefer praise but we have never praised anyone.[4]

To ask whether Gawar's political satire is revolutionary or an opiate of the people is somewhat like asking whether *Saturday Night Live* is going to topple the U.S. government or whether *Monty Python* will wreck the British parliament. Clearly Darid Laham's political satire attracts a large audience, no matter what the reason for his existence. Clearly he will not be the force to topple Arab governments; yet his productions are forces with which to reckon.

When I asked Darid Laham about his sharp political satire, he responded: "We have reached an audience who can protect us from any criticism." But, I pointed out, you are the only group that is allowed to operate in Syria. He shot back: "My lady, there is a difference between my saying 'You are wearing an ugly dress' and 'Your dress of yesterday is far prettier than that of today.' The second is a far gentler criticism." Darid Laham's view, then, is that he has developed a satirical style which is subtle enough to be permitted.

Whether or not Gawar is a tool of the Syrian regime, it is indisputable that he is also a beloved stage personality who holds a favored position similar to that of the hakawati and the shadow puppeteer of the past century. In short, he speaks to the hearts and to the trials of the Syrian and other Arab people in a language that they understand. His video plays and movies will be sell-outs in the Arab world for some time to come.

NOTES

1. Unless noted otherwise, passages directly quoting Darid Laham are excerpted from a series of interviews conducted by Evelyn A. Early in 1982.
2. Riad Ismat, "The Arab World's Comic Gadfly: Syria's Darid Laham," *The Middle East*, March 1980, pp. 52–54.
3. Dahabi, interview with Evelyn A. Early, 1982.
4. Ismat, "The Arab World's Comic Gadfly," p. 54.

"To Mount at-Tiyal He Declared": Some Poetry from the Yemeni Civil War

Steven C. Caton

The civil war in the Yemen Arab Republic (North Yemen) lasted from 1962, when a military coup put an end to a thousand-year-old imamate, until 1967. Gamal Abdul Nasser of Egypt supported the Republicans while King Faisal of Saudi Arabia supported the Royalists.

In 1967 South Yemen wrested power from the British colonists and established the Marxist-oriented People's Democratic Republic of Yemen. Skirmishes along the borders continued past the ceasefire and attested to political differences separating the two states although hopes for reunification were continually voiced. In 1990, the two Yemens, divided since the 1700s, reunified into one Yemeni state. —Eds.

At John F. Kennedy's inauguration in 1961, Robert Frost read a poem especially composed for the occasion, the opening lines of which are:

> Summoning artists to participate
> In the august occasions of the state
> Seems something artists ought to celebrate

When suddenly a gust of wind blew the piece of paper out of the poet's hands, the ceremony had to proceed without his being able to finish the prepared text. The event presaged what was to befall Kennedy's symbolic gesture of wedding poetry to power. Enthusiasm for this idea waned after the first few months of his presidency and he never referred to it again.

Adapted from Steven C. Caton, *Peaks of Yemen I Summon: Poetry As Cultural Practice in a North Yemeni Tribe*. Berkeley: University of California Press, 1990. Poems copyright © 1990 The Regents of the University of California; by permission of the University of California Press.

During the Kennedy era and long thereafter, a revolution and ensuing civil war broke out in North Yemen (southwestern Arabian Peninsula) where the association between poetry and power was not the exception but the norm of political rhetoric. Of course, poetry is only one of many verbal registers in which Yemenis tried to exhort or otherwise persuade their compatriots, but it was nevertheless one of the most important. In the dawn hours of September 26, 1962, Sanaa's radio listeners heard a tribal poet reciting his ode announcing the advent of the Revolution and a steady stream of verse was to issue thereafter on the civil war which lasted until approximately 1972. The following verses are only a small portion of that output but are nevertheless representative of a use of poetic discourse in marked contrast with our own sociolinguistic traditions.

To this day the most numerous and powerful element in Yemeni society is the sedentary, agricultural tribes. All the poetry in this section was composed by shaykhs from the area of Khawlan, whose territory stretches eastward from the capital Sanaa to the outskirts of Marib, site of the dam which was considered by the ancients as one of the "seven wonders" of the world.

The tribal shaykh is an important figure in Yemeni politics, though he is not an absolute ruler, having to shape consensus by persuasion rather than coercion. In times of crisis, however, such as intertribal war or the threat of foreign invasion, the tribe, probably an entire confederacy, might rally around an outstanding military leader and grant him considerable power. For example, Khawlan is composed of several tribes which are unwilling today to forfeit their independence to the authority of a "Shaykh of Shaykhs." This was not always the case. In the Yemeni civil war the Khawlanis elected one of their tribal shaykhs to head their joint armies—Naji bin Ali al-Ghadir—so renowned was he for his valor, wisdom, military prowess, and, as we shall see, poetic talent.

The one-thousand-year-old imamate was overthrown by army officers under the leadership of Salal, who was to become the first president of the Republic. Imam al-Badr, however, managed to escape to the northern part of the country, where he rallied the tribes in support of his cause. For the next ten years a costly and very bloody civil war inflicted deep wounds on Yemen which have still not healed.

Like other tribal areas, Khawlan was very fickle in its political allegiances during the conflict. A common joke of the era relates that they were Republicans by day and Royalists by night (the former maneuvering mainly in daylight whereas the latter's guerrilla forces carried out their operations under the cover of darkness). At the beginning of the revolution many tribesmen of the region were sympathetic to the new government because it promised to institute badly needed social, political, and economic reforms. But when Salal in the early days of his regime asked President Nasser to send troops and matériel (by mid-November of 1962 there were reportedly about ten thousand Egyptian troops on Yemeni soil), Republican Khawlanis such as Shaykh al-Ghadir balked at what seemed to them to be a foreign invasion of Yemen and they threw in their weight with the Royalists.

One of the greatest poems to come out of this early period of the civil war was composed by Shaykh al-Ghadir. In it he proclaimed his political position:

> To Mount at-Tiyal he declared and shouted to every peak
>   in Yemen//We will never join the Republic, though we be
>   snuffed out of the world forever,
> though yesterday were to return today and the sun rise from
>   the south//though earth were to consume fire and clouds
>   rain bullets.

The poem is of the type called *zamil*. Meter and rhyme are among its chief aesthetic features, a satisfactory discussion of which would be too technical here. Alliteration and sound-symbolism are also quite intricate and demonstrate the skill of the poet. His artistic ability in this regard reflects positively on his reputation for honor. As for the content, it has to be compressed into the space of only two lines, which readers can see approaches the compactness of aphorism. The most important aesthetic appeal of the lines above lies in the clever use of paradoxes. For example, the poet cites a series of impossible events ("though yesterday were to return today" and "though the earth were to consume fire") and declares that even if these should occur, his side would still not join the Republic. Hyperbole is to be found in poetry around the world as a device by which to express emotional emphasis.

Zamil poems may be linked as parts of exchanges between poets who challenge each other. Indeed, the poem above was a poetic challenge hurled at the Republicans, one of whose shaykhs, Salih bin ar-Royshan, took up the gauntlet. The respondent in such exchanges is required to compose at least an aesthetically equivalent poem or, better yet, top his opponent by surpassing his metaphorical, alliterative, and humorous flourishes. If the poet is not up to scratch, he loses face, and the honor of his group is in turn diminished. Let us now turn to ar-Royshan's composition to see whether it manages to meet al-Ghadir's challenge:

> Beg pardon of one who's wended a crooked course.//
>   The MiG, the Yushin, the helicopter and phantom jet—
> Fighter pilots are not stopped by M-1 rifles and cartridges//
>   Tell Hasan and Badr, O Naji, silver has turned to
>   brass.

To appreciate how good ar-Royshan's response is we must delve into its sound texture in more detail than most nonspecialists have patience for. Readers will have to take my word that its alliterations and sound symbolisms surpass the original. I cannot resist, however, pointing out one detail of this poet's superb craftsmanship, a stunning use of allusion which comes at the end of the poem. Al-Ghadir is commanded to tell the deposed imam and his right-hand man Prince Hasan that "silver has turned to brass" (silver having been a symbol of the imamate). Many times I asked listeners what this line meant and received various, but not necessarily contradictory, answers. One person told me it referred to the collapse of the monarchy's army, another said it simply meant that the value of the imamate had been debased, and still another had a different interpretation. If we saw in the previous poem how hyperbole was used to get the listener's attention, here the technique is subtlety. This way of talking "between the lines" is in fact greatly admired even in everyday language.

This stunning poem was not only a reply to a challenge, it provoked the following retort from Shaykh al-Ghadir:

> The Yushin won't do you a bit of good—we have the means to
> combat it. You're crazy!//
> The land mine is certain to leave the tank in pieces.
> Salal, the lunatic, won't help you, nor al-Amri Hasan.//
> O Satan, you're cursed! The curse is in a narrow grave.

While the meter, rhyme, and alliteration of the original are preserved, it does not match the sound symbolism of ar-Royshan's poem. It frankly deteriorates into name-calling against the president and his prime minister, al-Amri Hasan, and only partially succeeds in matching allusion with allusion at the end of the poem by a not-so-subtle reference to the death of the Republican soldiers. It nevertheless is judged by Yemenis to be a good, if not outstanding, zamil.

I was never able to elicit ar-Royshan's reply to this poem, if in fact one exists. Perhaps he thought it did not require one on the grounds that he had already won the zamil exchange with the second poem. However, he did produce another one on a different meter and rhyme scheme which was addressed to the Royalists:

> I ask you: where did the Imam go, the day the bullets
> riddled his house?//
> O you who say the people will never join the Republic:
> listen to the clamors and convulsions of its army.

The last line in Arabic is again sound-symbolic, the alliterations being eerily effective in mimicking the reports of guns on the battlefield.

One could add hundreds more examples of zamil poems, but those above are among the most famous ones remembered by Yemenis from this period of the civil war. Note that the poets are shaykhs, the political leaders of the tribes. Though any adult male may compose verse for various public occasions, the shaykh must cultivate the art for himself or prevail on one of his talented followers to perform the important routine of challenge-and-response. The exercise of power is commensurate with the practice of poetry. War is waged with words as well as with weapons.

Entertainment in the Marketplace

Philip D. Schuyler

Marketplaces have always attracted aspiring performers. In Western countries without the large market plaza, amateurs may take to the subways and street corners. In the Middle East, performers find ready audiences among customers and vendors waiting to buy and sell, or to fill time during the long market day. Philip D. Schuyler writes about contemporary markets in Morocco and the street performances there which constitute art and commerce at the same time. —Eds.

A market (*suq*) in Morocco overwhelms the senses with its profusion of goods, colors, characters, press of bodies, and the scents of mint and manure. Observers have often ignored, however, the market's tapestry of sound. Whether in a market in the old section of a city or at a weekly suq in the country, the air is filled with a rich blend of dramatic exchanges and musical strains. Merchants and craftsmen call to one another, asking to borrow a tool or a scale weight, or to make change. Each act of bargaining is a small drama in which buyer and seller perform their respective roles. Some merchants literally sing the praises of their wares. Dealers in medicines, potions, and insecticides are particularly given to long, and often amplified, accounts that extol the potency of their products, tell of successful applications, and include homilies about the good life. To demonstrate the success of their treatments, they display bottles of preserved scorpions or tapeworms, or piles of painlessly extracted teeth.

Musicians may wander among market stalls, performing a line or two in exchange for a few coins from merchants or customers. In both the city and the country, however, there is usually a section of the market set aside for more conventional entertainment, just as there are specialized areas for vegetables, livestock, hardware, and craft goods. The scope of entertainment ranges from one or two acts at a small country suq to as many as fifty different kinds of entertainment in Jamaa el Fna, the great square (and perpetual fair) in Marrakesh.

The variety of entertainment rivals the variety of goods in other parts of the market. Local musicians are joined by their itinerant colleagues who, in the old days at least, came from as far away as Algeria, offering novelty to the locals and a reminder of home to travelers and emigrants. There are also preachers, storytellers, and small comedy troupes, as well as acrobats (long a Moroccan export to international circuses), animal trainers, and an occasional trick bicyclist or fire eater. Other diversions include games of strength, skill, and chance: boxing matches, shooting galleries, muscle-testing machines, the wheel of fortune, three card monte, or the string game (where shils sometimes outnumber customers). It is rare to find all of these activities in one market, but it does happen in Jamaa el Fna or at the large festivals held during major pilgrimages to a saint's shrine. The pilgrimage sites may also draw small carnivals, with ferris wheels (sometimes hand-cranked) and other rides, as well as fancifully decorated tent theaters offering a full program of six or seven different acts for a dime.

Not so long ago, market performers served several vital functions in Moroccan society. The itinerant entertainers acted as journalists, carrying news from one market to the next. Public preachers offered moral guidance and explanations of religious texts to a largely illiterate public. Comedians provided political and social commentary. Storytellers gave lessons in history. Musicians put all these messages into song. Times have changed, of course. Public education has brought literacy to many. Radio, television, recordings, and films now provide entertainment and information. Yet street performances continue much as before, an important stage in the apprenticeship of many entertainers, a supplement to the income of journeymen and masters, and an honest way to earn a living for many down on their luck. The tradition is so entrenched that in more modern cities without public performance areas, such as Rabat and Casablanca, musicians perform in the aisles of intercity buses before departure.

Just as marketing has its elements of drama and music, so market and street performance has its elements of merchandizing. Except in tent theaters, the performers themselves are responsible for every aspect of the production: they must gather the crowd, manage the "stage," and collect the money. Attracting an audience is easy. As soon as entertainers unpack their equipment—musical instruments, trained animals, or simply a stool for a storyteller—spectators begin to gather. Performers announce the beginning of the show by pounding on drums or by shouting; the racket attracts more spectators. By showtime, the entertainer may have attracted a half-dozen to more than two-hundred onlookers.

The spectators naturally drift into an arc around the performance area. But some may hang back too far, leaving the circle ragged and open; others may crowd too close, leaving little room for the performance. The entertainers try to shape the crowd into an even circle.[1] A tight, well-organized cluster helps keep the audience in place, and makes the event look more intriguing to passersby. Women and children are encouraged to sit around the perimeter, to improve visibility for those behind and to give the circle more stability. The performers continually groom the crowd, squeezing out a troublemaker, making sure a favored patron gets a good view. In performance groups with more than three members, one may be delegated primarily to crowd management, which not only helps keep the circle in good order but also permits the performers to size up the audience. The spectators are not simply a boundary and stage backdrop, of course, but may be recruited as actors or as a chorus commenting on the events. Most important, each spectator is a potential contributor.

Like any other craftsmen or merchants, entertainers come to the market to make money. But unlike their colleagues, performers must give away their product before being paid. Thus, they rely on several strategies to hold the spectators' attention until they extract money from the audience. The first is the judicious use of suspense or teasing, a device as ancient as the One Thousand and One Nights and as modern as television. Market entertainers suddenly break off their act in the middle of a song or a story to make their pitch to the audience. If the spectators wish to hear the rest, it is suggested, they must first satisfy the performers (spare my head, buy my product, give me money). The transition from performance to pitch may be subtle indeed. Musicians may engage in a mock argument over the text or the rendition of a song. They may then hold a contest, in which the antagonists trade lines or dance steps. The audience is then invited to vote for their favorite by contributing to one side or the other. More often, however, the argument escalates into a slapstick routine, with performers pursuing each other around the circle, sometimes using spectators as a shield. Eventually, after much invective and many blows, one member of the group offers to mediate through prayer.

The introduction of prayer is a second fund-raising strategy: the attempt to divorce the appeal for money from entertainment. The performers' pleas may be cast entirely in religious formulae.[2] They invite the audience to join them in an invocation to God and the Prophet Muhammad, calling down their blessings on king and country, on the spectators, and on the performers themselves. The invocation is in part a sincere prayer for absolution from indulging in the spiritually suspect public performance, but it also changes the tone of the proceedings and demands the direct participation of the onlookers. The performers may claim that they seek, not money, but sustenance. Such requests appeal to the Muslim obligation of charity, but they also lead many Moroccans to consider street performers as no more than entertaining beggars.

Often, however, performers provide more than entertainment. Artistic ability is one of many manifestations of *baraka*, translated as "spiritual power" or "blessing." Indeed, many musicians make pilgrimages and sacrifices at saints' shrines in search of talent and inspiration. Baraka, once obtained, can be passed on to others. Thus, musicians, as bearers of baraka, have the capacity to bless others—their audience—and the blessing is worth money. A performer may, for example, put a knot in his sash and hold it out to the audience, offering a contributor the chance to undo the knot, and thus symbolically "untie" his personal problems. Each donation is met with praise and a prayer for the donor, and if someone should make a contribution in kind (a candle, some fruit, or a piece of cloth), the performer will extol both the giver and the gift, and then, having endowed the object with added baraka, offer to sell it to the highest bidder.

Once the appeal for money is underway the promise of "more to come" is frequently repeated in various forms, to keep the audience from drifting away. A particularly generous gift may be welcomed with a fragment of song. In larger groups, while one or two performers make the appeal and collect donations, others may tune up and play softly among themselves, suggesting that the next piece is coming almost immediately. Finally, the promise may be made explicit: periodically, those in charge of the appeal count up the take and announce the figure to the audience. "We have eight *dirhams* here, all we need is two more to make ten. Who will complete the ten *dirhams* for us?" In reality, the performers often do not announce the amount of the gifts as they come (so that the audience cannot keep count), and continue to collect as long as the spectators do not begin to slip away in too great numbers. Only then does the main entertainment begin again.

The performance as a whole is thus a kind of seamless, circular variety show. A comic routine interrupts song and dance, an invocation is used to mediate slapstick conflict, and music and ribald humor intrude on prayer. Almost every performer relies on the same basic repertory of devices; only the balance changes from group to group. Musicians make their pitch in the form of a sermon, just as preachers and storytellers often integrate songs into their performances, and punctuate their narratives with a slap on a drum. The mixture of elements helps the entertainers to engage the spectators and to keep them in suspense. Indeed, for many members of the audience, the sometimes scandalous comedy routines, and even the prayerful pleas for money, offer as much entertainment as the music itself. In short, while other media have usurped many of the traditional roles of market entertainers, the vitality and immediacy of their performances offer excitement that can be found in no other form.

NOTES

1. The name for the circle of spectators (*halqa*, plural *hlaqi*; literally "ring") has become the term for street performance in general. The term was originally applied to the circle of students that gathered around scholars in the great universities of the

Muslim world, such as Al-Azhar in Cairo or the Qarawiyin in Fez. Preachers are still a fixture in the market, and even the bawdiest comic halqa often has a high religious content.

2. The pitch itself is called *fatha*, from *Al-Fatiha*, the opening sura of the Quran. The fatha is much more than Quranic recitation or prayer, however. Some performers are highly esteemed for their ability to extemporize sermons on such mundane topics as a mosque light or a passing cloud, and to reach members of the audience individually by invoking their local patron saint.

Sad Songs of the Western Desert

Lila Abu-Lughod

Performances can be public events with vast crowds or private ones with a few observers as in the case of the Awlad 'Ali bedouin women of Egypt. In their personal discourse, the women sing short poems to articulate intimate feelings which they could not convey in normal conversation. The Egyptian bedouin women's poems express their problems in a cultural form specific to, and understood by, those sharing the same life situation. —Eds.

Living in camps and towns scattered throughout the coastal region of the Egyptian Western Desert, the bedouins known collectively as Awlad 'Ali are seminomadic pastoralists in the process of sedentarization. Their traditional economy was based on sheep and camel herding, supplemented by rain-fed barley cultivation and trade (recently replaced by smuggling and legal commercial ventures). Arabic speakers and Muslims who migrated from Cyrenaica (Eastern Libya) at least two hundred years ago, they proudly assert their separate identity within Egypt, where they are a minority living on the fringes of settled life. They differentiate themselves from the peasants and urbanites of the Nile Valley by the tribal ideology which shapes their social and political organization, not to mention interpersonal relations, and by their stricter adherence to a moral code of honor and modesty. Their cultural traditions are also distinct. They share with other bedouins a great love of poetry, which they use to express some of their most poignant sentiments.

During the nearly two years I lived in a small community of Awlad 'Ali Bedouins, I rarely tape-recorded anything but wedding festivities. Laughingly accusing my machine of being a tattler, people were loath to let me record their ordinary conversations and the songs or poems that frequently punctuated these. I was usually out of batteries anyway since people loved to listen to the tapes I had made. They enjoyed the wedding tapes even though the singing was barely audible over the din of multiple conversations, crying babies, and excited children. But one special tape was always requested. It had been recorded one afternoon when I happened to catch the spontaneous songs and conversation of two women sewing a tent. They were comfortable with me and with each other, and we were alone in the household. As they shredded fabric for the patchwork for the tent walls and sewed the pieces together, they talked and then began to sing short poems called "little songs" (*ghanaawy*, singular *ghinnaawa*) that I was beginning to discover were very important to the Awlad 'Ali. They took turns responding to each other's songs. 'Aziza initiated the singing with the following:

> Patience brought no fulfilled wishes
> I wearied and hope's door closed . . .

Her friend answered with a song implying that it was better for one to replace love with patience. 'Aziza rejoined with a song about the persistence of memories; her friend countered with an exhortation to forget those who cause pain.

Whenever I played this tape for women in the community, they sat quietly and listened intently. They always looked solemn and pained. Some shook their heads sadly and commented, "Her bad luck!" or "This is news that makes you cry." Some even wept. It took me a while to understand why.

The poems were sung mournfully and were not without the poetic graces of alliteration and internal rhymes. Yet the images in the poems were not remarkable, nor were the themes of patience and memories uncommon. What moved people who heard the songs was that they knew the difficult conditions under which 'Aziza lived, and they cared about her, having known her all their lives. She had been born in the community and had spent all but a few of her thirty-three years there. She had recurring problems with the moody and poverty-stricken brother with whom she lived. Barely able to support himself and unable to keep a wife, he resented having to support his divorced sister. Her marital history was sad. Her husband had taken a dislike to her shortly after their marriage and had become abusive. She escaped home only to be met with her father's death. After the funeral she was persuaded to return to her husband's household, where her sister-in-law (also her half-sister) mistreated her, and then got into trouble with her husband, who had been away in Libya. He divorced her and she never remarried. To make matters worse, she had a hideous and painful skin disease that had first manifested itself during the difficult period before the divorce and that broke out periodically. She conceded that her condition worsened whenever she dwelt too much on her misfortunes.

'Aziza's revelation of painful personal sentiments in poetry moved people. Knowing the circumstances of her life, they realized that the despair of her poems was due to her unhappy marriage, her illness, her poverty and loneliness. When she sang about memories and her inability to forget, they understood that despite the passage of time, she was still concerned with her ex-husband and wounded by his unfair treatment of her. By singing about patience, 'Aziza betrayed her hopes and her faith that some reward would come from her suffering. Her discouragement troubled the listeners, as well as her friend who gave her poetic comfort, because they knew how few signs of hope really existed.

'Aziza was not the only bedouin individual to use poetry in this way. Both men and women recite this type of oral lyric poetry in conversation with intimates or sing as they work alone. They admit that they sing about what is on their minds, and it was my impression that they sing more often when they are facing some personal crisis. Those who hear the poems appreciate them for what they reveal about the experiences of those reciting. Despite the intrinsic ambiguity of such condensed and formulaic poetic statements, they are easily interpretable because friends and relatives usually have such intimate knowledge of the particular circumstances of one another's lives.

Since I spent more of my time with women, I came to understand the relationship between their poems and their lives more clearly and will confine this description to them. Women are moved by the poems of other women because the contours of bedouin women's experiences are so similar. Their lives follow much the same pattern: they grow up with kin, marry (sometimes moving to another community, sometimes not), have many children, and grow old. With luck, they will be given to a good husband who will not mistreat them, their husband's kinswomen will be kind, their kin will support them, and their children will be healthy. Most likely, they will face a number of difficult experiences and will suffer. Women agree that their lives are hard. They work hard, often handicapped by poor health due to inadequate nutrition and constant childbearing. More trying are the hardships in the interpersonal sphere.

Separations from loved ones are a fact of life, especially in a society until recently nomadic. For women, the most difficult separations, after their own from their natal families at marriage, are those from their children. Daughters marry and leave to live with their husbands' families. Their daughters' departure is hard on mothers, who lose companionship and household help. But it is expected. With best wishes and prayers, daughters are sent off with songs like the following:

> The household and neighbors suffered
> when she left, the one with gazelle eyes . . .

When sons leave, mothers are heartbroken. One poor woman I knew had a son in Libya. He had gone there as a migrant laborer and then had been unable to return after the border closed in 1977. She had not seen him for five years. As she told me about him she began to weep and sang the following:

> If only you who're far away
> Despair could bring you close . . .

Her friend who was sitting with us responded with another song to comfort her:

> Nothing is odious but death
> In time hope brings the absent . . .

This sentiment was certainly felt by another woman I met. Her son had been killed recently in an altercation between some bedouin men and a group of Egyptian soldiers riding on a train through a bedouin area. She sang:

> A fog of despair shrouds the eye
> just when it starts to clear . . .

The intimacy of growing up in the same household and the central ideology of the primacy of blood ties combine to make bonds between brothers and sisters very close. These are intensified when a woman marries because she begins to depend on her brother for protection against mistreatment by her husband or his family. The loss of a brother leaves a woman feeling vulnerable. One young woman whose brother had died a few months earlier sang of her grief as she sat alone washing clothes:

> They shoved you between despair and fire
> you turned to ash, my little heart . . .

Women are also troubled by their relations to husbands. Most marriages are arranged by the families of the bride and groom. Although romantic love is glorified in stories, people think love marriages don't work out well, and they are not common. Nearly all brides are shy and won't admit to being happy about marrying, even if they are pleased. But some brides are genuinely unhappy with the mates chosen for them. One such bride, whose kinsmen were adamant that she accept the marriage they had arranged for her, could not express her objections without alienating her kinsmen or insulting the women in her new community, kinswomen of her husband. She rarely said much, but recited numerous poems and often sang to herself while she worked. One of the poems she recited was the following:

> On my breast I placed a tombstone
> though I was not dead, oh loved one . . .

More often, women have developed attachments to husbands to whom they have been married for years and are hurt if the men leave them or seem no longer to care. Women I knew who, in keeping with notions of modesty and social propriety, vehemently denied attachment to their spouses, professed a lack of concern with their marriages, and admitted no interest in sexual matters nonetheless recited poems expressing sentiments of attachment and emotional vulnerability to men.

A young widow whose husband had been killed in a fight did not speak of him. She was cheerful and her sense of humor endeared her to the community. She seemed content to forego remarriage, preferring to remain with her children and the women among whom she had grown up. One night she recited a number of poems, including the following, that saddened and moved the women who heard them.

> Drowning in despair
> the eye says, Oh my fate in love . . .

A married woman whose husband of fifteen years wished to take a second wife admitted no concern, expressing only anger at his failure to buy her the proper gifts and his unconventional decision to hold the wedding in his brother's house rather than her own. Yet she expressed the sense of hurt by myriad poems, including:

> Long shriveled from despair
> are the roots that fed my soul . . .

> Patience is my mourning for the loved one
> and your job, oh eyes, is to cry . . .

Other women in the community tried to console her by comparing her fate to that of other women ("Do you think you are the first woman whose husband ever took a second wife?"), cynically commenting that men are all like that (as soon as they can afford it, they seek another wife and more children), or telling her to be grateful for her six children. They indicated empathetic concern by reciting in her presence poems, such as the following, which voiced what they assumed she was feeling:

> Despair of them, dear one, made you
> a stray who wanders between watering places . . .

This poem evoked a despair so powerful it could drive someone to abandon human society and to roam outdoors like animal. By expressing sentiments from her point of view, rather than by offering advice, the woman's friends emphasized the sense of community and commonality of experience.

Bound by conventions and traditions, this oral folk poetry would seem to be a highly impersonal form of expression. Yet individuals use the poems to express the supremely personal, in the double sense of that which touches on their own experiences and that which is confidential, to be shared only with intimates. What is most interesting is that people express feelings they could not ordinarily express without compromising their social reputations and images as proud and independent. More often than not, the poems voice sentiments of sadness, unfulfilled longing, or suffering caused by a sense of abandonment. Bedouin women, like the men, have great pleasures in their lives, and their conversations are generally marked by humor and laughter. But as one old woman explained when I commented that most poems seemed so sad, "When a woman gets what she wants, she gets happy and shuts up."

A Folk Revival in Morocco

Philip D. Schuyler

The universal appeal of music is dramatically demonstrated in the Middle East. Popular vocalists and musical groups are superstars. The queen of the Arab music world was the Egyptian songstress Umm Kulthum, a middle-aged former Quran chanter with a deep, velvety voice. As she sang of lost love, millions of fans suffered with her. Her six-hour concerts were jammed although one ticket cost the equivalent of one-fourth of an average month's wages. Each song told a separate story of love and pain and ran the length of a long-playing record. She was adored during her lifetime and mourned greatly at her death.

Although much Middle Eastern music continues to use traditional melodic and rhythmic structures, many composers have, since the beginning of this century, borrowed elements of Western European style. The themes addressed have begun to change. Although unrequited love is always popular, contemporary music also raises issues of ethnicity and politics.

Philip D. Schuyler discusses the revival of folk music in Morocco by a group which has successfully fused Western, Middle Eastern, and traditional music to provide a genre of Moroccan folk music with which rural Moroccan immigrants identify. This new music is as authentically "Moroccan" as the songs crooned in Egyptian casinos, mentioned in the introduction to this section, are Egyptian. —Eds.

Music is an integral part of daily and ceremonial life in Morocco, from lavish weddings and royal receptions to storytellers in the market and religious processions winding through the streets. Each region, each city, and each social group has its own particular style of music, often performed on instruments unique to that group, with song texts sung in a highly specialized dialect.

Until recently, however, if one were to judge from what was available on the air, in the shops, and on the concert stage, one might think that Moroccan music was disappearing. During the 1950s and 1960s, the commercial music market in Morocco was dominated by popular stars from Egypt (Umm Kulthum and Farid al-Atrash), France (Johnny Hallyday), and the United States (James Brown). The most successful local recording artists were, for the most part, imitators of Egyptian film style or, more rarely, French pop and American soul. Traditional and regional music was not completely ignored on radio and television, but for the most part it was relegated to low-powered stations and limited programming time. Commercial recordings of traditional music seldom sold more than a few thousand copies, mostly among emigrant laborers nostalgic for the sounds of home. Recordings were, in any case, largely superfluous, since live performances were so readily available.

This situation is hardly uncommon among smaller nations. Indeed, some observers have predicted the replacement of traditional music around the world with homogenized popular music in the American style.[1] Change is inevitable, and the powerful influence of the West—economic, cultural, and technological—cannot be denied. But developments in Morocco (and elsewhere) in the early 1970s demonstrate that local traditions can give birth to new popular forms and that old styles can still be revived, and even strengthened.

In late 1971, a new wave of commercial music appeared in Morocco when several actors formed a group called Nass el-Ghiwane (People of Love, or People of Temptation). Within a few months another group, Jil Jilala (Generation of Jilala), had split off from the first and overtaken it in popularity. Together the two groups rapidly became the most successful in Morocco.[2] Soon after, they launched successful tours in the rest of North Africa, the Middle East, and Europe.

The new ensembles grew out of the theater troupe of Tayeb Sadiki, a Moroccan playwright and director. Like a number of other artists and intellectuals during the mid-1960s, Sadiki turned to Moroccan traditional culture for his subject matter, using characters and events from Moroccan history to comment on twentieth century society and politics. He also incorporated songs by mystical poets, such as Sidi Abderrahman el Mejdoub and Sidi Qaddur el Alami, into his plays. These songs met with such an enthusiastic reception that the actors-musicians were persuaded to turn exclusively toward music.

Although the groups may have grown out of an intellectual movement, they found their strongest supporters among the poor, and often uneducated, urban youth. As the country became more urbanized in the years after World War II and Independence (1956), many young people grew up cut off from their rural roots, but with no particular attachment to traditional urban culture. In fact, they constituted the first generation that could have a sense of national, as opposed to local or regional, identity. They identified readily, however, with the members of Nass el-Ghiwane and Jil Jilala, who came from the same background and spoke to their concerns.

The rise of the new groups might be compared to the appearance of folk-revival and, later, folk-rock bands in the United States and Europe in the 1950s and 1960s. In both cases, traditional songs and melodies were recast in a new form, designed to appeal to a modern audience. Nass el-Ghiwane and Jil Jilala were able to fuse elements of Western, and to a lesser extent Middle Eastern, performance with a repertory based on traditional Moroccan songs. The Moroccan elements, furthermore, were drawn from a variety of sources around the country. The resulting synthesis was undoubtedly Moroccan, without being tied to a specific regional or ethnic group. The identity of the groups was open to interpretation on the part of each observer. Like Morocco itself, they could seem by turns conservative and revolutionary, traditional and modern, Arab, African, and Western.

The strongest influence from the past was provided by religious brotherhoods, such as the Aissawa, Jilala, and Gnawa. The brotherhoods have for centuries occupied an important place in the music culture of Moroccan cities. They have at times also served as the focus for protest and resistance to the government. On these two counts, at least, they provided an ideal model for counterculture musical groups.[3]

A second source of inspiration came from the Euro-American counterculture. Many popular musicians visited Morocco during these years, and a few, such as the Rolling Stones and Led Zeppelin, even maintained houses for frequent or extended stays. While the stars were perhaps no less remote than the average tourist or expatriate, thousands of other world travelers were open and accessible.[4] Young Moroccans were thus exposed directly to counterculture fashions in music, dress, and philosophy. Indeed, the Western thirst for exoticism may have helped encourage younger Moroccans' revival of interest in their own traditions.

The influence of both Islam and world countercultures is immediately evident in the groups' names. The names themselves had strong religious associations: Jil Jilala (Generation of Jilala, or devotees of the mystic saint Moulay Abdelqader Jilali); Seba'tu Rijal (Seven Men, named for the seven patron saints of Marrakesh); Shab l-Hal (Friends of Trance), and so on. Nass el-Ghiwane even sought to capitalize on a similar trend among European youth by adopting for a time a second, Franco-American name: New Dervich.

At the same time, the use of group names distinguished the new bands from other popular ensembles in Morocco, which were generally identified by the name of the star performer. Group names projected a new image of collective consciousness and identity, not unlike the America and British rock bands of the late 1960s. In fact, the group concept went beyond the names alone. Members often collaborated in composition and production, while in performance, ensemble work was stressed and solos shared among the musicians. As time went on, individual personalities emerged, and one or another of the members became known as the composer or arranger, the songwriter, the charismatic leader, and so on; but collective identity remained paramount.

The style of presentation was even more clearly influenced by the West. In performance, the musicians spread themselves across the stage in the manner of rock bands, rather than clustering together, as did traditional Moroccan groups. Each singer and instrument had a separate microphone, and the groups were the first in the country to use sophisticated mixers and public address systems. Record covers were lettered in Arabic, but in many cases the graphic presentation was strongly reminiscent of album covers and posters from San Francisco. Even their clothing reflected the mixture of styles. Over boots and bluejeans or bellbottoms, the new musicians wore embroidered shirts and vests of Moroccan manufacture. While the cut of the clothes and the style or embroidery were based on traditional models, the specific combination of elements and colors was quite recent. Indeed, these garments were designed for (and often by) tourists, especially hippies.

The instrumentation of the new groups reflected a similar eclecticism. To carry the melodic lead, Nass el-Ghiwane and many of their emulators chose the banjo, while Jil Jilala used the *bouzoukee*. These instruments, of American and Greek origin respectively, were mildly exotic in a Moroccan context, but their sound and playing technique were quite similar to that of the small plucked lutes of many Moroccan folk ensembles. The lead instrument was supported by a *gnbri*, a three-stringed lute used by the Gnawa, a religious association with strong West African connections. The deep, rich sound of the gnbri made it an ideal complement to the higher-pitched lead instrument.

The other two or three members of the ensemble played a variety of drums. Some of these, such as the *ta'arija* (a small, vase-shaped drum) and the *bendir* (a round frame drum), have traditionally been used in a variety of different contexts, both sacred and secular; others, such as the *herrazi* (a large, single-headed, cylindrical drum) and the *tbila* (a pair of pottery kettle drums), on the other hand, have been used primarily in the ceremonies of religious brotherhoods. The association with religious brotherhoods was enhanced by Jil Jilala's occasional use of the *qaraqeb*, double castanets of iron used by the Gnawa.

The content of the recordings and live concerts was almost purely Moroccan. Texts, melodies, and drum patterns were borrowed from a variety of traditional sources, including urban popular songs of the seventeenth to nineteenth centuries, rural communal dance styles from around the country, and especially the repertories of various religious brotherhoods, such as the Aissawa and the Gnawa. The groups also used new texts, composed by members or their friends. But all of the texts expressed a kind of nostalgia for the past, either in manifest content or in their archaic vocabulary. The reinterpretation of historical texts permitted the groups to comment on political and social issues in a way that would not normally have been acceptable to the government.[5] The obscurity of vocabulary, even in the modern texts, created ambiguity that allowed each listener to create his or her own meaning.

The musicians adapted—or rather transformed—their material in a number of ways. Tests and music from different regions and social groups were strung together in a single song, creating a mosaic effect. Ensemble singing was often arranged in patterns derived from Western harmony. The musicians also used novel playing techniques on their instruments. The tbila, for example, would normally be beaten with sticks, but the new groups played it with their hands, more like a set of bongos than a traditional Moroccan drum. Furthermore, the ensemble as a whole contained instruments that would not be found together in a traditional context. The Gnawa gnbri, for example, is traditionally accompanied only by the double castanets; one would not expect to find it in combination with drums and other stringed instruments. Indeed, the overall configuration of instruments—lead string instrument, bass, and drums—resembled nothing so much as the English and American "power trios" such as Led Zeppelin and the Jimi Hendrix Experience.

The folk revival seems to have taken root as a new tradition. Less than two years after the appearance of the Nass el-Ghiwane and Jil Jilala, one journalist estimated that there were over two thousand groups copying their style (Mohamed 1976:13). Such groups now appear frequently in traditional contexts such as weddings and, occasionally, in public markets like Jamaa el Fna, the great square in Marrakesh. Although most of the copy groups have followed the original model, a few have struck out in new directions. Several groups have added electric instruments, such as the guitar and organ. A number of groups now sing in one of Morocco's Berber dialects, in an attempt to encourage young people not be become totally assimilated into the Arabic-speaking environment of the cities. But all the new groups convey the message that it is possible to be modern and maintain traditions at the same time.

The influence of Nass el-Ghiwane and Jil Jilala has extended to other areas of Moroccan musical life. Since the mid-1970s, imitators of Middle Eastern popular music have incorporated more and more Moroccan elements into their performances. A number of traditional musicians have also begun imitating the folk revivalists, consciously borrowing instruments and melodies from other ethnic groups to create their own eclectic style. But lest we fear homogenization of a different sort, it should be pointed out that the borrowing is truly eclectic, ranging as far afield as Hindi film music. The results may not always be felicitous, but it does seem, in a few cases at least, that the trend has rejuvenated some nearly moribund styles.

One of the most admirable results of the folk revival—beyond the fine music that has come out of it—has been an increased interest in the traditions that inspired the movement in the first place. The tendency toward cultural nationalism and the low cost of producing and distributing music on cassettes have both contributed greatly to this trend. But Nass el-Ghiwane and Jil Jilala also deserve credit for drawing popular attention to traditional music. Indeed, Jil Jilala has invited a number of traditional musicians to perform with them in the studio and on stage, and they have also produced recordings of traditional musicians, such as the Gnawa, that were previously unavailable on Moroccan labels.

Most important of all, however, has been the influence of the new groups on their original audience. The groups' success in Europe and the Middle East has given their fans a sense of pride. The songs themselves have given the audience a better understanding, or at least curiosity, about their own history and traditions. And, because the music is simple enough and the instruments inexpensive enough to be played by amateurs, the folk revival has kept the audience from becoming mere consumers of other people's music. It has made them again active participants in their own music culture.

NOTES

1. Alan Lomax (1976:10), for example, refers to the possibility of a "cultural grey-out." Wallis and Malm (1984) are scarcely less pessimistic, although the data in their fine, detailed study presents a more balanced view of the actual situation in the record industry in small countries.

2. For example, one of Jil Jilala's early records was reported to have sold 50,000 copies in a single week; that is roughly equivalent to selling 500,000 copies in the American market, a figure made still more impressive by the lower per capita distribution of record players in Morocco and the lack of advertising.

3. As Cornell (1983) points out, Western scholars have tended to overemphasize both the autonomy of saintly lineages and the extent of their dissidence. Nevertheless, many Moroccans accept the notion of the brotherhoods as a kind of counterculture, and it is that perception that is relevant here. As one member of the Heddawa, a loosely organized mendicant order, put it, "Nass el-Ghiwane? Where do you think they got their stuff? We were the original hippies" (field notes, 9/75).

4. A sizable contingent from Julian Beck's Living Theater was resident in the town of Essaouria for several months in 1969. Their presence (as well as the beauty of the town and its low cost of living) was a magnet for other world travelers, who virtually colonized the nearby village of Diabet. Abderrahman Paco, a member of Nass el-Ghiwane and a native of Essaouira, was still living in the town at the time. Similar concentrations of hippies could be found in Tangier, Marrakesh, and on the beaches near Agadir.

5. For example, Nass el-Ghiwane's first big hit, "*As-Siniya*" ("The Tea Tray"), describes the tray with the pot in the middle, surrounded by tea glasses. When the singer demanded to know why his glass had not been filled, listeners understood that he was accusing the king of monopolizing rights and material goods in the country, distributing them only to whom he chose.

REFERENCES

Cornell, Vincent J. 1983. "The Logic of Analogy and the Role of the Sufi Shaykh in Post-Marinid Morocco." *International Journal of Middle East Studies* 15:67–93.

Lomax, Alan. 1976. *Cantometrics: An Approach to the Anthropology of Music.* Berkeley: University of California Extension Media Center.

Mohamed, Jibril. 1976. "Nass el Ghiwane-Jil Jilala: les limites d'une experience." *Lamalif* (Casablanca) 81:12–18.

Wallis, Roger, and Krister Malm. 1984. *Big Sounds from Little Peoples: The Music Industry in Small Countries.* New York: Pendragon.

GLOSSARY

Arabic (A)
Persian (P)
Turkish (T)

adha (A). Harm, filthy.

ʿadul (A). Notary.

aghawat (plural), singular **agha** (P, here borrowed into Arabic). Persian title of rank, status.

ahl al-sunna wal-jamaʿa (A). The people of the Prophet's sunna. The term **sunnis** comes from this nomenclature.

ahli (A). Family.

ʿaib (A). Shame, disgrace.

Aissawa. North African religious brotherhood.

Ali. The son-in-law and cousin of the Prophet Muhammad; the fourth caliph of Islam for Sunni Muslims and the first Imam for the Shiʿites

ʿalim, plural **ʿulama.** A scholar, especially of Islam; a Muslim religious authority.

Allah (A). God; literally, "the God."

Antar. Arab hero noted for courage and heroism. Stories about Antar stem from pre-Islamic epics.

ʿaqid (A). Contract.

arak (A). A strong, colorless liquor.

ʿasaba (A). Family relationship in the paternal line.

asl (A). Descent.

'azl (A). Coitus interruptus.

baladi (A). Local, authentic, as opposed to foreign, inauthentic.

baraka (A). (Persian barakat). The blessing and grace of God.

batin (A). Inner, inside; term from vocabulary of mysticism meaning real, actual.

bay'a (A) Oath or pledge of allegiance to a sovereign.

bayt al-mal (A). Public treasury.

bedouin. Anglicized plural of bedu (badawiyin), nomad. Although taken from the plural, in English bedouin means a nomad.

bendir (A). A round frame drum, shaped much like a tambourine.

bey (T, borrowed into Arabic). A Turkish title of rank; indicates status; a polite term of address.

boozoukee (borrowed from Greek). Stringed musical instrument, resembling a mandolin.

caid (A, borrowed into French). Traditionally a tribal chief; now a governor or high-ranked government administrator (French transliteration).

caravanserai (P). Lodging place for caravans; an inn with adequate space for pack animals.

chadaris (P). Ankle-length veils worn in Afghanistan (in Iran, chador).

chap (P). Left, off the mark.

couscous (A). Dish made of semolina topped with a stew (Egyptian koskossi).

darar (A). Harm.

dawla (A). State.

dawwa (A). Medicine.

derb (A). Street, alley.

dhaif (A). Guest.

Dhu al-hijjah (A). The month when the pilgrimage is made. Muslims use a lunar calendar.

dillal (A). Auction (Moroccan usage).

din (A). Religion.

dirham (A). Piece of money; monetary unit used in Morocco, roughly equivalent to the French franc.

dlaal (A). Auctioneer (Moroccan usage).

duʿa (A). Personal prayer.

dukhun (A). Smoke.

effendi (T, borrowed into Arabic). A Turkish title of respect, ranks below bey; a polite term of address.

ʿeris (A). Wedding (Sudanese usage).

al-fajr (A). The dawn; name of the major Arabic-language newspaper in Jerusalem (also has an English edition).

Fatah (A). The largest constituent group of the Palestine Liberation Organization, headed by Yasir Arafat.

fellah, plural **fellahin** (A). Peasant.

fidya (A). Ransom.

fitiwwa (A). Neighborhood tough (Egyptian usage).

fitna (A). Temptation, charm, fascination.

fqih, plural **fuqaha** (A). A person somewhat learned in Islamic religion and law; a neighborhood or village religious leader (Moroccan pronunciation).

fuʿala (A). The ritual use of food, coffee, and perfumes.

gadaʾ (A). Young man possessed of manly virtues (Egyptian usage).

gallabiya (A). Long outer robe worn by men (see **jellaba**) (Egyptian usage).

ghayla (A). Harming of the child in the womb by nursing an infant while pregnant.

ghder (A). Betrayal, treachery (Moroccan usage).

ghinnaawa, plural ghanaawy (A). Little song; a short poem.

ghulam (A). A young boy.

ghusl (A). A washing of the whole body; a major ritual ablution.

Gnawa. A religious brotherhood prominent in Morocco; origin from West Africa.

gnbri. A three-string lute.

habous (A). Endowment property or funds.

hadana (A). Child custody.

hadith (A). A written account telling of the Prophet Muhammad or the early Muslim community.

hajj (A). The pilgrimage to Mecca. A person who has made the pilgrimage to Mecca will take the title **hajj** (m.) or **hajja** (f.).

hajji (A). A person who is making the pilgrimage.

hakawati (A). Storyteller.

halqa (A). Circle; used for circle of students or of spectators.

halva (P; A, **halwa**). A sweet made from a sesame seed paste.

Hanifi (A). One of the four schools of Islamic law; prevalent in areas formerly controlled by the Ottoman Empire, Pakistan, India.

haqq (A). Right, correct, proper.

hara (A). Quarter of an urban neighborhood.

haram (A). Forbidden, prohibited.

haramlik (T). The women's section of the house.

harim (A). A sacred place; harem, female members of the family.

harira (A). A thick soup.

henna (A). A plant which when powdered yields a red dye used on hair, hands, and feet. Henna can be drawn into intricate designs and is used for festive occasions such as weddings.

herrazi (A). Large, single-headed, cylindrical drum (Morocco).

hija' (A). Satire, ridicule.

hilm (A). Forbearance.

hshuma (A). Shame, modesty, politeness (Moroccan usage).

hsim (A). To be modest, polite, know your proper place (Moroccan usage).

Hussein. Grandson of Prophet Muhammad, third Imam of Shi'i community martyred at Karbala.

ibn (A). Son (of).

ibn al-balad (A). A local guy, a city man, as opposed to a rural dweller.

ʿid al-Adha (A). The Feast of Sacrifice, the greatest festival of Islam.

ʿid as-seghir (A). The feast of cakes which immediately follows the end of Ramadan.

ihmal (A). Irresponsibility.

ihram (A). The white robes worn when performing the hajj.

imam (A, P). In Shiʿi Islam, the head of the Muslim community; in Sunni Islam, a prayer leader.

imamzadeh (P). Descendant of the imams.

Islam (A). The religion which stems from the revelations Muhammad received from the Angel Gabriel, now contained in the Quran. Islam literally means submission, with the sense of submission to a higher power, here, God.

istibraʾ (A). Washing with water after urinating.

istinjaʾ (A). Washing with water after defecating.

ʿitra (A). A powerful neighborhood tough.

ʿizz (A). Prestige.

jellaba (A). Long, hooded robe worn as an outer garment by both men and women.

jinn, plural **jnoun** (A). Spirits made from smokeless fire, demons, either harmful or helpful, often mischievous spirits.

kaʿba (A). Sacred shrine at Mecca. The site has been revered from pre-Islamic times. Literally, a cube.

karikos (Greek). Shadow puppets.

kazzabin (A). Liars (Lebanese/Egyptian usage).

khaf (A). Fear.

khais (A). Dirt.

khalifa (A). An administrative title, indicating the head or leader; caliph.

khaluq (A). A mixture of saffron and other scents.

kif (A). A variety of hashish (hallucinatory hemp).

kizb (A). Lie, deceit, falsehood.

ma'azun (A). Registrar of marriages and divorces (Sudanese usage).

mabruk (A). Blessed.

madina (A). Literally, city. Today madina is used to indicate the old, densely populated section of the city.

mahr (A). Bride price, dower.

majlis (A). A session, gathering, meeting; also, the term for parliament, national assembly.

makhluʿ (A). Reckless, asocial.

makhzen (A). The central government (North African usage).

maktub (A). Written, fated.

malang (P). A person, possibly with divine power, who has withdrawn from the world (Afghanistan); a highly marginalized person often thought to be a pretender or illegitimate (Afghanistan and South Asia).

Maliki (A). One of the four major schools of Islamic law; prevalent in North Africa.

malʿun (A). Cursed.

maʿmur (A). Police officer in charge of a district, captain.

manzul (A). Compound of opium, hashish, and spices.

marabit, plural **marabitiin** (also **marabout**) (A). A saint or holy man; the tomb of a pious or holy man or woman which is visited to ask for aid or blessings.

al-Masʿa (A). "The Place of Running," corridor appended to the Sacred Mosque in Mecca where the saʾy is performed.

mawlid (A). Anniversary of a saint.

mawwal (A). Folk tales.

minbar (A). The pulpit in the mosque from where the sermon is delivered.

mkhammariya (A). A reddish mixture constituted of costly oils and scents—aloewood, saffron oils, civet, and ambergris. It is an indispensable ingredient of all festive rituals in the Gulf.

mosque. Anglicized. A structure housing a meetingplace for Muslims, designed for community prayer.

mousem (A). A festival (usually held annually) honoring a saint.

muallima (A). An "in-charge" woman, often with a smart mouth (Egyptian usage).

Mu'awiya. The fifth caliph, the founder of the Omayyad dynasty.

muezzin. Anglicized. The person who calls Muslims to prayer five times a day from the minaret (anglicized).

mujawwad (A). A style of reading or chanting the Quran.

mukhtar (A). Mayor.

mullah (P). A religious authority, generally in the town or village.

murafiq, plural **murafiqin** (A). Companion, bodyguard, follower, servant.

mushahara (A). Infertility; inability to breastfeed a child well.

muslim (A). One who submits to the will of God; the proper term for an adherent to the faith of Islam.

mutasawwuf (A). Sufi, mystic.

mutawwif (A). Guide for pilgrims in Mecca.

muwashahat (A). Lyrical poem set to music.

nadhir (A). Administrator, overseer.

nafaqa (A). Support.

nasib (A). Fate.

nazafah (A). Cleanliness.

nuqta (A). Joke.

nūshūz (A). Violation of legal duties on the part of either the husband or the wife.

pasha (T, borrowed into Arabic). Turkish title of rank and status for high officials, governors; a notch higher than bey.

piastre (Egyptian Arabic, borrowed from Italian). Monetary unit.

qabadi, plural **qabidiyat** (A). Real man, man of valor (Lebanese usage).

qadar (A). Fate.

qadi (A). Shari'a court judge.

qahwa (A). Coffee or coffee shop.

qaleh (P). Fortified private residence (Afghanistan).

qareqeb (A). Iron castanets.

qasbah (A). Fortified stronghold.

qassima (A). Contract of marriage

qawm (A). Group, nation.

qazi (P, borrowed from Arabic). Shari'a court judge.

'qel (A). Mind, reason.

qeran (P). Coin (Afghanistan).

Quran (A). The Muslim sacred scripture which records the 114 revelations to Muhammad revealed through the Angel Gabriel.

ra'i (A). Host.

Ramadan (A). The Muslim month of fasting.

rizq (A). Sustenance supplied by God.

rujula (A). Manliness.

salat (A). Prayer; the formal ritual prayer performed five times a day.

samovar (P). Large brass container which heats water for tea.

sa'y (A). "The Running," ritual of the pilgrimage which reenacts Hagar's search for water for the infant Ishmael.

seghir (A). Small (**sghir,** Moroccan usage).

shahada (A). The creed, statement of belief for Islam: There is no god but God and Muhammad is the messenger of God.

shari'a (A). Islamic law.

sharif, plural **shurfa** (A). Descendant of the Prophet Muhammad. A sharif is believed to command baraka by his descent.

shaykh, fem. **shaykha** (A). Respected man, often older; the head of the tribe.

sheikh, fem. **sheikha.** Anglicized shaykh.

shi'at Ali (A). The sect of Ali; Shi'ites.

shi'i (adj.), **shi'ite** (noun), **shi'a** (collective noun) (A). Sectarian; the second largest sect of Islam who follow Ali and his sons as Imams (leaders) of the Muslim community.

sigheh (P). Temporary marriage contracted by participants, dissolved after a set term.

solafah (A). Gossip.

sufi. Anglicized. A Muslim mystic.

sulha (A). Conciliation, arbitration, peace meeting.

sunna (A). The practice of the Prophet Muhammad or his community.

sunni (A). The most numerous sect of Muslims

suq (A). Market; marketplace.

ta'arija (A). A vase-shaped drum.

tahar (A). Circumcision.

tahara (A). Purification, purified.

tahdid al-nasl (A). Birth control.

tahkim (A). Marriage arbitration.

tajwid (A). A code of rules defining how to read the Quran aloud.

takhtit al-'a'ili. Family planning.

talaq (A). Repudiation, divorce.

tanzim al-usra (A). Family planning.

tariqa (A). Sufi order; literally, "the way, the path."

tasawwuf (A). Mysticism, sufism.

tawaf (A). Making the seven circumambulations around the Ka'bah.

ta'ziyeh (P). Shi'ite passion play commemorating the martyrdom of Hussein at Karbala; performed annually during Muharram.

tbila (A). Pair of pottery kettle drums (Moroccan usage).

tib (A). Perfume, scent.

tibb rawhani (A). Islamic medicine.

toman (P). An Iranian monetary unit.

'ulama, singular **'alim** (A). Scholars, specifically those learned in the Islamic sciences; Muslim religious authorities.

umma (A). The Muslim community.

umra (A). The shorter form of the pilgrimage; the lesser pilgrimage.

waʿd (A). Exposure of a newborn girl; a type of infanticide which reflects greater valuation of sons.

wadi, or **wad** (A). Valley (literally, a dry river valley); in North Africa, river.

wali (A). Saint; guardian.

waqf, plural awqaf (A). Endowment properties or funds.

waritha (A). Inheritance.

watan (A). Nation.

wilaya (A). Guardianship; legal power.

wuduʾ (A). Ritual ablution before prayer; purity, cleanliness.

wuquf (A). "The Standing," a ritual part of the pilgrimage which involves standing on the plain of Arafat, facing Mecca.

Zainab. Daughter of Ali and Fatima (Muhammad's daughter), sister of Hussein; often referred to as Our Lady (Sayyida) Zainab.

zajal (A). Folk tales.

zakat (A). Tithes.

zamil (A). A poetic form.

zar (A). Ceremony which releases the demons (jinn) from a possessed person.

zawiya (A). An Islamic brotherhood.

ziarat (P). Visit paid to a shrine (Iran).

zinah (A). Decoration, beauty.

zuwaj (A). Marriage

SELECTED READINGS

This section is designed to guide readers new to the area to basic works on aspects of everyday life in the Middle East. We concentrate here on works that address the themes and subjects that are the focus of this book. The list is, of necessity, selective.

BACKGROUND ON THE MIDDLE EAST AND ISLAM

Any in-depth understanding of the Middle East requires a sense of the area's history and Islamic principles. Two provocative histories are Sydney N. Fisher and William Ochsenwald, *The Middle East: A History*, fourth edition (New York: McGraw-Hill, 1990), and Albert Hourani, *A History of the Arab Peoples* (Cambridge: Harvard University Press, 1990). Hourani's *Arabic Thought in the Liberal Age, 1798–1939* (Cambridge: Cambridge University Press, 1983) presents an important window on the interactions between the Middle East and the West in the nineteenth and early twentieth centuries. Don Peretz, *The Middle East Today*, fourth edition (New York: Praeger, 1983) is a useful general history and survey of the Middle East. A good source for the geography of the region is Colbert C. Held, *Middle East Patterns: Places, Peoples and Politics* (Boulder: Westview Press, 1989).

While the politics of the Middle East are outside the purview of this volume, understanding political dynamics and institutions is useful. An excellent introduction is James Bill and Robert Springbord, *Politics in the Middle East*, third edition (New York: HarperCollins, 1990). Fouad Ajami, *The Arab Predicament* (Cambridge: Cambridge University Press, 1981) presents a thoughtful look at political and philosophical trends in the Middle East. *The Middle East*, seventh edition (Washington, D.C.: Congressional Quarterly Press, 1991), compiled by the publisher, is a detailed sourcebook; chapters introduce such topics as Middle East arms sales, Islam, country profiles, and a chronology. Two books give a particularly good sense of the Israeli-Palestinian conflict and the people involved: David Shipler, *Arab and Jew: Wounded Spirits in a Promised Land* (New York: Penguin Books, 1986) and Thomas Friedman,

From Beirut to Jerusalem (New York: Farrar Straus Giroux, 1989). A good general text is Charles D. Smith, *Palestine and the Arab-Israeli Conflict*, second edition (New York: St. Martin's Press, 1992).

The primary source on Islam is, of course, the Quran itself. The Muslim scriptures are available in a variety of translations, although, as Muslims state, the language of the original can never be adequately replicated in any translation. N. J. Dawood, *The Quran* (London: Penguin Books, 1956) is readable and widely available. Its peculiarity is the arrangement of the surahs (chapters) in a nontraditional order. Mohammed Marmaduke Pickthall, *The Meaning of the Glorious Koran* (New York: Mentor Books, Penguin Books, n.d.) presents a methodical translation which owes more to accuracy than to lilt of language. A. J. Arberry, *The Koran Interpreted* (New York: Macmillan Press, 1969) gives a sense of the flow and tone of the original Arabic. Two excellent general presentations of Islam in practice are John L. Esposito, *Islam: The Straight Path* (New York: Oxford University Press, 1988) and Frederick M. Denny, *An Introduction to Islam* (New York: Macmillan, 1985). Esposito's work is a concise, synthetic overview of the major tenets, organization, and movements of Islam. Denny considers both Islamic principles and contemporary religious practices. A more detailed look at Islam is Fazlur Rahman, *Islam* (Chicago: University of Chicago Press, 1966, 1979). An original, widely studied work on the history and practice of Islam in Morocco and Indonesia is Clifford Geertz, *Islam Observed* (Chicago: University of Chicago Press, 1968).

Questions raised by the intersection of Islam and politics are considered in John L. Esposito, *Islam and Politics*, third edition (Syracuse: Syracuse University Press, 1991). Other volumes on related subjects are James P. Piscatori, ed., *Islam in the Political Process* (Cambridge: Cambridge University Press, 1983); John L. Esposito, ed., *Voices of Resurgent Islam* (Oxford: Oxford University Press, 1983); John J. Donohue and John L. Esposito, eds., *Islam in Transition: Muslim Perspectives* (Oxford: Oxford University Press, 1982); and Ali E. Hillal Dessouki, ed., *Islamic Resurgence in the Arab World* (New York: Praeger, 1982). Islamic fundamentalism or activism is surveyed in Henry Munson, *Islam and Revolution in the Middle East* (New Haven: Yale University Press, 1988); Emmanuel Sivan, *Radical Islam* (New Haven: Yale University Press, 1985); and Barbara F. Stowasser, ed., *The Islamic Impulse*, (Washington, D.C.: Center for Contemporary Arab Studies, 1987). Nazih Ayubi, *Political Islam* (London: Routledge, 1991) examines the Islamist claim to Islam as a government.

Anthropological surveys which give a good sense of the pluralistic Middle Eastern society and culture include Louise Sweet, ed., *Peoples and Cultures of the Middle East*, two volumes (Garden City, N.Y.: Natural History Press, 1970); Daniel Bates and Amal Rassam, *Peoples and Cultures of the Middle East* (Englewood Cliffs, N.J.: Prentice Hall, 1983); and Dale Eickelman, *The Middle East: An Anthropological Approach*, second edition (Englewood Cliffs, New

Jersey: Prentice Hall, 1989). A useful reader is Nicholas S. Hopkins and Saad Eddin Ibrahim, eds., Arab Society in Transition, (Cairo: AUC Press, 1977).

MIDDLE EASTERN LITERATURE

Perhaps the best sources of material on Middle Eastern life are novels, essays, biographical accounts, stories, and poetry written by Middle Easterners. A brief selection of works available in English translation is listed here. The Middle East's most celebrated is Nobel Prize–winner Naguib Mahfouz (Mahfuz). A number of Mahfouz's novels are in English translation. Among his best known are *Children of Gebelawi,* trans. Philip Stewart (Washington D.C.: Three Continents Press, 1981); *Midaq Alley,* trans. Trevor Le Gassick (London: Heinemann Educational Books, 1975); *Miramar,* trans. John Fowles (London: Heinemann, 1978); and *Mirrors,* trans. Roger Allen (Minneapolis and Chicago: Bibliotheca Islamica, 1977). Anchor Books (Doubleday) has made the following works by Mahfouz available: *Autumn Quail; The Beggar; The Beginning and the End; Midaq Alley; Respected Sir; The Search; The Thief and the Dogs;* and *Wedding Song.* Mahfouz's most famous work in Arabic is his trilogy, translated into English by William Hutchins: *Palace Walk* (New York: Anchor Books, Doubleday, 1990); *Palace of Desire* (New York: Anchor Books, Doubleday, 1992); and *Sugar Street* (New York: Doubleday, 1992). The Egyptian Tawfiq al-Hakim is a prolific and well-respected playwright and author. His translated works include a collection of plays, *Fate of a Cockroach,* trans. Denys Johnson-Davies (London: Heinemann, 1973), which contains "Song of Death," and *Maze of Justice,* trans. Abba Eban (Austin: University of Texas Press, 1947, 1989), an autobiographical account of time spent as a local prosecutor in the Egyptian countryside.

English translations of other well-known Middle Eastern authors include Aziz Nesin, *Istanbul Boy,* trans. Joseph Jacobson, three parts (Austin, Texas: Center for Middle Eastern Studies, 1977–1990); Sadiq Hidayat, *Haji Agha: Portrait of an Iranian Confidence Man,* trans. G. M. Wickens (Austin: University of Texas Press, 1979), *The Blind Owl,* trans. D. P. Costello (New York: Grove Press, 1957), and *Sadeq Hedayat: An Anthology* (Boulder, Col., Westview Press, 1979); and Jalal Al-e Ahmad, *The School Principal,* trans. John K. Newton (Minneapolis and Chicago: Bibliotheca Islamica, 1974), *Lost in the Crowd* (Washington: Three Continents Press, 1985), and *Gharbzadegi (Weststruckness)* (Lexington, Ky: Mazda Publishers, 1982). The Moroccan writer Driss Chraibi has written numerous works, including *Heirs to the Past,* trans. Len Ortzen (London: Heineman, 1972) and *Flutes of Death,* trans. Robin Roosevelt, *The Butts,* trans. Hugh Harter, and *The Simple Past,* trans. Hugh Harter (all published by Three Continents Press). Other translated works are Ghassan Kanafani, *Men in the Sun* trans. Hilary Kilpatrick (Washington, D.C.:

Three Continents Press, 1984); Yusuf Idris, *The Cheapest Nights*, trans. Wadida Wassef, and *The Sinners*, trans. Kristin Peterson-Ishaq (both published by Three Continents Press); and Fathy Ghanem, *The Man who Lost his Shadow*, trans. Desmond Stewart (London: Heinemann, 1966). A major Turkish author is Yasar Kemal, three of whose works are *Anatolian Tales*, trans. Thilda Kemal (New York: Dodd, Mead, 1969), *Memed, My Hawk*, trans. Edouard Roditi (New York: Pantheon Books, 1961), and *The Wind from the Plain*, trans. Thilda Kemal (New York: Dodd, Mead, 1969).

Significant contemporary novels include Ali Ghanem, *A Wife for My Son*, trans. G. Koziolas (Chicago: Banner Press, 1984); Gamal al-Ghitani, *Zayni Barakat*, trans. Farouk Abdel Wahab (London: Penguin Books, 1988); Emile Habiby, *The Secret Life of Saeed The Pesoptimist*, trans. Salma K. Jayyusi and Trevor LeGassick (London: Zed Books, 1985); and Abdelrahman Munif, *Cities of Salt*, trans. Peter Theroux (New York: Vintage, 1989), which tells of life in the Persian Gulf Emirates. Among various anthologies which present the works of these and other authors is Salma Jayyusi, ed. and trans., *The Literature of Modern Arabia: An Anthology* (London, New York: Kegan Paul International, 1988).

Inea Bushnaq, *Arab Folktales* (New York: Pantheon Books, 1986) is a collection of tales told and retold in Middle Eastern families. Margaret Mills examines Afghani folklore in *Rhetoric and Politics in Afghan Traditional Storytelling* (Philadelphia: University of Pennsylvania Press, 1991). Sabra J. Webber looks at North African folklore in *Romancing the Real: Folklore and Ethnographic Representation in North Africa* (Philadelphia: University of Pennsylvania Press, 1991).

Poetry has traditionally been the primary literature of the Middle East. Pre-Islamic poetry, long epic poems telling of Arab heroes, their thoughts, environment, and battles, is the source of all other literary works. Although various translations of the odes (*muallaqat*) exist, a good starting point is the translations of selected odes in Jacques Berque, *Cultural Expression in Arab Society Today*, trans. Robert W. Stookey, poetry trans. Basima Bezirgan and Elizabeth Fernea (Austin: University of Texas Press, 1978). Collections of more contemporary material include Salma Jayyusi, ed. and trans., *Modern Arabic Poetry: An Anthology* (New York: Columbia University Press, 1987) and Miriam Cooke, *War's Other Voices: Women Writers on the Lebanese Civil War* (Cambridge: Cambridge University Press, 1987).

Three anthropologists take a new approach to literary expression. Steven C. Caton's work on Yemen, *Peaks of Yemen I Summon: Poetry as Cultural Practice in a North Yemeni Tribe* (Berkeley: University of California Press, 1990), looks at poetry from a practical and political as well as an aesthetic viewpoint. Like Caton, Michael Meeker, in *Literature and Violence in North Arabia* (Cambridge: Cambridge University Press, 1979), links poetry to the political and conflict-ridden aspects of tribal life. Looking at women's songs, Lila Abu Lughod, in *Veiled Sentiments: Honor and Poetry in a Bedouin Society* (Berkeley:

University of California Press, 1986), sees poetry as expressive of interpersonal concerns and relations.

FAMILY AND COMMUNITY

Books about the family include Elizabeth W. Fernea, ed., *Women and the Family in the Middle East: New Voices of Change* (Austin: University of Texas Press, 1985); Andrea Rugh, *Family in Contemporary Egypt* (Syracuse, Syracuse University Press, 1984); and Said K. Aburish, *Children of Bethany: The Story of a Palestinian Family* (Bloomington: Indiana University Press, 1988).

Ethnographies of Middle Eastern tribal life are relatively plentiful. Some of the most recent to focus on the question of change and adaptation are Lois Beck, *The Qashqai of Iran* (New Haven: Yale University Press, 1986) and *Nomad: A Year in the Life of a Qashqai Tribesman in Iran* (Berkeley: University of California Press, 1991); Donald Cole, *Nomads of the Nomads* (Arlington Heights, Ill.: AHM Publishing, 1975); and William Lancaster, *The Rwala Bedouin Today* (Cambridge: Cambridge University Press, 1981). An older but generally popular work which conveys the traditional Western romanticism of the Middle East is Wilfred Thesiger, *Arabian Sands* (New York: E. P. Dutton, 1959). A valuable source book on the bedouin and the fellahin is Cynthia Nelson, ed., *The Desert and the Sown* (Berkeley: Institute of International Studies, University of California, 1973). A different approach to tribal lineage is taken in Ernest Gellner, *Saints of the Atlas* (Chicago: University of Chicago Press, 1969).

Studies of communities often address rural-village–urban ties. Jean Duvignaud, *Change at Shebika* (Austin: University of Texas Press, 1977) recounts the struggle of a small Tunisian town to adapt to modern techniques and practices. Lawrence Rosen, *Bargaining for Reality: The Construction of Social Relations in a Muslim Community* (Chicago: University of Chicago Press, 1984) and Clifford Geertz, Hildred Geertz, and Lawrence Rosen, *Meaning and Order in Moroccan Society* (Cambridge: Cambridge University Press, 1979) look at a Moroccan town, Sefrou. Susan Schaefer Davis and Douglas A. Davis, *Adolescence in a Moroccan Town* (New Brunswick, N.J.: Rutgers University Press, 1989) study how social change distances teenagers from the world of their parents and grandparents. John Waterbury, in two books, *Egypt: Burdens of the Past, Options for the Future* (Bloomington: Indiana University Press, 1978) and *North for the Trade* (Berkeley: University of California Press, 1972), considers life in the twentieth-century Middle East—in *Egypt* from a macrodevelopmental perspective and in *North for the Trade* from the personal viewpoint of a successful Muslim merchant. Kevin Dwyer, *Moroccan Dialogues* (Baltimore: Johns Hopkins University Press, 1982) and Henry Munson, *The House of Si Abd Allah* (New Haven: Yale University Press, 1984) concentrate on narratives of individuals. Studies on agriculture and community development include James A. Miller, *Imlil: A Moroccan Mountain Community in Change* (Boulder, Col.: Westview, 1984) and Nicholas S. Hopkins, *Agrarian Transformation in Egypt* (Boulder, Col.: Westview, 1978).

In *Samed: Journal of a West Bank Palestinian* (New York: Adama Books, 1984), Raja Shehadeh documents life in limbo among the Palestinians on the West Bank caught between their aspirations and the reality of Israeli rule. *The Arab World: Personal Encounters* (Garden City, New York: Anchor Press/Doubleday, 1985) by Elizabeth W. Fernea and Robert A. Fernea compares Middle Eastern countries over time, from the authors' first visits to Iraq in the 1950s to the present day.

A number of significant studies look at specific aspects of Middle Eastern life. Aida Kanafani, *Aesthetics and Ritual in the United Arab Emirates* (Beirut: American University in Beirut, 1983) lays out the design of food and adornment in Middle Eastern life. Andrea Rugh, *Reveal and Conceal: Dress in Contemporary Egypt* (Syracuse: Syracuse University Press, 1986) studies Egyptian modes of dress. William O. Beeman, *Language, Status, and Power in Iran* (Bloomington: Indiana University Press, 1986) delineates the relationship of linguistic forms and language to action. Juan E. Campo discusses homes, space, and Islam in *The Other Sides of Paradise: Explorations into the Religious Meanings of Domestic Space in Islam* (Columbia: University of South Carolina Press, 1990).

Works on religion and community include Vincent Crapanzano, *The Hamadsha: A Study in Moroccan Ethnopsychiatry* (Berkeley: University of California Press, 1973); Michael M. J. Fischer and Mehdi Abedi, *Debating Muslims: Cultural Dialogues in Postmodernity and Tradition* (Madison: University of Wisconsin Press, 1990); Michael Gilsenan, *Saint and Sufi in Modern Egypt: An Essay in the Sociology of Religion* (Oxford: Clarendon Press, 1973) and *Recognizing Islam* (London: Croom Helma, 1982); Kristina Nelson, *The Art of Reciting the Qur'an* (Austin: University of Texas Press, 1986); and Earle H. Waugh, *The Munshidin of Egypt: Their World and Their Song* (Columbia: University of South Carolina Press, 1989). Carolyn Fluehr-Lobban, *Islamic Law and Society in the Sudan,* (London: Frank Cass, 1987) studies the linkage between Islamic law and society. Dale Eickelman looks at the interplay of education, lineage, and religion in *Moroccan Islam* (Austin: University of Texas Press, 1976) and *Knowledge and Power in Morocco* (Princeton: Princeton University Press, 1985). Eickelman has edited a volume on Muslim pilgrimage with James Piscatori, *Muslim Travellers* (London: Routledge, 1990).

WOMEN

The study of women in the Middle East has boomed over the past decade and a half. Where once scholars were hard pressed to find material on women's lives and experiences, now studies branch out beyond basic ethnography to specific studies of locales, classes, and interests.

The first important books on women in the Middle East are still highly useful: Elizabeth W. Fernea, *Guests of the Sheik* (Garden City, N.Y.: Doubleday, 1965); *A Street in Marrakech* (Garden City, N.Y.: Anchor Press, 1976); Elizabeth W. Fernea and Basima Q. Bezirgan, eds., *Middle Eastern Muslim Women Speak* (Austin: University of Texas Press, 1977); and Lois Beck and Nikki Keddie, *Women in the Muslim World* (Cambridge: Harvard University Press, 1978). Fernea's accounts of her family life in the Middle East are highly accessible and generally popular studies which focus on women's relations, but they are moreover studies by an outsider attempting to enter Middle Eastern society. Fernea and Bezirgan and Beck and Keddie presented some of the first collections of material about women. In the former, women recount their own lives; in the latter, scholars present studies on women in the Middle East. Nikki Keddie and Beth Baron, eds., *Women in Middle Eastern History: Shifting Boundaries in Sex and Gender,* (New Haven: Yale University Press, 1991) is a new volume on women in Middle Eastern history.

Middle Eastern women have produced critical works on women's place in Middle Eastern and Islamic society. Nawal El Saadawi's books—novels, short stories, autobiography, studies—such as *Women at Point Zero*, trans. Sherif Hetata (London: Zed Press, 1983), a novel, and *The Hidden Face of Eve*, trans. Sherif Hetata (London: Zed Press, 1980) a study of women in the Arab world, are good examples, as are Fatima Mernissi, *Beyond the Veil: Male-Female Dynamics in Modern Muslim Society*, revised edition (Bloomington: Indiana University Press, 1987) and *Doing Daily Battle*, trans. Mary Jo Lakeland (New Brunswick, N.J.: Rutgers University Press, 1989). Mernissi's latest work, *The Veil and the Male Elite* (Reading, Mass.: Addison-Wesley, 1991), examines the interaction of historical Muslim leaders and women's status. Margot Badran and Miriam Cooke, eds., *Opening the Gates: A Century of Arab Feminist Writing* (Bloomington: University of Indiana Press, 1990) presents feminist perspectives over the past century. Other works include Guity Nashat, ed., *Women and Revolution in Iran* (Boulder: Westview Press, 1983); Nahid Toubia, ed., *Women of the Arab World: The Coming Challenge*, trans. Nahed El Gamal (London: Zed Press, 1988); and Leila Ahmed's *Women and Gender in Islam: Historical Roots of a Modern Dilemma* (New Haven: Yale University Press, 1992). Fedwa Malti-Douglas, *Woman's Body, Woman's Word: Gender and Discourse in Arabo-Islamic Writing* (Princeton: Princeton University Press, 1991) surveys Arabic literature for attitudes toward women.

Erika Friedl, *Women of Deh Koh* (Washington, D.C.: Smithsonian Institution Press, 1989) relates stories of the author's friends in an Iranian village gathered over decades of acquaintance. Studies of women situated in the family and society include Daisy H. Dwyer, *Images and Self-Images* (New York: Columbia University Press, 1978); Susan Dorsky, *Women of Amran* (Salt

Lake City: University of Utah Press, 1986); Christine Eickelman, *Women and Community in Oman* (New York: New York University Press, 1984); Veronica Doubleday, *Three Women of Herat* (Austin: University of Texas Press, 1990); Soraya Altorki, *Women in Saudi Arabia: Ideology and Behavior among the Elite* (New York: Columbia University Press, 1986); Vanessa Maher, *Women and Property in Morocco* (London: Cambridge University Press, 1974); Arlene E. Macleod, *Accommodating Protest: Working Women, the New Veiling, and Change in Cairo* (New York: Columbia University Press, 1991); Anne Cloudsley, *Women of Omdurman: Life, Love and the Cult of Virginity* (New York: St. Martin's Press, 1984); Evelyn A. Early, *Baladi Women of Cairo: Playing with an Egg and a Stone* (Boulder, Col.: Lynne Rienner, 1993); Carla Makhlouf, *Changing Veils: Women and Modernisation in North Yemen* (London: Croom Helm, 1979); Judith Tucker, *Women in Nineteenth-Century Egypt* (Cambridge: Cambridge University Press, 1985); Unni Wikan, *Life among the Poor in Cairo* (London: Tavistock, 1980) and *Behind the Veil in Arabia: Women in Oman* (Baltimore: Johns Hopkins University Press, 1982); and Nancy Tapper, *Bartered Brides: Politics, Gender, and Marriage in an Afghan Tribal Society (Cambridge: Cambridge University Press, 1991).*

Middle Eastern women's accounts of their own lives are increasingly being written and translated. Leila Abuzeid, in *The Year of the Elephant* (Austin, Texas: Center for Middle Eastern Studies, 1989), writes of her own experiences. Nayra Atiya, in *Khul-Khaal: Five Egyptian Women Tell Their Stories* (Syracuse: Syracuse University Press, 1982), presents accounts of women's lives in Egypt. Another work of note is Bouthaina Shaaban, *Both Right and Left Handed: Arab Women Talk about Their Lives* (Bloomington: Indiana University Press, 1991). Stories written by Iranian women are translated for Western readers in Soraya Paknazar Sullivan, *Stories by Iranian Women since the Revolution* (Austin: University of Texas Press, 1990).

NOTES ON CONTRIBUTORS

MUHAMMAD FAHMI ABDUL, author of the booklet *Sayyida Zainab: The Chosen of Bani Hashim*, is a writer who popularizes Islamic history for the lay reader.

LILA ABU-LUGHOD is Associate Professor of Anthropology at New York University. She is the author of *Veiled Sentiments: Honor and Poetry in a Bedouin Society* and *Writing Women's Worlds: Bedouin Stories*, two studies of the Awlad 'Ali of the Western Desert of Egypt.

BISHARA BAHBAH is the author of many articles on Middle Eastern politics and the book *Israel and Latin America: The Military Connection*. A member of the Executive Committee of the Center for Policy Analysis on Palestine, he is Adjunct Professor of Political Science at Brigham Young University and Senior Fellow at the Institute for Social and Economic Development in the Middle East at the Kennedy School of Government, Harvard University. In April 1992 he was appointed as member of the Palestinian peace delegation to the Middle East Multilateral Working Group on Arms Control and Regional Security.

LOUISE BERDAL, a graduate of the University of Rheims in nursing, volunteered with the international group Doctors Without Borders to serve as a nurse in Beirut, Lebanon, in 1982 during the Siege of Beirut and in Afghanistan for six months in 1984. She works for the Council of Europe in Brussels.

ANNE H. BETTERIDGE is Executive Secretary of the Middle East Studies Association. She has conducted extensive research in Iran and has written articles on the anthropology of religion and symbolism as well as on women in the Middle East.

DONNA LEE BOWEN is Associate Professor of Political Science and Associate Director of the Womens' Research Center at Brigham Young University. Her publications concern family planning and Islam and regional development patterns in the Moroccan south.

JUAN E. CAMPO is Associate Professor in the Department of Religious Studies at the University of California, Santa Barbara. He is the author of *The Other*

Sides of Paradise: Explorations into the Religious Meanings of Domestic Space in Islam.

ROBERT L. CANFIELD, Professor of Anthropology at Washington University, has researched and written widely on Afghanistan. His edited volumes include *Turko-Persia in Historical Perspective, Afghanistan and the Soviet Union* (with Milan Hauner) and *Revolutions and Rebellions in Afghanistan: Anthropological Perspectives* (with Nazif Shahrani).

STEVEN C. CATON is an anthropologist who lived and worked in North Yemen from 1978 to 1981. He is Associate Professor of Anthropology at the University of California, Santa Cruz, and the author of *Peaks of Yemen I Summon: Poetry As Cultural Practice in a North Yemeni Tribe.*

DRISS CHRAIBI is a popular Moroccan novelist who lives in Paris and writes in French about the contradictory emotions of longing and alienation which many North African immigrants there feel for their countries. His novels include *The Simple Past, Flutes of Death, Mother Courage,* and *Night in Tangiers,* for which he received the coveted French literary prize, the Golden Palm.

SUSAN SCHAEFER DAVIS is an independent scholar and consultant with extensive experience in North Africa. She is the author of *Patience and Power: Women's Lives in a Moroccan Village, Adolescence in a Moroccan Town* (with her husband, Douglas A. Davis), and many articles.

DOUGLAS A. DAVIS is Professor of Psychology at Haverford College with interests in culture and personality and psychoanalytic psychology. His work in Morocco has produced *Adolescence in a Moroccan Town* (with his wife, Susan S. Davis), a volume in the series Adolescents in a Changing World, and "Formal Operational Thought and the Moroccan Adolescent" in *Child Development in a Cultural Context,* edited by Jann Valsiner.

EVELYN A. EARLY, a symbolic medical anthropologist who has written on popular medicine, everyday narratives, and informal business, has researched in Egypt, Lebanon, and Syria. Currently the U.S. press attaché in Rabat, Morocco, she is author of *Baladi Women of Cairo: Playing with an Egg and a Stone* and various articles including "Catharsis and Creation: The Everyday Narratives of Baladi Women of Cairo" and "Traditions of Nationalism in Syrian Performance."

ELIZABETH W. FERNEA is Professor of English and Middle Eastern Studies at the University of Texas at Austin. Her many publications include *Guests of the Sheik, A Street in Marrakech, Middle Eastern Muslim Women Speak* (co-edited with Basima Bezirgan), and *Women and the Family in the Middle East.* Her films include "Some Women of Marrakesh," "Price of Change," "The Veiled Revolution," "Women under Siege," and "The Struggle for Peace: Israelis and Palestinians" (with Steven Talley). Her next book will be on children in the Middle East.

ROBERT FERNEA, Professor of Anthropology at the University of Texas at Austin, has conducted research in Iraq, Egypt, Afghanistan, Saudi Arabia, and Morocco. His works include *Shaykh and Effendi*, based on his research in an Iraqi village in the late 1950s, *Nubians in Egypt: Peaceful People*, and *The Arab World: Personal Encounters*, written with Elizabeth W. Fernea on their research and experiences in the Middle East.

CAROLYN FLUEHR-LOBBAN is Professor of Anthropology at Rhode Island College and has conducted extensive fieldwork in the Sudan, Tunisia, and Egypt. Her books include *Ethics and the Profession of Anthropology* and *Islamic Law and Society in the Sudan*.

ERIKA FRIEDL is Professor of Anthropology at Western Michigan University. She and her family have lived with the Boir Ahmad for more than five of the last twenty-five years during frequent visits, most recently in summer 1989. Dr. Friedl's latest work is *Women of Deh Koh: Lives in an Iranian Village*.

MICHAEL GILSENAN is a social anthropologist at Oxford University. His research in Egypt and Lebanon has produced such works as *Saint and Sufi in Modern Egypt* and *Recognizing Islam*.

MICHAEL E. JANSEN, an American convert to Islam after years of study of the religion, was possibly the first American woman to undertake and then write about the *hajj*.

AIDA KANAFANI received her Ph.D. in Anthropology from the University of Texas. She is a professor at the American University of Beirut. Her research in the Arab Gulf area has been published in *Aesthetics and Ritual in the UAE*.

AFAF LUTFI AL-SAYYID MARSOT is Professor of History at the University of California, Los Angeles. A well-respected scholar of Middle Eastern history, she has published numerous works, including *Egypt's Liberal Experiment, 1922–1936*.

JAMES A. MILLER, a cultural geographer, is Associate Professor of History at Clemson University. His book, *Imlil: A Moroccan Mountain Community in Change*, is the product of extended fieldwork in Morocco.

MARGARET A. MILLS, Associate Professor of Folklore and Folklife at the University of Pennsylvania, has conducted extensive fieldwork in Afghanistan and Pakistan. She is the author of *Rhetoric and Politics in Traditional Afghan Storytelling*.

KRISTINA NELSON, an ethnomusicologist and arabist, is the author of *The Art of Reciting the Qur'an*.

EVERETT K. ROWSON is Associate Professor of Arabic and Islamics at the University of Pennsylvania. His writings focus on intellectual and social history of the Middle East.

NAWAL EL SAADAWI, an Egyptian gynecologist and prominent feminist, has written many books on the status of women, including *Woman at Point Zero*. Her selection in this book is from *Women and Sex*, her first book on the situation of women in Egypt.

TAYEB SALIH is Sudan's most famous novelist and story writer. He was educated in Britain as well as in Sudan. His most celebrated works include *Wedding of Zein* and *Season of Migration to the North*.

PHILIP D. SCHUYLER, Assistant Professor of Music at the University of Maryland, has conducted ethnomusicological research in Morocco and Yemen. He has published articles on traditional music and on the revival of folk music and has produced recordings of Middle Eastern music.

ABDEL-SALAM AL UJAILI, a Syrian physician, has written several books on the history of Raqqa, Syria, and the surrounding area. He has served in various ministerial posts in Syria, including that of Minister of Culture.

JOHN WATERBURY is Professor of Politics and International Relations at the Woodrow Wilson School, Princeton University. He is the author of many works on Middle Eastern politics, including *The Commander of the Faithful*, *The Egypt of Nasser and Sadat: The Political Economy of Two Regimes*, and *The Political Economy of the Middle East* (with Alan Richards).

INDEX